## ALSO BY GARY VAYNERCHUK

CRUSH IT!

THE THANK YOU ECONOMY

JAB, JAB, JAB, RIGHT HOOK

**#ASKGARYVEE**

# #ASKGARYVEE

## ONE ENTREPRENEUR'S TAKE ON LEADERSHIP, SOCIAL MEDIA & SELF-AWARENESS

▶ ▶▶ ◀) 5:43 / 20:19

## GARY VAYNERCHUK

18 17

HARPER
BUSINESS

*An Imprint of HarperCollinsPublishers*

Frontispiece © VaynerMedia

HarperCollins books may be purchased for educational, business, or sales promotional use. For information, please e-mail the Special Markets Department at SPsales@harpercollins.com.

FIRST EDITION

Designed by William Ruoto

Library of Congress Cataloging-in-Publication Data has been applied for.

ISBN: 978-0-06-227312-3

ISBN: 978-0-06-247001-0 (B&N Signed Edition)

17 18 19 20    OV/RRD    10 9 8

TO THE VAYNIACS AND THE
VAYNER NATION, AND ALL THE
PEOPLE WHO HAVE WATCHED
EVEN ONE VIDEO OVER THE
LAST TEN YEARS. YOUR
ATTENTION IS MY OXYGEN.

# ✔ CONTENTS

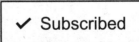

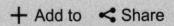

## ▶ ACKNOWLEDGMENTS

Nothing I do is possible without the support of my family. My heart belongs to my wife, Lizzie, and my kids, Misha and Xander. As always, tremendous thanks also goes to the rest of my family: my parents, Tamara and Sasha; my sister, Liz, and her wonderful husband, Justin, and their kids, Hannah and Max; my brother, AJ, and his wife, Ali; my grandma Esther, my fantastic brother-in-law, Alex, and his wife, Sandy, and their kids, Zach and Dylan; and my mother- and father-in-law, Anne and Peter Klein.

A huge thank-you to my team, aka the Dope Den: Steve Unwin, Zak Moy, David Rock, India Kieser, Alex De Simone, Andy Krainak, Andrew Greif, Staphon Lawrence, Brittany Hoffman, Siddharth Astir, and Rebecca Wright.

My gratitude also goes out to the whole team at HarperBusiness. And especially to Hollis Heimbouch, who says this is the best book I've written. Thank you for your consistent support and allowing me to roll the way I need to.

Finally, thanks again to my writer, Stephanie Land, who beside my brother and dad has been my closest partner in business. I can't believe this is book number four!

## ▶ INTRODUCTION

On February 21, 2006, on a YouTube channel with zero follow-ers, the world's first wine video blog launched. Without fanfare, it opened on a guy in a blue sweater—maybe it was black, the bad lighting made it hard to tell—seated in front of a blank beige wall. On the table in front of him rested three wine bottles and a small, dark bucket that looked like it might have once held a potted plant. His skin was sallow in the sickly fluorescent light that barely il-luminated his face, but he had a wide, optimistic smile. Looking straight into the Flip cam, he announced himself to his nonexistent audience in a subdued, serious, but friendly voice: "Hello, every-body, and welcome to the very first episode of *Wine Library TV.* I'm Gary Vaynerchuk." The echo was so intense he might have been filming inside a cave.

Over time the show got more dynamic and exciting. The host started to let his huge personality shine. He wore Jets shirts. He paired wines with Lucky Charms and described flavor profiles in colorful, colloquial language, like grape-flavored Nerd candy and dead deer mixed with cherries.

He filmed another 999 episodes before announcing on March 14, 2011, that the show was over.

Well, not quite over. On that same day he launched *Daily Grape*, a kind of *Wine Library TV 2.0* for the mobile era. That lasted eighty-nine episodes. And then he realized he really was done. He loved wine but he was an entrepreneur first, and there were just too many other things to do.

That character was me, of course. At the time I really did think I was done with daily video blogging forever. I could imagine the occasional interview or one-off video (have you ever seen my "Monday Morning Motivational" spot?), but a full show was too much. There was only one thing I didn't count on: you, Vayner Nation. I missed you! I missed talking to you every day. I mean, sure I could talk to you anytime I wanted to on Twitter, Instagram, or Facebook, but video elicits a different energy and encourages a spontaneity and vibrancy that can't be replicated on any other platform. I should have known that something was missing in my world when I realized that during every forty-five-minute speaking engagement the part I most looked forward to was the last fifteen minutes of Q&A. In fact, at one point I seriously considered making my whole presentation nothing but Q&A forever.

Meanwhile, the emails kept pouring in. Despite access to three books and hundreds of videos, people still had questions about how to successfully use social media—the new platforms and the old standbys—to build their brands, or how to market with native content, or even just how I do what I do. There was so much content I wanted to put out to help them, but with all my other obligations at VaynerMedia and elsewhere I just couldn't get to it.

Then DRock emailed me. DRock is David Rock, and he wanted to make a short film about me. The story of what he did to convince me to agree shows up somewhere later in this book, and it's a good one—a classic example of how to get yourself to the next professional level. He followed me around for a day and produced a gorgeous short film that perfectly encapsulates my entire philosophy about business and entrepreneurship. It's called "Clouds and Dirt." I enjoyed working with DRock so much I hired him to create videos for me full-time.

Then I looked around and saw that by bringing him on board I had accidentally formed the perfect content creation team—David for video, Steve Unwin for copy (a job eventually shared with India Kieser), and Zak Moy for design. On a whim, I pulled them aside and announced that I wanted to film a video, and they were going to help me.

And that's how on July 31, 2014, on a YouTube channel with 30,000 subscribers, one of the world's first business Q&A video blogs was launched. It opened on a guy in a blue-striped golf shirt smiling into the camera: "Hello, everyone, and welcome to the first *#AskGaryVee*." Though the first episode started off almost as low-key as its wine-themed predecessors, by the second, the light and sound quality were professional grade and the host was bringing hard energy and straight thunder. He started posing weird random objects, Jets paraphernalia, and eighties collectible toys on the sleek blond wood table in front of him as he answered his viewers' questions about social media, marketing, branding, and more. Subscriptions to the channel and eventually to the accompanying podcast ballooned as viewers kept asking questions, and he kept answering them.

At first I thought the show might be an every-now-and-then thing, but it was like riding a bike—as soon as I filmed the first episode, I wanted to do more. And so we did (DRock, Steve, and Zak didn't know what hit them). It's a challenge, of course. The world is much more mobile and much smarter than it was in 2006, when I started *WLTV*, and there is a lot more competition for eyeballs even than in 2011, when we finished *Daily Grape*. Which means I have to be even better. And I think I am, because I'm speaking from five more years of experience. That's five more years of watching new technologies rise and fall, experimenting with platforms, advising clients, and talking to people about their dreams and goals.

That's one of the things I love best about *The #AskGaryVee Show*. It's not a platform from which I talk about things that are important to me; it's a place where I talk about things that are important to you. You, the viewers, entrepreneurs, executives, and dreamers are the inspiration for the show just as the wines were the inspiration for *WLTV* and *Daily Grape*. And just as I could never run out of new wines to taste, there will never be a day when there's nothing new to say about the state of business. It's a constantly evolving and growing topic.

The other thing I love about this show is that in the end, I really did figure out a way to extend my favorite part of my keynote speeches. If you've never seen me onstage, I model my performance after the comedians I idolized in my youth, like Eddie Murphy, Chris Rock, and Richard Pryor. My presentations are salty and brash, but even as they shock they tend to make people laugh. Hopefully, they also make people think. I like the Q&A part best because that's the moment when people realize that I'm not a clever speaker with a few good ideas, but a devout practitioner with endless ideas. I can literally see the skeptics' expressions switch from cynicism to admiration and respect as they realize that they can ask me anything—anything!—and I won't dodge and I won't rehash and I will do my absolute best to give them detailed, tactical answers they can start using right away.

*The #AskGaryVee Show* allows me to do that for people every day. I love the community that has developed around it. I love that it has become an integral part of my life. I love that it has introduced a new cast of VaynerMedia characters to the world. And I love that together our little team has created the apex of modern marketing—an ultimate jab-and-content distributor.

While the vast majority of questions lobbed at me have to do with launching start-ups, building personal brands, leveraging social media, and deconstructing platforms, I also get asked about leadership, hiring and firing, public speaking, and the perks and perils of mixing family and business. Also the Jets. And parenting in the digital era. And my thoughts on the value of traditional education. And my biggest mistakes. I tell it as I see it, with the benefit of a broader perspective than I had even just a few years ago. I've always known what it takes to succeed in the trenches, but now with the hands-on experience of growing two businesses, one from scratch, I also know what the aerial view looks like, and what works best when you're responsible for creating culture, developing careers, and managing clients in a company that seems to double in size by the day.

I've been stunned at people's appetite for this content, especially the Millennials. We're increasingly reaching a young audience. It reaffirms my belief that there are gaping holes in the educational system, and entrepreneurs and innovators tend to fall through them, especially at the college level. They don't need theory. They need practical, tactical information, stuff they can hear one minute and start applying the next—real-world advice that can be adapted and reshaped as the winds of commerce and culture shift.

Already I'm getting emails from people who have taken the advice offered on the show and are getting good results. I don't think there's any better measure of its worth. On the other hand, the show's popularity also gives me a chance to see how many people say they understand hustle, and engagement, and biz dev, and jabbing, right hooking, and prioritization, but actually don't. On a car ride to Philadelphia I decided to look up the accounts of the people who watch the show the most. Of the fifteen people I tracked down, fourteen haven't changed a damn thing about how they communicate or do business since they started watching. So what are they getting from tuning in every few days? Maybe just the inspiration and motivation to keep trying. And maybe that means there's someone out there whom I haven't met yet, someone who hasn't commented or sent in a question, one of those lurkers who drive me crazy with their silence . . . maybe someone reading this book . . . and that person will come across a thought or rant or piece of advice that will help her see her path to success. In episode 63, @bluearcherpgh asked me what I'd title a college or high school course if I could teach one. I am teaching it, right here and now. Consider *#AskGaryVee* my marketing master class. The difference between it and anything you might have studied in school is that I don't want you to regurgitate what you learn; I want you to act on it right now.

▶

So why a book now when the show and podcast are still going strong? We cover an incredible amount of ground per episode, and as they added up it led me to realize that if we consolidated all the information and ideas we discuss into one easily accessible package, you'd have a complete blueprint to what makes me and other successful entrepreneurs tick. And that's exciting to me, and offers you something of value, and is therefore worthy of a book. And then there are a few other good reasons:

1. At the time of this writing, we have loaded 157 episodes on YouTube. Because they run 12–25 minutes each, it will take you hours to catch up if you've never watched them before. If you're hustling the way you're supposed to, you don't have that kind of time to spare. And if you've already watched them all, unless you are one of a few rare and particularly skilled individuals, a little review won't hurt you. Now you've got all those hours' worth of information in one handy package you can finish on an airplane ride.

2. The world moves quickly. When it comes to tech or media, what was true only six months ago may not be true anymore. This is my chance to update my answers. And in many cases, though I stand by my original response, in the time since it aired I've been able to think deeper about certain subjects and have taken the opportunity to expand my thoughts on them or adjust to changes in the market.

3. My last few books have been narrowly focused on sharing with you the marketing strategies and tactics that work, and documenting the growth and development of social media. This book will also cover all the most up-to-date information on platforms and tech, and how to create native content that gets people's attention. But it will go broader and deeper as well, revealing what I've learned not just in my role as entrepreneur and marketer, but as a leader, manager, and family man. I hope this book will offer

a perfect blend of motivation, inspiration, data, strategy, and executable information.

4. We've also included many brand-new questions and answers pulled from fans across our channels as well as from our own employees. So you'll find some familiar stuff in this book, and a lot that is new. Some questions have been consolidated or rephrased for clarity. Some are short and simple and silly, but I wanted to capture some of the fun we have on the show! All the topics are timeless, however, and you'll find that even the most specific answers can frequently be adapted in all kinds of ways for almost every industry, service, and product. Now, you might be wondering if that's a good thing. What could someone else's question about optimizing social for the elevator industry, or the future value of Instagram, or Disney's billion-dollar MagicBand possibly have to do with you?

5. Everything. Because a discussion of Disney's MagicBand leads to a debate over the future of wearable tech, which leads to Amazon's Dash Button, which makes it possible to reorder consumable products literally at the touch of a button adhered to household items. Imagine, just as you pour the last drop of detergent into the laundry reservoir, you can lean over and tap the detergent button affixed to your washing machine, and just like that, a new container is ordered and on its way. It doesn't take a genius to see how that development might impact every single business on the planet. And if you read my answers to the questions about making great content for the elevator industry, how musicians can make a better living, or why Instagram is going to be worth a bazillion dollars soon, you'll see that that information has everything to do with you, too.

My hope is that after you read this you'll feel empowered and armed with a deeper understanding of the current business environment, including the ins and outs; the black, the white, and the gray; the IQ and the EQ; the details and the big picture surrounding everything it takes to be a successful entrepreneur, executive, CEO, and manager. I've been spending a ton of hours on Instagram, Facebook, Pinterest, Snapchat, Meerkat, Periscope, LinkedIn, and many other platforms, and from this man's point of view we are living in an unbelievably interesting time. I haven't felt this sense of disruption since 2006–2007, when Facebook and Twitter started to eat away at Friendster and MySpace. The stakes and the opportunities are high, and the next thirty-six months of hustle might just pay off more than usual for those people willing to put in the time and effort. See, many people are only just settling into Facebook or Twitter, not realizing that the world has already embraced other opportunities as well. The advantage is yours if you want it.

And now, let's get on with the booooooooooooooooook!*

---

* Don't get the joke? Come by and watch the shoooooooooow!

# CHAPTER 1
# CLOUDS AND DIRT

---

## IN THIS CHAPTER I TALK ABOUT PRIORITIZING, THE OXYGEN OF YOUR BUSINESS, AND WHY THE MIDDLE SUCKS.

---

I spend all my time in the clouds and the dirt.

The clouds are the high-end philosophy and beliefs that are at the heart of everything I am personally and everything I do professionally.

Personally, it's really simple: family first. Nothing else really matters.

Professionally, it's not much different. That's what I often tell my staff at VaynerMedia—99 percent of what we deal with every day in business doesn't matter. This usually gets me a mix of confused, curious, and even disdainful looks from my new top execs or employees hearing it for the first time because of course they think that to do their job well, *everything* has to matter. But it's just not true. If you religiously follow just the few core business philosophies that mean the most to you, and spend all your time there, everything else will naturally fall into place. My clouds are extremely simple, and might sound familiar to anyone who has been following me for a while:

**Bring value to the customer.**

**Provide 51 percent of the value in a relationship, whether it's with an employee, a client, or a stranger.**

**Always play the long game of lifetime value.**

**Smart work will never replace hard work; it only supplements it.**

**People are your most important commodity.**

**Patience matters.**

**Never be romantic about how you make your money.**

**Try to put yourself out of business daily.**

These are my commandments.

So you see, the clouds don't just represent the big picture; they represent the huge picture, the everything. They are not goals. Goals can be achieved and set aside or moved. I'm Going to Buy the Jets is a goal. It drives me, too, but it's not at the core of how I run my businesses.

The dirt is about being a practitioner and executing toward those clouds. It's the hard work. On a personal level, my dirt is making sure I communicate well with my loved ones, that I show up and stay present, that I apologize when I mess up and that I make sure it doesn't happen too often. You know, the stuff of being a good spouse, parent, son, sibling, and friend. Professionally, it's knowing my craft. It's knowing there is a fifteen-person limit to an Instagram chat and that infographics overindex on Pinterest. It's understanding Facebook ads and the ROI of Vine. It's noticing changes and trends and figuring out how to take advantage of them before anybody else.

The vast majority of people tend to play to the middle, which is why they usually only succeed up to a certain level and then plateau. Alternatively, they get stuck in one or the other, getting so bogged down by minutiae or politics they lose sight of the clouds, or so into the clouds they lose the appetite or neglect the skills they need to execute successfully. Ideas are worthless without the execution; execution is pointless without the ideas. You have to learn to prioritize properly and quickly identify what's going to move you further ahead and what's going to make you stall.

I saw how these tendencies played out early in my career in the wine industry. I encountered a lot of amazing wine people with brilliant palates whose businesses stunk because they weren't good at that part. Conversely, I'd meet with some of the best wine retailers in the country and be shocked to find that their actual knowledge about wine was incredibly limited. A great wine merchant has to be a businessperson first and a wine person second, for sure, but that second part really did matter. I always thought the reason the success of my family wine business, Wine Library, accelerated so quickly once I got involved was that I took both seriously. I knew my business, but I also knew my craft, and that practitionership—loving wine, tasting as many as I could, and caring about the regions and producers—created tremendous value for my customers and ridiculous ROI for me.

I see a similar phenomenon in today's marketing world. At this point in my career I have sat down hundreds of times to meet with people claiming to be social media experts, only to discover they have gaping holes in their knowledge about the platforms and little idea of how they have changed over time. This is why I feel justified telling potential clients that if they work with me, they'll be working with the best social media practitioner at the best social agency in the country. Because at VaynerMedia, the clouds matter, and the dirt matters, and nothing else.

There are too many people who are average at what they do, and then confused by their average results. Everyone has their own definition of clouds and dirt, but if there's any advice I can offer you that will change the entire trajectory of your career, *it's to start pushing on both edges*. Raise the bar on your business philosophy, dig deeper into your craft. You want to be an equally good architect as you are a mason. You've got to be able to simultaneously think at a high level and get your hands dirty.

---

▶ Can you elaborate on what the middle is and why it sucks?

---

To be in the middle is to be like everybody else. It's a start-up that pitches me by saying: "We're going to do something in the photo app space." You mean like everybody has been doing for the past five years? It's commodity work. It's not influential and it's not special. It's safe.

On any given day, I sit through four or more pitches. And the pitch I usually end up liking? The one where the players are actually doing the work. They're in the trenches. They're not just doing the big holistic thinking or the higher-level branding; they're just at a raw level, executing. They're engaging like mad and experimenting on platforms and trying things that risk getting them ridiculed in the trades. There really aren't that many people who are hard practitioners like that. There also aren't that many people who are looking far into the future. I'm talking 2025 and 2030. Everyone is hanging in the middle space, trying to get the most in the short term out of their new app instead of trying to build something that lasts.

Let me put it this way: If you have pages and pages of notes, but no product, you've got nothing. If you can't tell me how you're going to build your product, you've got nothing. And if you are only thinking three years into the future, you've got a huge vulnerability. That's what people in the middle are doing. The middle keeps everything going the way it always has. The clouds and the dirt break things.

All the best apps, companies, and products have broken the way we live life, transformed how we communicate, and changed our day-to-day. Good products evolve us.

You're surrounded by the middle for 99.9 percent of your life. Most things are unremarkable. I want you to lose yourself in the clouds and the dirt and figure out what you can make that changes the game.

Vagueness sucks. Lack of drive sucks. Half-assing things sucks. And so does the middle.

---

▶ How do you know how much time to give to clouds versus dirt? Should you base your decision on your personality? Your strengths?

---

You need a healthy balance. If you're leaning too far one way or the other that's a problem. I'd be uncomfortable if you were 70/30 in any direction. That should be your absolute minimum.

You do also need to map your DNA. If you're a big-picture thinker, make sure you're still spending 30 percent of your time honing your practitioner skills. If grinding and hustling is more your thing and where you want to spend 70 percent of your time, that's cool, but keep at least 30 percent of your time reserved for getting in those trenches and seeing how your ideas actually play out in the real world. And there will be an ebb and flow. Sometimes you'll have to switch from 70/30 to 30/70 because you were doing something right, and now you have to make sure all parts of the business, from the strategy to the operations, is caught up and heading in the same direction. At the time this question was asked, I was actually thinking that I would have to move into a 90/10 division of thinking versus execution because for the nine months prior I spent the majority of my time executing, and in that time I had spotted opportunities to rechart the company.

There's no perfect breakdown of clouds and dirt, but they always need to be in play. You have to make a commitment to strategy and execution and think of them holistically. There are too many prima donnas out there who think that as the brains of the business they don't have to get their hands dirty.

---

▶ When is the long tail actually just moving the goalpost?

---

As most of my followers know, I want to buy the Jets. I've wanted to buy the Jets since I was a little kid. Three decades later, I'm still at it, but I'm not tired. That's how long-term I am. Owning the Jets will be a by-product of ignoring anything other than the clouds and dirt. I consider every decision I make—from launching VaynerMedia to writing books to public speaking to doing a podcast and show—as a chess move, and I don't make it unless it gets me closer to owning the Jets one day.

But I suspect what you're thinking is, big picture is great but if you're ignoring all the little stuff in the short term, will you ever really reach your goal? I say yes, because when you have a big picture, a north star, a truly long-term vision, something interesting happens: You stop stressing the dumb little shit day in and day out because you're playing the big game. So the short-term angst, which is really just a by-product of the friction caused by growth, becomes a little more manageable. And when you're not stressing, you've got a whole lot more energy to go all in. If you're single-mindedly focused on your long-term goal, you'll be more effective in the short term and get there faster.

---

▶ Where do you see yourself in five years?

---

I have no idea. I'm not a planner and don't have a five-year plan. Five years ago Instagram and Snapchat didn't exist, nor did GoPro.

Netflix wasn't what it is today. The world is changing too fast to be able to predict where I will be professionally. Personally I will be in better shape, I will spend more time with my family. I'll be going to tee-ball games and ballets and shows and hacking my life to have better balance. Professionally I will be doing what I always do—listening to the marketplace and adjusting on the fly in real time, running a business, and marketing like it's 2021, 2022, 2027, or whatever year you're reading this in.

I am a "halftime adjustments head coach." If I'm down 23–21 at the end of the second quarter, I've got fifteen minutes of halftime to figure out how to turn things around for my team, using what I've learned, tracking the patterns, and adapting in the moment. In the words of Missy Elliott, I'm gonna drop down, flip it, and reverse it. And that's how I come out winning 35–24. That is who I am as an entrepreneur. I improvise and adapt to new realities on the ground while always keeping my eye on the clouds.

---

▶ What's the biggest lesson you learned this year?

---

This question was posed in 2014, when I was twenty-six days into a new diet and workout regimen designed by the personal trainer I hired to help me get back in shape. I had realized I wasn't accountable to myself when it came to health, so if I was going to make a change I would need to become accountable to someone else. It worked. At the time, I'd made it to the gym twenty-six times and eaten seventy-eight healthy meals in a row without cheating. Since then I've kept it up. I feel so accomplished. I'm also grateful that I figured the solution out at a young enough age that will allow me to reap the benefits for decades to come.

So the biggest thing I learned that year hands down was that prioritizing my health is a really good idea. My energy level was down while because I had been living on sugar. But after just a few weeks, I felt like a different person. Making my health a priority has changed my life. And remember what I said about how everything I do is a chess move that gets me closer to owning the Jets? This change isn't just good for my health or my family; I will be able to build businesses and invest and do what I love to do longer because of it. It's cloud thinking, which is win-win all the way around.

▶ **What is an area in life where you haven't given it your fullest efforts?**

There were once two places where I wasn't giving my all. One was in the nonprofit/NGO space. I was giving my dollars but my effort and time were reserved for my family. Now I'm a proud member of the board of Pencils of Promise, which does require a time commitment, as well as several other organizations to which I donate both time and money. The other was my health. Between kids and businesses and volunteering and working out, it's hard to find Gary time, and I haven't figured out how to hack that yet. In September during football season I always get several hours on Sundays. Maybe I should find something just for me that I enjoy during the rest of the year, too, but that doesn't feel right to me while the kids are still so young.

▶ **What motivates you to continue any project without seeing any significant growth prior?**

I believe in my purpose. I'm blown away by how people are crippled by a project that doesn't go the way they wanted it to. I have a clear vision professionally where I want to go and so I am willing to be very patient along the way because I have conviction and remember why I believed in doing it in the first place. Otherwise I just want to be a good human being, do business the right way, and hustle. I control all of that. If I don't get results then it's because I made a wrong strategic decision. But that doesn't cripple me, either, because I know where I'm going. For the one or two times I invest poorly or get involved in the wrong thing I'm going to figure out a win alongside of that. I understand in those losses that I am gaining valuable experience.

---

▶ Does VaynerMedia focus much energy on winning awards and what's your take on the ad industry's obsession with awards in general?

---

I think awards are horsecrap. The reason agencies want to win them is twofold: They use it to recruit talent, and they use it to get more business. They're putting out work for clients that's geared toward getting awards instead of trying to sell something. I understand the business rationale, but it takes your eye off the prize, which is to do something for business. At VaynerMedia, our work is the word of mouth of our business. I think awards are an energy sucker away from what matters, which is selling the product for the client. Old-school reporting and awards have been the justification for many agencies. I am excitedly waiting for technology to catch up and create more black-and-white data that will prove the results of marketing activities and campaigns.

▶ If you had a seven-acre vineyard, how would you sell lots of wine?
How would you do things differently compared to all the other
vineyards out there?

Clouds and dirt. Or as I used to say to my dad, big and small. If I
had a small parcel in New Zealand and wasn't making that much
wine, here's what I would do:

Small: hand sell. I would fly to the big cities in Australia and
New Zealand and walk around to visit restaurant sommeliers. I'd
go restaurant by restaurant, retailer by retailer, and try to get in
their door. I'd offer tastes and sell to every individual, thus scaling
the unscalable.

Big: become a media company. I did that in 2006, and it's what
I've been saying everyone should do for years, no matter what their
business. While working at Wine Library I was doing the small
stuff—the tactical email service, the website, working the floor on
a Saturday. But then I started doing the big things, like *Wine Library TV*. You, small New Zealand winery, need to become the
authority on New Zealand food and wine. Put out written or video
content on as many channels as you can and start talking. Talk
about your products. Talk about your competitors. Talk about what
goes with wine, and why we drink wine, and why New Zealand
grows great wine grapes, and what to eat with wine. Talk wine, talk
New Zealand, talk with passion, confidence, and expertise. There's
room for everyone at your level. Become bigger than you are.

Small: Don't get caught up in the glam. When *Wine Library TV*
took off I started getting interview requests and media coverage,
appearing on *Conan* and *Ellen* and *Jim Cramer*. But the whole time
I was still downstairs hustling, still trying to get a good deal on
Barolo, still answering emails and engaging with people on Twitter, and trying to sell another bottle. Even as you start to taste
success, you have to have the humility to get on a middle-aisle seat

to the Philippines and sell a few bottles of wine to some random restaurant.

---

▶ **What would you prioritize as a one-person business?**

---

The answer is the same whether you're a solopreneur or part of a team running a small business.

In the beginning of any venture, it can be difficult to predict your cash cycle and know what to prioritize because everything feels imperative. Customer satisfaction is huge, as are issues like establishing company culture, budget, marketing, and hiring.

But there is one thing that always transcends everything else: *Cash. It is the oxygen of your business.*

You can make the greatest cup of coffee, the greatest sneaker, the greatest TV show, or the greatest work of art ever, but if you can't sell your product you are out of business. So your first priority is sales because it generates cash, and cash is what allows you to do everything else. Without it you're a fish out of water, gasping for breath.

I can't say it enough times: Cash is oxygen.

---

▶ **If "Cash is oxygen" is your priority as a one-person business, what's second? Product, team, or service?**

---

There is no second.

That doesn't mean there aren't other things you need to concern yourself with that will affect the success or failure of your venture. Ignoring customer service or your product quality or company culture is a very bad idea that will ultimately sink your business. It's just that ignoring them will probably sink it a little more slowly than running out of cash will. Your business isn't that much different from a human body. It will run on sugar and caffeine. It will run even better if you give it water, vegetables, and a workout. But it won't last five minutes without oxygen.

So let's say you've got a good handle on your cash flow. How do you figure out what's next?

Focus on your strengths. What else are you really good at? Design? Growth hacking? Nail these skills down, and then drill deep with them. If cash is your company's oxygen, your strongest skills are its DNA. Develop and cultivate them because they will be the hallmark of your company.

For example, I'm really good at growing top-line revenue, so that's what I focused on in the early days of both Wine Library and VaynerMedia. It was only later that I worked on driving profit back up.

This moment when you decide what to focus on next is crucial not only because it's going to help you grow, but also because it could be what allows you to bring in more key players, people who may not be great at selling but are overwhelmingly talented at something else—something else that complements your own talents.

Bet on your strengths. It's an underrated business strategy in a world where so many people are obsessed with fixing their weaknesses they give short shrift to the skills they were born with.

# CHAPTER 2
# STARTING OUT

---

## IN THIS CHAPTER I TALK ABOUT CHOOSING A NAME FOR YOUR COMPANY, MAKING YOUR MARKET CARE ABOUT YOU, AND STANDING UP TO YOUR MOM.

---

Sometimes kids ask me questions on *The #AskGaryVee Show,* and I'm always struck at how much they take all the opportunities at their fingertips for granted. Of course they can get two thousand views for their makeup shows shot from their bedroom. Of course they can just reach out to a seasoned entrepreneur and ask him a direct question. Every time I see their happy, hopeful faces I want to scream, "Do you know how lucky you are? Do you know how much closer I'd be to owning the Jets right now if I'd had access to the Internet back when I was your age?" My God, the things I could have done.

And now more people than ever are doing those things, because that's the kind of change the Internet has brought on our society. It's why so many of us can start building something incredible even when we're just sitting at a makeshift desk in a broom closet. It's why we're able to talk to each other, network, reach influencers, find inspiration, and engage at a level unseen in human history. We are all so, so lucky. It's such an exciting time to be an entrepreneur—heck, to be a human being!—and I'm pumped at how many people are going out into the world with their ideas and their hustle.

I get a lot of questions from entrepreneurial newbies and re-starters looking for everything from nuts-and-bolts platform ex-planations to reassurance that they've actually got what it takes to succeed. I try to answer as many as I can because if there's anyone I know I can help, it's this group. I often say there are two core things that bring people value: 1) entertainment, and 2) utility. I know this chapter falls in the latter category, and not only for the en-trepreneurs just starting out. Old-timers, pros, and establishment icons, don't pass up this opportunity to see what's on the mind of the new generation. Even if you think you already know all the an-swers, you might be surprised. And their questions—not to men-tion their eagerness, their fears, and their sheer excitement—can be good reminders as to why you decided to hop on this awesome, crazy train in the first place.

---

▶ Finding a marketing job out of college is tough, especially one that's not sketchy. How do you find a job that is the right fit?

---

What's a sketchy marketing job? I can only imagine you're talking about the lowest common denominator stuff out there, like MLM (multilevel marketing), which relies on a pyramid scheme, or creat-ing landing pages, selling overpriced e-books, or hawking supple-ments that haven't been vetted. I can see why you'd think that was dark, bad stuff.

But most of the marketing world isn't like that. There are plenty of reputable marketing and social media agencies looking for talent, so you need to recalibrate and raise the bar on your search. If you can't find a quality company to pay you to work for them, apply for an internship so you can prove your chops. At VaynerMedia we've been able to offer many of our interns permanent jobs. We're growing fast so we've needed to fill positions, but we also hire when someone proves themselves to us through hustle.

Many internships pay, but if you can't find a paying position, consider working pro bono and turning that into a great opportunity. You can read about how DRock, my videographer and director, did it in this book. Don't want to work for free? Well, it seems to me that if you've been struggling to get a job for three or four months, it's a lot more productive than sitting around doing nothing. I mean, who's paying you to do that? Take a pro bono half day in a place where you can pick up skills, network, learn your craft, and get an employer's attention (or at least guilt her into recommending you to someone else). Unless you are literally sending out résumés and interviewing eighteen hours straight per day, you've got time to volunteer your professional talent somewhere. Find a place where you think you can make doors open, and put your skills into action. We have become too entitled. Go out and earn that job.

---

▶ How or should the length limitations inherent on Twitter/Vine/ Instagram affect a start-up when choosing its name?

---

I frequently get questions from people wanting to know the science to coming up with a great business name. Science? There is no science. People will agonize for hours, weeks, months, trying to figure out the name for their start-up, hunting for that perfect, zingy, creative name that allows them to "stand out" and "disrupt the category." You want to know how you stand out and disrupt the category? It has nothing to do with your name.

Just stand out and disrupt the category.

Are you going to tell me that "Apple" or "Vine" is an earth-shatteringly clever name? Or "Snapchat" or "Reddit"? Do you know how many people tell me they wish they had a different last name so they could use it for their company? They're talking to a guy named Vaynerchuk! "Oh, but that's unique and cool and . . ." No, it's really not. My name is "good" because I made something out of it.

What did "Google" or "Facebook" mean to anybody when they weren't the household names we know today? You want people to recognize and remember your name? Earn it. Of course serendipity and good timing can play a big part in any product or start-up's success, but none of that is even possible without a whole lot of hustle and sweat first.

If you're really worried about your name taking up too much space in this short-form era, go with an abbreviation. No one seems to care that I'm often signing off as GaryVee nowadays. You can also let your audience abbreviate for you. People will help you evolve your name so long as whatever you deliver brings them value.

Here's my two cents: Stop worrying about coming up with the perfect name. Yes, a good name carries some marketing power, but at the end of the day if the product sucks, the name means nothing. If you have a clever name, people might stop and notice. If you don't, they really won't care. They're going to assign it meaning based on the experience they have with your brand. So please, stop worrying about your name and start worrying about your product.

---

▶ What was the hardest thing about starting up VaynerMedia from scratch?

---

I'm asked this all the time, and the answer might surprise you.

It wasn't leaving Wine Library.

It wasn't launching a new business with another family member.

It wasn't jumping into the agency world with zero experience.

It was all the options I had at my disposal.

During the first nine months we were launching the agency I was troubled by the fact that there were about eight hundred other things my brother, AJ, and I could have done together, and it was hard not to look back at all those opportunities and wonder, did we do the right thing? In addition, that same year my daughter Misha was born and I published my first business book, *Crush It*. There was so much going on—was this venture the best use of my time? The second-guessing was brutal.

You've surely experienced this kind of buyer's remorse after making a big decision. Almost everyone has. Kids when they finally pick a college. Managers when they make a hire. Entrepreneurs when they invest. Because you know that there's always that chance you messed up and missed the next big thing. The perfect school. The perfect hire. The monster dividends. We all have our #onealmond moment. (Not familiar with it? I talk about it in Chapter 16, on investing.)

At some point, however, you've got to hike up your big-boy pants, accept the decision you've made, and move on. After all, you made your decision for a reason, so trust your judgment. There's no point in looking back. Even if you discover you made a mistake, you'll be okay, because every option will get you something. It might be a return on an investment, or it might be a lesson learned. Sometimes it's hard to tell right away which is going to be the more valuable. Either way, so long as you don't shy away from making decisions, so long as you aren't content to sit and dither, you will never be left with zero. Suck it up. Make the call. And remember: Be grateful if you're lucky enough to have too many options. It's a blessing and a half.

▶ How much of success is confidence, how much is skill, and how much is luck? You seem to have a lot of the first.

I have been lucky, that's for sure. I could have been born two decades earlier in the Soviet Union and spent my formative years going insane locked behind a communistic regime until I got to the United States in my early twenties, and thus had a twenty-year delay trying to accomplish everything I've set out to do. Heck, I could have been born a bus!* Instead I was born during the Cold War at a time when Israel and America teamed up to make a deal with Russia that traded people seeking political asylum for wheat. (Yes, that's right, I was traded to the States for *wheat.*) And so I moved here when I was three years old and had every opportunity to live the American Dream. If that isn't luck, I don't know what is.

So luck is a really good thing to have, and maybe I've had more than my fair share. But it's not the main ingredient to success. Not at all. As has been pointed out, I have a lot of confidence and bravado. But those wouldn't be worth much if I didn't also have the skills and the hustle mentality to execute. I suppose one could argue that even getting the good DNA that allowed me to have confidence and hustle could be considered lucky. And yet, there are plenty of people who start out without much confidence, or who aren't taught a good work ethic, and they come into it on their own and win.

So it seems to me that success—my success in particular, and I suspect most people's success in general—is a well-balanced blend—a nice little Meritage, if you will—of luck, DNA, confidence, and hustle.

---

* **Don't know what I mean? Google my "Monday Morning Motivational video."**

▶ How long is too long for a fiscally responsible entrepreneur to stay in a safe full-time job? At what point do you have to accept that it's not going to happen. Is it ever too late to start?

These are going to be some hard words for some of you to hear:

If you have a full-time job, you're not an entrepreneur. You may have aspirations of being an entrepreneur, and you may have entrepreneurial tendencies, but if you are born to be an entrepreneur you will not be able to breathe for more than ten minutes in a "real" job.

If you've been going along fine for a few years in a full-time job and not had the urge to gnaw your leg off like a fox caught in a trap, you're probably doing what you're supposed to be doing.

But. If you are between the ages of eighteen and twenty-nine, and you are miserable whenever you work for anyone but yourself, and you feel restless, and you believe in your bones that you've got what it takes to run your own show, go do it. Go do it before you take on the responsibilities of a mortgage or a family, before your parents start to need you or you adopt a dog. Do it now while the only person you have to worry about is you.

The best way to become something is to do the work required to become something. Sell, sell, sell. Figure out what it takes to provide value. Learn how to communicate your value proposition. Engage with your customers. Find mentors. Go work for free and under people who can show you the ropes and serve as that point of contact when you need it. Learn the hustle and taste the game. Put yourself in the position to win. You can read as many books as you'd like (ahem . . .) but they're not going to make you an entrepreneur. What is it Yoda said? There is no try, only do.

Stop waiting for the perfect moment to jump, because it will never come. If you want to be an artist, make art. Want to open a pizza place? Go work in a pizza joint and learn the business. Build an app and stop waiting for Mashable to write about it because they aren't going to give a crap about it until you put in the hard work of proving it solves a problem, serves a need, and makes people happy.

Start doing whatever it takes. Even if that means selling the very shirt off your back.

PETE BROWN
@pbrown76

▶ Do you think giving up a secure job for a new and exciting opportunity is irresponsible when you are the sole provider for your family?

You know, my gut reaction to this kind of question would usually be to say that you're being irresponsible if you *don't* take a chance to follow your passion and be a happier person. If you have a working partner, you could have a conversation about whether you could maintain your lifestyle on a single salary or what you'd need to do to downsize. But when you're the main breadwinner of a family? Quite frankly it would be irresponsible to walk away from your steady income unless you have enough savings, a trust fund, rich parents, or some other cushion to help maintain your lifestyle for at least two years after you begin your new journey. I'd say you should absolutely go for it, *but only if the decision comes at the expense of luxuries, not at the expense of rent or food.* It's one thing for you to willingly eat Vienna sausages every night for a year, but it's not okay to put kids in that position.

There are a lot of people who are able to enjoy being hobby entrepreneurs because their joy is in the process, not in the outcome. So they make maybe $10–40K on the side doing something they love, and they're satisfied with that because they don't need to make a billion dollars to be happy. If you've gotten to a point in your life where you can't ditch everything to follow your dreams, being a hobbyist can often give you the best of both worlds.

---

▶ I love my job but I want to do my own blog and my own hustle. But I'm crippled when it comes to executing.

---

One of the hardest things about making your dream, or your small business, or your blog, or whatever is just *doing* it. Taking that first step can often be the only thing standing in your way, because once you start getting shit done, the momentum just carries you forward.

There's no doubt that taking that first step can be terrifying. I get it. I really do. But I also have to wonder, would you be so afraid if you knew no one was watching? See, I think what really scares people is not fear of failure, *but fear of failing in front of someone who matters.* Like your mom or dad. Your best friend. A sibling. A mentor. A spouse. None of us wants to disappoint someone we admire.

But if you want to be an entrepreneur—if that's what you really, really want—you cannot give a shit about what other people think of you. Not even your parents.

I won't lie—people will criticize you. They will say mean things, maybe even hateful things, often because they're jealous that you had the guts to get out there and do your thing, or because they love you very much and are scared for you. And that's okay. If you truly trust and believe in yourself, you will learn to ignore them and they will learn to accept your decisions. And if you fail and people laugh at you, they're not worth your time. Ignore them.

If fear is holding you back, think about whose opinion matters the most to you, and then sit down with that person or those people face-to-face. And this is what you say: "I'm about to do this thing, and the only reason I haven't yet is because I don't want to let you down. This is a long journey and I know I'm going to make it in the end, but I need to know that if I stumble, you won't think less of me or turn away. Because that would crush me."

Anyone with a heart would be touched by such vulnerability and show of respect. Who wouldn't be honored to learn that his or her opinion meant that much to you? Chances are good they'll promise to have your back. And hopefully that's all you'll need to take the next step. You want to surround yourself with people who are going to stand by you and encourage you to get back up, not keep you down.

---

▶ What's the best way to deal with someone who is negative about entrepreneurship? What if it's your mom?

---

You know what's great about entrepreneurship? At the end of the day, one of you is going to be right. Who's it going to be? The best way to handle this is to stick it to your mom. Go out and execute and enjoy saying, "I told you so."

Because you must know that her negativity doesn't mean that she doesn't believe in entrepreneurship—it's that she doesn't believe in you. That probably hurts. I hope it also pisses you off. Nothing gets me more worked up than someone who doesn't believe in me.

Now, maybe your mom is right. Maybe you are delusional. You need to go talk to other people in your ecosystem and find out what they have to say. If they concur with your mom, you might think

twice about your ambitions. If they're supportive and you can ⸻
they're sincere, that should help boost your confidence.

Most important, you have to ask yourself: Do you believe in you?
If you believe you're an entrepreneur, then no one else's opinion really
matters. Prove them right or prove them wrong—either way, you're
better off for trying. If you're asking this question, it might mean that
you've put weight into your mom's opinion. I put zero weight into
anyone's opinion about me because I know exactly who I am. Can
you say the same? When you can, you'll know exactly what to do.

---

▶ How do you make your market embrace your product or ideas
   when it just doesn't care about them yet?

---

I get asked a version of this pretty frequently, which boils down
to: How do you take someone from "maybe" to "yes"? How do you
make them buy in?

You don't.

I don't try to convert anyone. No one! None of the content,
none of the things I do—books, keynotes, videos, T-shirts—are
done in the hope they will convert a single person. I speak only to
the already converted, and you should do the same.

This question applies to much more than just social. It applies
to whatever thing you are trying to sell. Period. If you sell fax machines, and your market doesn't believe in fax machines, don't try to
convince them to buy fax machines! Go find the people who have
bought into the fax machine idea and sell to them. Because if you're
too early in a business or a theory where there's no buy-in, you've lost.

People are always marveling at how I manage to get into markets just ahead of the mainstream, but as I always say, I'm not Nos-
tradamus. What I am is practical. I spend zero time convincing
people to believe what I believe in. Up-and-coming wines. The

Internet and email marketing back in 1997. Google AdWords in 2000. Snapchat two years ago. There were even plenty of people who didn't believe the market was ready in 2009 when I started VaynerMedia with AJ, but in fact there was just enough for us to build a business, and we grew into it. You need a few people waiting at the end if you're going to survive, and they were there. That's how we knew we'd be okay if we skated to where the puck was going to be, not where it already was.

Apply your time and energy to where there is fertile ground. It might take a lot of work to find your customer base, but it sure beats wasting your breath on people who are never going to help you out.

I promise you, the more you reach out, the more opportunities to make new connections will arise. Put in an extra one or two hours every day to go beyond the place you've already been looking. It'll be worth it.

BOOK WINNER!

CHEF LIZETTE
@CHEFLIZETTE1
cheflizette.com

---

▶ When trying to create a new media property (say, something at the intersection of food and tech, with no real precedents), how do you find and forge the right partnerships, that is, people with resources *and* access?

---

Everybody always has something to offer. When I biz-dev from a zero-starting place, which seems to be where this question is coming from, and I'm looking to extend my reach and resources, I'm always trying to reverse-engineer the most valuable thing I can give to those people.

I think the way to do it would be with something I call shock and awe. I would reach out to as many of these people as I could, as often as possible. But instead of asking them to do something for me, I'd ask what I could do for them. It would be about following them on social or in the media, not about reaching out and asking directly, because let's face it, these kinds of people are usually busy. It would be about asking what value props you can bring to them.

I'm an enormous believer in spec work. I know it has a bad name, but if you're looking to get something from someone, there are other ways you can pay them besides money, and providing your service or your product for free is a great way to build up points you can cash in.

For example, I'm always the cheapest, or the most vulnerable, when I'm promoting a book. So for anybody reading this who bought 25–2,000 books in exchange for my time, I think you got a good deal. I discounted my time and my impact in order to make this book a success. So when you assess the fifty people you want to reach, you need to look at them and understand their vulnerabilities to see where you might get them at a discount. Now, if they don't have those vulnerabilities, figure out how to provide disproportionate value by listening and asking directly.

---

▶ Who would you recommend pitching an app idea to? What steps would you recommend?

---

At first I was like, what kind of question is this? If you have an idea and you can't code, you pitch a cofounder or a dev shop to build it. If you need money, you pitch it to money people. When you need to sell it you pitch to a strategic buyer. If you need press, you pitch it to the media and influencers. Who do you pitch it to? Whomever you need at that moment!

Then Steve Unwin (an amazing cast member from the shooooooow) explained to me that anyone who knew I invested in apps might wonder who might have a shot if they came to me. For example, I invested in the wine app Delectable. How did that deal happen? Well, a VC for Delectable knew I had a wine background. He pitched Phil Toronto, who vets my deals, and sure enough when I learned about it I thought it was intriguing. It's strategic to consider an investor's history if you want to predict their interests in the future. But then, every single decision you make in your business life needs to be strategic.

---

▶ How do I get the first ten customers for a creative service start-up?

---

I once made a video where I showed the visitors to garyvaynerchuk.com how to cold-call potential customers on the air and get people to consider doing business with me. I had no script, other than to articulate exactly what kind of value I thought my blog could bring to anyone who might advertise on my site. It was a short, pleasant conversation that ended with the potential customer agreeing to review some ideas if I ever put them to paper and sent them to him. I'd call that a productive phone call. If I had been a new entrepreneur trying to find those first customers, I would have immediately picked up the phone again and dialed a new potential customer. And then I'd have done it again, and again, and again, for as long as I could that day, and the next, and the next.

To get those first ten customers, you have to grind. You can't be shy, my friends. Just roll up to every single person in the world who might possibly buy your stuff (meaning who already buys into at least the concept of your idea or product; see two questions up) and ask them to buy your stuff.

WARREN WEEKS
FOUNDER, THE ART OF THE GREAT MEDIA INTERVIEW
@ElevenPR

▶ PR firms offer media training for executives but the quality varies
a lot. A lot of companies have grown complacent and just hire
the same firms over and over. How do I get on the radar of
decision makers (who aren't actively looking, either because
of complacency or because they think all media trainers are
essentially the same)?

First and foremost, this is an excuse as much as it is a question.
When I started VaynerMedia, plenty of our prospective clients
were in the habit of hiring other, more established agencies. Every
industry has its market leaders—companies who have done good
work in the past and have become the default solution for their
client base. Your goal is to become one of those leaders who are au-
tomatic go-tos. So first you have to get over your resentment of the
competition and realize that you haven't done crap to establish your
brand. The way you can overcome that, in my opinion, is to deliver
great work and start creating word of mouth. It's just grinding and
going through the process.

Now, if you're asking me how to get your first client, you might
just have to come in cheaper than you want to. You've got to do a lot
more business development, networking, advertising, and putting
out content. These are the classic, tried-and-true ways for a B2B
company like yours to get business. Put out content on LinkedIn
and SlideShare. Go to YPO meetings and industry events for the
organizations you're targeting. Or just cold-call and offer your

services at prices low enough to bring on clients who can then start recommending you based on the quality of your work.

This is really, really, black-and-white stuff. It comes down to pure execution. If your work is great, that becomes your reputation, and that becomes the gateway drug to bring in business to your sales funnel. You may call the incumbents lazy, but I call it an earned reputation.

---

▶ Why do you focus on top-line revenue?

---

A lot of first-time entrepreneurs try driving margins and profit very early on. I do not. At both my dad's wine shop and VaynerMedia, I focused on top-line revenue. Why? Because you can always drive your profits, but there's a very small window in which to focus on the top line.

When I run a business, I tend to innovate and be ahead of the market, and so I want to run fast and grab as many customers as I can while I'm still slightly ahead. It also gives me the ability to bring in the people who will keep things running in the background, freeing me up to play offense and concentrate on building my brand and gaining leverage as fast as possible. Because eventually, the market will catch up with me, and that's when things get interesting and exciting. That's when people start believing in what I'm doing, be it wines, e-commerce, video blogging, or social media. Three, four, five years down the line, after I've already established my brand and gained customer loyalty, then I can start to drive profit. You can always start cutting costs or raising prices at any time, but land-grabbing more customers gives you the leverage and the scale you need to ultimately convert once the time is right. Of course it takes a certain skill to balance your expenses and sales so you don't go out of business, but I've made a good career of pushing those limits. I think my stomach for top-line revenue is why I now have a second business under my belt that grew from $3 million to $50 million within five years.

I understand the desire to play things safe and guarantee you make payroll, but remember, if you take too long to grow someone else is going to come along and eat you up.

---

▶ I have an app idea, with my target market willing to test it, but I need to create the app and I'm not a programmer. Any advice?

---

It's the simplest thing to do in the world. MeetUp.com, for instance, has eight hundred different developer meetups. Find the closest one, even if it's far away, and go find your developer.

I get so many questions like this every day: "Hey, Gary, how do I hire a business partner/developer/assistant?" If you aren't capable of figuring out something so basic all by yourself, how the hell are you going to make it in that business? Ideas are shit. Execution is the name of the game. Just. Make. It. Happen.

You know, seriously, if you have to ask this question, you're probably out of business before you even start. Think about that before you invest a single minute more into your endeavor. For real.

---

▶ I'm building an app that is probably six months away from a working prototype. What would you suggest I start doing now to build it up so that when it is time for release we'll have plenty of users?

---

That's a tricky one that lots of developers have to figure out every day: How can you promote a product months ahead of the launch date when you're not even sure what the product itself is going to look like?

The answer is a terrific tactic that works on everything: content, content, content, content, content, content.

Let's say you're putting out a productivity app. Go reserve something like dailytimemanagement.com, and then use that domain throughout the months leading up to the launch. Start putting out content for Medium or your blog or RebelMouse that will draw like-minded people interested in that topic and lifestyle, people who are most likely to use the app. Do everything you can to create a hub and community around the very thing your product was built to address.

Then when the app comes out, you pound that community with it. Shout at them. Ask them to test it out. Give them free trials or limited access so they can experiment with it. If they love it, they'll start marketing it for you with word of mouth. You'll know very quickly what works, what doesn't, and what you need to focus on next.

You know what we call this? That's right. This is a classic example of using jabs and right hooks to build a brand. Flooding your community with quality content and earning their trust until the day you're ready to make the ask is a tactic that works for *everything*. Give consumers a place where they can go to learn, discuss, meet other people, and be a part of something. Then hit them really, really hard.

---

▶ What is the biggest obstacle to success: lack of time or lack of capital?

---

The obstacle would be assuming that lack of time or capital is an obstacle. What you're talking about is excuses.

There are a million things that can stop your success. Your family's health and welfare. The country where you live or where you're trying to set up a business. A competitor with a billion dollars and mega skills who punches you out and drops you in the first round.

Bad media coverage. A random moment in time. If I were to look down at my phone while driving and kill somebody it would ruin me. There are a million reasons you can find to stop building a business, but almost every time, the real reason why you will stop is not that you don't have time or money, *but that it's hard.*

To be a successful entrepreneur, you have to be an optimist. A lack of time is just incentive to be more efficient with the time you do have. Insufficient capital is a game to see who can find the most creative way to get more. You don't see obstacles—you see opportunities. Optimists accept that obstacles will be in their path, and assume they'll figure out a way around them. Which is not to say the grind isn't hard for optimists, too. It is. *They just like it.*

If you don't, maybe you're not cut out for entrepreneurship. Or at least you don't have the stomach to do what it takes to be No. 1. And you know what? That's okay. Thriving at No. 7 instead of stressing at No. 1 would be something to be proud of, and a great way to live.

---

▶ **What should I look for in a cofounder?**

---

First look at yourself. You have to be self-aware and honest about your weaknesses, and find someone who can make up for them. When you're considering a candidate, ask yourself if she provides the black-and-white to your gray. Does she love HR when you don't care? You want to cover the core things that drive a business—a team, a product that works, a revenue model, sales, retention, vision, and execution.

When people go wrong, it's because they weren't willing to be honest enough with themselves. They think, Oh, I can get by with my accounting skills. Oh, I'll figure the legal stuff out as I go along. Um, no. There is something to be said for being intrepid and willing to problem-solve and learn, but you want a rock-solid foundation for your business. Ideally, together you and your cofounder will be a million times stronger than when you are apart.

---

▶ What came first at VaynerMedia: clients or employees? And did you ever do the work by yourself?

---

About two or three months before AJ graduated from college I brought in our first client. We made that customer pay for the whole project up front, which we then used to pay our first five or six employees, all of whom still work here. AJ and I did actually do a lot of the early work on that first project by ourselves. We're good in the trenches.

I hope you'll remember that anecdote. One of the reasons so many people go out of business is that they don't know how to manage their cash flow. You think you're going to make $80K so it's okay to have $70K in expenses. But shit happens, and if there's any kind of a hiccup and the money doesn't come in when you think it will, you've got no buffer and you're suddenly in trouble. Tech people often assume they're going to keep raising incredible amounts of money, not realizing that once you're a real company people start making decisions based on what you're doing, not what you promised you'd do. So anytime you can sell ahead of your expenses, do it.

---

▶ What are your tips for teenage bloggers to show brands they mean business?

---

Do you have traffic? Followers? Content? Engagement? Brands don't care if you're 14, 41, or 4,000 years old so long as you show results. They may underestimate you at first, but numbers don't lie.

---

▶ How can I filter years of exciting adventures and experiences into value that someone would actually be interested in?

---

I don't know. Are your seventy-one years of experience interesting? Will anyone care about what you've done?

I'm a person who will automatically value the life advice from someone who has lived seventy-one years, but the rest of the world isn't like me. So to reach those people, the first thing you need to figure out is the best method to communicate. How are you going to storytell? Do you want to put out a show? Write articles? Blog? Tweet? Podcast? And then once you've perfected your medium, how will you monetize it? You could sell advertising, subscriptions, coaching, content. You could organize a community and put on a conference. Tell your story, establish your cred, make your story relevant, build your brand, and the monetization opportunities will come. Humans of New York was simply a Facebook page before it became a cultural phenomenon and landed Brandon Stanton a book deal.

I'm the poster child for how to make money without directly selling. A lot of my contemporaries sell e-books or white papers. I do none of those things. For years I put out my content at scale and built my brand. Eventually, I built up enough leverage that people wanted to hear me speak, and I could charge good money for my time. They wanted me to write books, which I was able to sell to a big fan base. I was able to start a social media agency. I provided value with the content that I relentlessly pump out. You need to do the same.

> ▶ When you have a new business idea, how long does it take to implement? Do you run with it? Strategize for a while? Consult with others?

So you've decided to take the leap on a business idea. Congratulations! Taking that first step forward is one of the hardest parts of the process.

Now what? How fast do you need to move? Well, that depends. I have sat on businesses for an insanely long time, years even, before I executed on them. Before we started VaynerMedia, AJ and I thought about it for ten or eleven months to make sure we were making the right decision. You could say we let the idea marinate. In the meantime, we almost decided to move forward with a fantasy sports site. But in the end, VaynerMedia won out.

And then there was the time Jérôme Jarre and I had dinner, and literally the next day we had formed a talent agency for Vine stars called GrapeStory.

The key is to make sure you look at your idea from lots of different angles and ask the important questions. If you're working with a partner, you should be communicating constantly and hitting your ideas, concerns, and thoughts back and forth until you're both satisfied with the answers.

One thing to which all entrepreneurs should pay close attention is the timing of an idea. Ask yourself (and your business partner, if you have one): Am I ready? Do I have the time to do this right? The biggest failures in my business career have been when I bit off more than I could chew. I've mentioned I had an intensely busy 2009 (new baby, new agency, new book). Because of those obligations I wasn't able to give my full attention to the online wine review website Cork'd, which I'd bought in 2006. It didn't see the end of 2009.

So choose your battles. Don't rush anything. Map your life and make sure this is going to get you where you want to be. And stay open to serendipity. You never know what can happen before that one idea comes to fruition.

---

▶ How do you avoid letting a new business run its new social media plan by itself?

---

Well, that's easy. This is a continuous game. I face this all the time, but I'm not worried. I know everything about Snapchat stories. I know what's evolving on Facebook. I guarantee my clients will never know as much about social media as I do. The best way to stay indispensable is to stay ahead of your clients and always have something more to give.

---

▶ What is the best way to scale a business with an inherently low profit margin?

---

I answered this question with Jack and Suzy Welch when they were guests on the show, and we were all in agreement. You need new products, new innovations, and a new angle. Take the assets you have and deploy them to grow the business—just make it a better business, even a different business, than the one you started with.

This is what I did when I went into my dad's business at $3 million in revenue and made 10 percent gross profit before expenses. The liquor business is notoriously hard because there's a wholesaler in the middle that takes 25 percent of the 50 percent that a retailer normally takes. So here's what I did. I took the low-margin items that were driving the store's business and bet on them. I took all the Santa Margaritas, the Kendall Jacksons, the liquor items that were low margin, and used them as marketing lures to get people into the store. Those low-profit-margin items were the honey. But then I merchandized the store and built a brand. Customers came in to buy a bottle of Kendall Jackson, but then I sold them a different, higher-margin chardonnay because it was a better wine. They liked it. They came back for more. And while they were there they noticed other higher-margin items, and tried those, too.

Use your low-margin items to drive your business, then use those pennies to invest in advertising and build from there.

---

▶ What's your best piece of advice for a first-generation American entrepreneur, venturing out on her own, away from her family business?

---

I have two pieces of advice.

1.  Be practical. How much money do you have to stay alive, and for how long? Do you have enough money to cover rent, expenses (anticipated and unexpected), and overhead for a year? You should.

2.  Be prepared to sacrifice. The minute you decide to launch a new business, you also make the decision to do nothing else but that for the next year, and maybe even two years, but build your business. Every minute of every eighteen-hour day should be dedicated to this endeavor. Your business success will come at the expense of family time, friend time, vacations, and any other hobbies or activities you once enjoyed. This business has to be your entire life, or it will die.

I think a lot of people go into business for themselves underestimating how hard it really is to make your dreams come true.

DAWN SWICK-RENSHAW
@DAWNSWICK
www.stoneycreeksocialmedia.com/

▶ If you could go back to any time in your life and know then what you know now, when would that be and what one thing would you change in your business life?

This is something I rarely think about, so it's nice that writing this book gives me the opportunity to go back and address it. I would probably go back to the early 2000s when I was buying "wine" and many other words on Google AdWords. Looking back, I would probably have spent 90 percent less money on ads in *Wine Spectator*, billboards, and radio, and I would have poured it all into Google AdWords. Most people weren't paying any attention back then, the inventory was wildly underpriced, and the demand curve was in my favor. Even back then, there was enormous customer activity on Google that led to transactions, and I feel like I left way too much money on the table. It's why I've been so emphatic about Facebook ads during this generation. This, too, will go away.

I'd also go back to that moment for another reason (and this is something I don't think I've ever even said out loud). A lot of the applications that Eric Kastner and I created in Wine Library's early days—things like emailing people with abandoned shopping carts, or targeting emails based on user's searches on the site—became industry standards half a decade later. What's more is that a lot of the companies who built the tools for other companies to execute on those ideas went on to become $500 million or even billion-dollar companies. Many of my own actions were so early that if I'd been smart enough to turn them into products or services instead of just in-house tools for Wine Library, I might own the Jets right now.

---

▶ What are the biggest mistakes you see young entrepreneurs make?

---

It might take the rest of my life to list them all.

Okay, I'm joking. Sort of. No, seriously, I see many Millennials doing great things. But I also see a lot of you making one mistake in particular that I think is making you dangerously vulnerable, and it's this: You're building businesses that only work during best-case market scenarios.

It's not entirely your fault. If you are twenty-one years old today, the last real economic downturn was in 2008—when you were four-teen. You've never had to do business in any economic landscape but one on the upswing, in which it is super-easy to raise money to build a business. You've been trained as excellent peacetime generals.

The problem with that is that today's current market conditions are not allowing young entrepreneurs to cultivate strong business discipline. This is a great time to be starting a business and try-ing to sell it, but what happens when the bad times eventually roll around again? The best businesspeople aren't just good peacetime generals, they're fierce wartime generals, too.

So how do you prepare for war during peaceful times? Start thinking worst-case scenarios. Imagine a stock market collapse. What will you do if all of a sudden everyone snaps their wallets shut because they're too scared to invest?

Protect yourself before you have to face that situation. Here is what young entrepreneurs must do ahead of time if they want to build a business that can weather every storm.

**1.** Build solid teams. In the midst of rapid growth, don't lose sight
of the importance of longevity. Invest in your teams, celebrate
their victories, listen, and be a good boss so that when rough
winds hit, you can rely on their skills, loyalty, and intellectual
capital to help you keep the ship upright.

**2.** Build good products.

**3.** Excel at sales.

Without sales you've got nothing, in good times or in bad. Do
whatever you need to do to build the most kick-ass sales department you can find.

Young entrepreneurs are operating during a very sunshiny moment
in time. Don't let your skill set be limited by it. Because bad times are
coming. The good news is that good times will follow. And then the
bad ones will return. And then get chased away by the good.

Get it? Be ready for every possible outcome. Only entrepreneurs
with the grit will rise to the top, and stay there.

---

▶ How do I overcome the perception of being "too young" when I'm
pitching VCs?

---

I have no pity for any young person coming into the business world
today. Twenty years ago the only thing you would have been allowed to do in the business arena was serve coffee. That all changed
because of tech. No one today is going to dismiss a young person
unless that young person hasn't got the goods.

The secret to raising money is to sell your idea to people willing
to buy. If you've been told you'll get forty-five minutes for a VC
pitch, and you can feel it isn't happening, cut things short and leave.

You have better things to do with those thirty minutes. And once you leave that office where you were basically told you couldn't win, get out there and prove them wrong.

Let me assure you of one thing, however. If someone tells you they're not giving you money because they think you're too young to do what you say you can, they're not telling you the truth. They're being nice. Every VC in the game will be pumped to give a twenty-year-old money if they believe in that twenty-year-old. If they don't, it means they see a flaw in your idea or your execution. What you do with that feedback is up to you.

---

▶ As a successful solo entrepreneur, do I have to grow my business bigger than I can handle alone?

---

Depends on what you want in life. Are you fulfilled and making the money you want? Not everyone is a good manager. Plenty of entrepreneurs have grown their businesses only to realize that once the scope of their role changes they aren't enjoying themselves anymore. You don't want to make more money just to give up your happiness. There's got to be a sweet spot in your growth where your money and happiness are aligned. I'm lucky—what I love creates a lot of wealth. But lots of people would hate living the way I do. So figure out what you need to be happy, and grow your business just enough to get you there.

---

▶ What fundamental skill do many entry-level marketers lack?

---

Who cares? I never worry about what you don't have, but about what you do. Because I believe in betting on your strengths. Everyone is different, and everyone will bring a different set of skills to the table. If you're trying to get an entry-level position, you have to figure out what skills you have that will bring value to your employer, and then hone those skills to the best of your ability. If you get an interview, go in knowing who you are and spend all your time talking about how you can bring value to a brand, company, or department. Someone is going to see you've got what he or she needs.

▶ How can I converge my vision of being a YouTuber with my parents' vision of me getting a university degree?

Once you graduate, people will be interested to know what school you attended, but very few will ever, ever ask you to tell them your GPA. Do what you must to make sure you meet all the requirements to graduate and focus the rest of your time on building your brand, so that once you've got that diploma in hand, you'll feel good knowing your parents can sleep at night, and you'll have laid the groundwork to becoming a YouTube sensation.

BOOK WINNER!

KEVIN ASP
President of InboundMed.com

▶ If you have a Plan B, does that mean you are setting yourself up for failure? Should you never have a Plan B because you should be confident in your Plan A?

I believe in having a hard-core Plan A alongside a deeply practical Plan B. You'd be crazy not to at least consider what you would do should your entrepreneurial venture fall apart. After all, you've got to eat. For most people, the solution would be something very ordinary like going back to school, taking a boring day job, or moving back in with your parents. And that's fine.

You shouldn't go into your Plan A with blind faith, but I wonder if sometimes the people who fall short of their dreams didn't take too much comfort in their Plan B. If I had to break down the energy I have and have witnessed in other successful people, I'd probably say we allocate something like 97 percent into our Plan A, and 3 percent into Plan B. A lot of people who want to play things safe probably invest their energy more 75/25, or even 50/50. And that's deadly. Forgive me for sounding kind of Zen, but if you're focusing that much on your backup plan, you're putting out too much failing energy.

What was my Plan B? I think in the back of my mind I knew I could always make a living buying stuff at garage sales and selling it on eBay.

Although, when I say the thought was in the back of my mind, I mean it was way back there, in the deep dark place where I dumped every Spanish verb I never learned. Because if I'm totally honest, I was always sure I'd win.

# CHAPTER 3
# EDUCATION

---

**IN THIS CHAPTER, WE'LL TALK ABOUT THE CLASS I'D LIKE TO TEACH, THE VALUE OF AN MBA, HOW TO GET A MENTOR, AND WHAT PROFESSORS CAN DO, IF ANYTHING, TO ENGAGE THEIR STUDENTS.**

---

The answers to the questions in this chapter might make you think that I'm not a fan of the current education system. You're going to think I don't see any value in it because I was a bad student, and there's probably some truth to that. It is deliciously ironic that I, an F student, have received invitations to speak at Harvard, Yale, and Stanford.

School was never my thing. That's an unusual thing for an immigrant to say, especially a Jewish immigrant. Traditionally education was my people's (and most people's) ticket out of the ghetto. But I sucked at it. We're not talking B's and C's with the occasional D popping up its ugly head. We're talking a long, remarkably consistent stream of D's and F's. There were just so many more interesting things to think about than the Pythagorean theorem or grammar, like the ton of cash I was making selling baseball cards. I just didn't have the patience or the interest to study what was in my books. I knew that wasn't where I was going to learn what I needed to know to succeed.

If only more people had the same self-awareness and self-confidence. As a forty-year-old man today who spends most of his time with successful entrepreneurs and professionals, I'm fascinated at how little parallel there can be between one's level of education and success in the modern business world. I would never be so naïve or misguided as to suggest that time spent in a top university can't help get you closer to financial success, and I know that diplomas are entry-level requirements for thousands of jobs. But I passionately, emphatically believe that the American university system has lost its value proposition in face of the speed and intensity of the current business marketplace. When you also factor in the unfair debt structure of college loans and how severely they can set young people back, I think it's time we really start having conversations about whether a college degree is appropriate for everyone.

It's a hard conversation to have because the American college dream has been so well branded. Even when kids know in their souls that they don't belong in school, parents can't let it go. Many grew up hearing that a college degree is necessary for any upward mobility or interesting career, and they are terrified their kids will find their options limited without those degrees in hand. They haven't yet recognized the massive changes that have occurred in the business place. You also have other scenarios where parents are at a total loss on how to guide their kid because he got a great-grandmother's entrepreneurial DNA instead of their own more traditionally inclined DNA. But what pisses me off is how often parents' self-esteem is unhealthily attached to the accomplishments of their kids. They force their kids into an inhospitable educational ecosystem and terrible debt just so they can get their hands on the right bumper sticker. That's despicable, and I hope anyone strug-

gling against this will read this chapter and th.
strike out on their own and follow their heart. I an.
entrepreneur but I have no interest in making either of th.
become one. If they choose to go a more traditional route, I'll support them. Truly, though, by the time my kids will be college-age,
the free education that will be available on the Internet will be incredible. My kids' generation may be the last generation that holds
university to such high esteem.

If you're lucky enough that you can afford to go to school just
to soak up the experience, network, or expand your horizons and
ideas, be my guest. But today you can go to an incubator to network and you can travel to expand your horizons. Why do you
have to incur debt—debt that you cannot even declare bankruptcy
against—to do those things? You might even be able to get paid to
do it! One thing is certain: College will not properly train you to be
a prime-time player in today's business environment and anything
you might learn there about marketing or social media is already on
its way to obsolescence. The entire market moves at such a speed
that even great entrepreneurs have a hard time keeping up. Within
a month of your graduation, there will always be a new platform, a
new app, a new channel for doing business that didn't exist before.
Nothing except hustle, prescience, good instincts, time, and patience is going to help you master them. And none of those things
can be taught anywhere except the School of Life.

▶ If you could create and teach your own college (or high school)
course, what would the name of the class be? How would you
teach it?

It would be called "Why You Shouldn't Have Signed Up for This
Course in the First Place," and it would explore the disconnect be-

tween school and the entrepreneurial world. It's one thing to learn from books and study history and write papers analyzing why one marketing campaign might have worked better for a brand than another. But being able to repeat what you've learned, and being able to actually apply that learning to the real world, are two totally different skills and I'm not sure your performance in any course can predict how well you'll do at the latter.

If I were to teach a course, the last thing I'd want is for my students to regurgitate my words. I can't tell you how many people I see repeating my hyperbole but not actually acting on my recommendations. They're automating, for Pete's sake! You know why that pisses me off? Is it because they're hurting themselves? No. If they're not going to hustle I can't control what happens to them. It's because they make me look bad. If you Regram one of my posts about hustling, anyone who sees it is going to presume that you hustle, too. But you're not. You're playing Call of Duty a few hours per day, watching *The Walking Dead*, and taking half-day Fridays. The outside world doesn't know that, though, so when people see you're getting nowhere, to them it will look like my advice doesn't actually work. Sometimes I'll confront people about this at a conference or through a direct message, and it's been fun for me to watch people admit they've been talking the talk but not walking the walk. It's nice to be vindicated, for sure, but more important, acknowledging their mistake usually gets them going again in the right direction.

You can't nod your head when I tell you to hustle and then not hustle. You can't retweet inspiring posts about good listening and then not engage. I can't believe how few of my followers write articles on Medium when it's the one platform that offers virality to people who have no audience. I'm there often and I have an audience. Why do I bother? Because it gives me a bigger audience! That's why I do everything I do.

You don't need a twelve-week course to digest my biggest piece of advice: *Don't be a student, be a practitioner.*

▶ I am a fourteen-year-old. I want to be an entrepreneur but I don't know where to start. What actions should I be taking as a kid?

Wanting to be an entrepreneur and being one are two different things. If I were you, I'd sell the shirt off your back to another kid. I'd find some rocks and sell them to a nine-year-old girl. The best way to become an entrepreneur is to behave like one. Entrepreneurs sell, so start a business or start selling things. If you're still not sure how to begin, find a young entrepreneur in your neighborhood who's doing something like what you'd want to do and ask if you can help. Learn the ropes. There's no reading about this stuff—only doing. Drop this book or Kindle right now, kid, and look around, pick something up, and post it on eBay . . . GO!

▶ I read *Think and Grow Rich* and it changed my life in a positive way. Have you read any books that influenced you?

No. I've written four books, one about wine, and three about business. When I have written my eighth, I will have written more books than I have read. A lot of people think that one of my weaknesses is that I don't read, and I waver between believing they're right or they're full of it. The truth is that I do read; I just don't read the things other people like to read. I read up on baseball cards before selling them. I memorized the wine trades and used what I learned to help me sell on the floor of Wine Library, even before I could drink. I read in short, easily digestible formats about what interests me and what's practical for me to know.

Actually, I've read two business books, if you call the biography of Steve Jobs by Walter Isaacson a business book; the other was by John Battelle, called *The Search*, about Google. And then another favorite was called *The Nine*, about the Supreme Court, by Jeffrey Toobin.

---

▶ What advice would you give a high school senior in America who is trying to decide whether or not to go to college, and which one?

---

Casey Neistat is a filmmaker who has done everything from Internet video storytelling, to ad work for companies like Nike, Mercedes-Benz, and J.Crew, to a film for the *New York Times*. When Casey and I did an episode together we got the chance to have a long discussion over the value of a university degree. I thought he had some really good things to say.

He answered (reprinted here with minor tweaks for length and clarity), "In life you should only be doing two things ever: discovering your passion and then realizing it. So if you know what you want to do and that trajectory doesn't necessitate a college education, then skip it. Chances are you don't know what you want to do or you wouldn't be asking this question. And if you don't, your responsibility is to figure it out. College is one of the best atmospheres and environments to be in to figure out your passion, purpose, and calling."

I agreed, but I pointed out that taking on $200K in debt to find your passion might not be the most practical choice. Today there are other places besides universities where people can congregate, learn, and find the mentors who will help them figure out their path in life without holding them hostage to debt for the first ten years of their career. In 2015, college is not always the answer.

Some of my contemporaries say that the university degree will meet its demise in about ten years, but I don't see it happening that fast. There are still too many kids going to college merely to avoid disappointing their parents. I have a kindergartner and I talk to a lot of the parents who send their children to her school. Their views on the importance of college haven't changed even though there is evidence all around us that a degree will not get their kids what a degree got them, or even their own parents. And they're still wrapping their own ego up in their children's accomplishments, so they will push the kids to aim for the Ivies because it will be proof of their good parenting. Until that changes, colleges will still be able to sucker young people and their families out of a tremendous amount of money for very little practical value in return.

Casey and I got lucky. We figured out our passion and we had the talent to make a career out of it. There are a lot of people who try the same thing and they suck at it. Just watch the auditions for *American Idol*, or the wannabe NBA players. So I asked Casey, what if you suck at your passion?

Casey answered by paraphrasing Anaïs Nin: "Anyone's life shrinks and expands on the proportion of your willingness to take risks and try new things." He goes on: "And that's why I think an academic environment is a great place to try new things and experiment. So if your passion is painting and you're a terrible painter, maybe spending time at university will open your eyes to graphic design, which doesn't require a paintbrush, and you can make a great living and still live out an artistic passion. Of course, college can be a huge waste of time and money if you go for the wrong reasons. Some other opportunities might be as practical as an academic education. What you can't count on is that going to college will get you something in return, especially success. One thing that is more and more true especially as tech opens new means of sharing and transmitting information is that there is no defined path. If there were a defined path to success, especially in creative endeavors, everyone would follow it. College can be a great way to find one of those paths, but it's not the only way, and it's certainly not a guarantee once you get there."

---

Jack and Suzy Welch had more to add to this conversation when I invited them onto the show for episode 89 to share their incredible wisdom and talk about their new book, *The Real-Life MBA*. They wrote it for people already in the workforce who might have gotten really good at one thing, but wished they could take a 360-degree view of their career. They might want to brush up on skills, learn new things, or reevaluate their options without giving up two years of their life and going into debt. We answered a number of questions from the Vayner Nation during this episode that appear throughout this book, but I had a couple of questions of my own that I wanted answered (reproduced here with minor tweaks for clarity):

**GV:** Do you believe a top 25 or 50 business school MBA is as valuable in the marketplace in 2015 as it was five, ten, or twenty years ago?

**JW:** Only the top ten. The value slides pretty quickly. With the top ten you've got McKinsey and Booz lined up waiting for you when you walk out the door. So if you attend a top ten school you're putting out a huge $300K investment, but the returns are pretty good.

**GV:** I'm spending a lot of time with those kids now, and many of them want to become start-up entrepreneurs. Do you believe the ROI of that $300K is equally good for them if they choose that path instead of the one that takes them to Bain or McKinsey? Should they go big salary and bonuses at Booz (and drive down their debt) or go out on their own?

**JW:** It depends on the quality of the idea. Entrepreneur is not a profession like a lawyer or doctor. What is your idea? What is the value proposition? Can you win?

▶ I feel as though online courses are usurping traditional education
in a big way. Do you see this happening, and is there money to be
made?

Yes, such as Skillshare, the Kahn Academy, and Chase Jarvis's
CreativeLive. When I'm trying to learn something I go to You-
Tube and look for a one-minute how-to video. Information is a
commodity and the Internet has given us the platform to learn
that way. I don't need a teacher, no matter how charismatic, to
tell me basic information. What matters, and where the experts
can offer value, is in opinions, interpretations, and context. Take
my show, for instance. My base information isn't always vastly
different from what you might hear elsewhere (though I'm im-
modest enough to think I might have introduced some of that
information and over time it has trickled down into the mainstream and become public domain). What matters and is far
more interesting is the context and examples I provide. No one
can re-create that.

The changes you're seeing today in the educational landscape
is nothing compared to the disruption you're going to see over the
next twenty years.

▶ What's the last new skill you learned as a result of taking an
interest in someone else's passion, hobby, or job?

Golf? My brother, AJ, fell in love with it, but as much as I like it I
can't commit to the five hours it takes to play, so that's the end of
that. Aside from that, I'd probably say respecting data. Weird answer, right? I believe in data because when Eric Kastner and John
Kassimatis started as Wine Library's developers they showed me

the other side of marketing—the data targeting and CRM (Customer Relationship Management system).

The power that data could deploy at the time was mind-blowing. It was the year 2000 and much of what we think of as the Internet wasn't common practice yet or even invented. Between Eric's and John's computer skills and my marketing skills, we created the foundation for WineLibrary.com, which massively helped grow our business.

---

▶ I'm a self-taught media marketer. Is it worth taking courses before applying for jobs?

---

There are too many variables for me to be able to judge whether it would benefit you to take a course. Are the courses good? Are you the type who can learn in an academic environment? Or do you learn better by doing? Social media and modern digital marketing is in an early awkward stage; the people teaching courses right now are the early players of 1995–2003 marketing, and quite frankly many of them are spewing a lot of crap. In five years, when a new generation of instructors with more advanced perspectives on how business should be done has taken over, I might feel a whole lot better about you taking that course. But even so, I'm worried that the modern Web-based business world will always move too fast for traditional education formats to keep up.

---

▶ Any tips on how to get a mentor?

---

I've never wanted a mentor. Even when I had one in my father I pushed against it. My dad used to joke that I wanted to be a Cabbage Patch Kid, born from nowhere, because I was so independent when it came to business. If you want a mentor, I think you have to go and get one. But you'll have to do more than just ask people to let you follow them around or learn from them. People are busy, and mentoring people properly takes time. Even the most generous, kindest person is going to think twice before taking on the responsibility of mentoring someone else, especially someone they don't know well. Which is why your first step shouldn't be to ask people to be your mentor. Your first step should be to show them that you could provide them with something of value. In other words, that they will benefit from having you around.

For example, David Rock (aka DRock) is known as the director, producer, and editor of *#AskGaryVee*. He's also one of the reasons the show exists. One day out of the blue he contacted me. And unlike many people, he didn't ask for a job, or an investment, or an introduction to someone else, or a motivational chat. Instead, he told me he wanted to make a long-form piece of content, and he wanted to make it about me. That became the five-minute film called "Clouds and Dirt." In other words, he asked for my time and energy, but he offered me something equally valuable in return. After that, he didn't have to ask me for a job. I saw the beautiful end result and knew I'd be crazy if I didn't hire him to do more. I wanted to have him around.

If you want someone to be your mentor, you have to make him or her feel the same way about you.

---

▶ What advice do you have for professors to engage college
students in the classroom? What about outside of class?

---

I'm going to say this as respectfully as I can: Today more than ever, many professors aren't relevant to their students. I get emails all the time from people actually listening to my podcast while sitting in class at major universities telling me that what their professor is saying up at the front makes no sense. "They're telling me there is no ROI in social media!" So your biggest challenge is to be relevant. If you're a professor, especially if you're teaching marketing or communications, and you're not jamming on Snapchat and the Insta, you're making a huge mistake. You're out of touch and a step behind your students. You have to know their world and speak their language in order to reach them. Maybe you want to roll your eyes at the bad grammar and the poor spelling and the addictive nature of social media, but your students are rolling their eyes at you, too. If you aren't factoring in how these tools are changing communication in our society and their disproportionate impact on your students lives, you aren't providing them the most value you can.

You can't be romantic about how things should be. To be effective and have an impact on your students, you have to join and even embrace the world that actually is.

▶ I'm ten years old. Which one of your books should I read first and when should I read it? I can't decide!

Start with *Jab, Jab, Jab, Right Hook*. In a lot of ways it's a modern execution of *Crush It*, though less inspirational. That said, *The Thank You Economy* is the one you should take the most to heart because it has the most long-term soul and depth to it. The others are heavily tactical, but *TYE* is the philosophy and the religion. You'll probably understand *JJJRH* better than many people in the Vayner Nation because you're growing up native to social media. You've never known any other way to communicate.

Oh, and I hope the young person who asked this question is reading right now. I want you to know you are epic! Ten years old and on it! I am impressed. For all of you reading this with young children, ten is a super age to really start focusing your business skills.

---

▶ Morale in public education is at an all-time low right now. How do we create a thank-you-economy culture despite government mandates, curricula that aren't effective today, no funding, and, most of all, high stress and pressure on teachers?

---

You can't. The machine is too big and broken. With all my charisma, and energy, and clout, I can't move Fortune 500 orgs into modern marketing, and you want to try to move the entire academic infrastructure? Not gonna happen. What you can do as an individual is what I'm doing with *The #AskGaryVee Show*. You can put out great content, use the platforms that can reach people, and teach. You might like the slide deck format and use SlideShare, or prefer video and use Khan Academy. Play in the white space. *Work around the system, not within it.*

You can't make a huge impact on anything by trying to fix it within the rules of the current game. Change always comes as a result of reexamining the infrastructure and creating so much pressure against the machine, it *has* to change.

# CHAPTER 4
# FAMILY BUSINESS

---

## IN THIS CHAPTER, I TALK ABOUT FAMILY, FORGIVENESS, FAIRNESS, AND THE BEST DECISION YOU'LL EVER MAKE.

---

I write books for many different reasons, including the financial incentive, the extra exposure it offers . . . and okay, yes, my ego. But one of my driving forces when I get an idea for a book is: Can this actually help somebody? Could it change the course of someone's life? *Crush It!* did that. Seven years after its publication, I still get hundreds of emails from people telling me how that book inspired them to follow their dreams. I hope this chapter could be that powerful for anyone in a family business or considering going into one.

I've run two family businesses, the first with my father and the second with my brother. They're as complicated as business gets. One of my favorite cautionary pieces of advice is that one of the best ways to go out of business is to make emotional decisions, to get romantic about how you make your money, or to let your emotions get in the way of the task at hand (see Chapter 10 on Facebook ads for an example of how emotions can hold people back and create openings for other, less emotional operators). I say that, and yet I know there is nothing more emotional than dealing with the conflicts that arise within family businesses. There isn't a week I don't get emails asking, "How can I get Dad to let me try something new?" Or, "How do I convince my mom to join the twenty-first century?" Believe me, I've been there and I feel you.

I try to tread lightly because every situation has its own dynamics and variables, but there is one thing I can say that I hope is universally helpful no matter what kind of situation you're in: If you and your family love each other more than you love the business, you will succeed. There's no question in my mind that that has been the bedrock of why it worked out so well for us. In addition, we've put a lot of hard work into the relationships themselves. I often wonder what my relationship with my dad and brother would look like if we weren't in businesses together. I know no other way of relating to my father, but there was a time when we were growing up that my brother and I had a more carefree dynamic than we do now that we're in the trenches together. At one point we had to start scheduling non-work-related meetings to rekindle our brotherly relationship away from the workplace.

Most people will advise families not to risk family harmony by going into business together. I totally disagree. I say if you have the opportunity, go in headfirst. I'm passionate about this topic and have spoken to a lot of people about it over the years, and even the five to seven dozen I've met whose foray into business caused their families to explode like atomic bombs—to the point where they weren't speaking to each other, sometimes for years—even they eventually admitted that they were grateful for the time they had gotten to spend day in and day out with those family members. For that reason, I feel comfortable telling you that if you're debating whether to take the leap, it's a good decision and you will not regret it.

I can honestly say that there's nothing I'm more grateful for in my professional life than the opportunity I've had to work with two of the people I love the most in the world. It hasn't always been easy. It has taken a ton of emotional equity and enormous amounts of empathy, self-awareness, and compassion. But it has also honed my communication skills in a way I can't even quantify. Who needs Stanford or Wharton when you've got a family business to school you? Despite the days I cried in my dad's office, despite the hard conversations I've had to have with my brother, I think I'm the luckiest man alive to have what I have with them.

▶ Will you force your children to partake in the business like your dad? Will you be disappointed if they don't want to?

From the very beginning, I was a crap student and a great salesman. My dad knew what he was doing when he dragged me into the store at the age of fourteen. That said, if I had hated it and told my parents it wasn't what I wanted to do with my life, they would not have forced me to stay. My brother, AJ, worked in the store for only one summer, because it was obvious to my parents it wasn't for him. Plus he was a great student.

My parents were all about giving me opportunities to bet on my strengths, and that's the kind of parent I hope to be, too. I want to put my kids in a position to succeed, and I think sometimes that will mean challenging them. They need to know success doesn't come easy. For example, when my son, Xander, was two and a half years old, he had a basketball net in the living room. I used to play with him, but then he started to cry every time I picked up the ball because he knew I was going to block him. That's right, I wouldn't let my toddler son score (not even one basket) at living room basketball. Because I want him to learn that anything he wants in life, *he's going to have to earn it.*

Maybe my kids will become powerful businesspeople. Maybe we'll go into business together. And maybe they'll turn out to be schlemiels who couldn't sell water in the desert. I won't care. Lizzie and I will love them unconditionally. All we'll ask is that whatever it is they choose to do, they give it all their heart and do it to the best of their abilities. If they decide their life's work is in saving the one-legged butterfly, then I will do whatever I can to help them do that. Our job isn't to prepare our children to live our dreams, but to live their own.

---

▶ How important is it for your significant other to share your entrepreneurial vision? What was Lizzie's impact on building your empire?

---

Growing up I would always roll my eyes when I'd hear the classic adage "Behind every great man is a great woman." It didn't make sense to me. I was on the front lines hustling my face off and doing great with no woman backing me up (except my mom, which is a totally different relationship). Who needed 'em?

Then I fell in love. I matured, I became a man, and I realized how wrong I was. I'm absolutely flabbergasted by Lizzie's impact on my career. Her support, her complete and utter 100,000 percent support, is what gives me the headspace I need to be all in and do my thing at VaynerMedia.

I don't mean to say that I wouldn't have been successful without her. Without a doubt I would have. But I'm sure I would have been an unhappier person, less healthy, and less fulfilled. She makes my life whole, which means I'm not spending any brainpower worrying about the stuff in my life that isn't great—it's all great. My personal happiness means that unless I'm with her and the kids, all of my energy can be devoted 100 percent to my businesses. And I can do that for enormous amounts of time every day because of Lizzie and the way she supports me.

It's absolutely crucial for entrepreneurs to have as much freedom to execute on their vision as possible. But sometimes when you're in a relationship or you have family obligations you can only give 70 percent of your time. Or 50 percent. That's totally fine. Success is not a game of absolutes. You can still win; it just might take you more time than you hoped. Regardless of your situation, building a business is without a doubt a huge time and energy commitment, and you and your spouse or partner need to be realistic about that. However you conduct your life and business, make sure you're both on the same page. Keep your communication lines strong and open.

That said, if you love someone he or she needs to take precedence over everything else. And that's okay; it just means your career may have to go at a different pace or take a different path, because otherwise there will always be friction between your two loves.

Having a supportive significant other is not the only thing you need to succeed as an entrepreneur, of course, but it will make the whole endeavor go a lot faster. And it's definitely a lot more fun.

---

▶ How did you deal with the specific challenges of working in a family business?

---

Carefully. Family businesses are difficult because of the emotions and history that inevitably come into play. Yet now I'm in my second one, and I hope to run one with my kids one day. I think the reason I've had a good experience working in family businesses is that my mom and dad taught us that our love for one another should always trump our pride and competitiveness. We fought a lot, especially over our vision for the business, but we never allowed ourselves to go to sleep really angry after a blowup. Somehow we always managed to settle our differences before the day was done.

In every family business, you have to create an environment where the family's love for each other matters more than anyone getting their way.

---

▶ Has any business challenge ever tested your relationship with AJ, and if so, how did you work through it?

---

I've struggled a lot less working with AJ than I ever did with my dad. Their personalities are different, and my role in the business was different. I started off as No. 2 at Wine Library, but at VaynerMedia I'm No. 1. AJ is very good at telling things like it is and not backing down. When he was nine and I was twenty we started an eBay business together. It originally started at 70/30, but then one day he came to me and told me the split would have to be 50/50 because he believed the work he was putting in was worth half even though I'd put up all the money and had taught him the game. And when we started VaynerMedia, even though I was already in the market and had all the leverage, and a lot of the business was built on my personal brand, we decided that again it was important that we go in 50/50 to start the business out on the right foot.

We've disagreed, of course. He was absolutely convinced that we couldn't ask clients for a fourth of the retainer fee we get paid now. I enjoyed proving him wrong on that. And I'm sure if he were writing this book he could include a few stories where he proved me wrong. But overall, we are perfect partners. He's the straight man to my magic, but beneath the quiet surface there's an extraordinary maturity and self-awareness that serves him very well. Plus he's got his own brand of magic that brings tremendous value to our company. Six years into this venture, and we've never had a massive blowout.

Here's the thing to remember if you're going into business with a family member you love: Be the bigger man or woman. It always works. No matter what the disagreement, no matter how heated the fight, make sure to say "I love you." Those words are what keeps family businesses alive.

---

▶ What do you think AJ has learned from you in business?

---

I let AJ answer this one and was touched by his response. What struck me is that the lessons he's taken away from working with me are exactly the same lessons I try to teach all of our employees and everyone in the Vayner Nation. Say what you will about me, I'm consistent.

So what did AJ say he had learned?

1. Keep things in perspective. In the course of building a business fast there's a lot that gets thrown at you, some good, some bad. You have to keep the highs from taking you too high and the lows from dragging you too low.
2. Focus on what's important and on the big picture, and don't stress out over the rest.
3. Personalize your interaction with your employees. Some companies stick close to the HR book to protect themselves and make processes faster and more efficient, but we don't use a cookie-cutter system. Every situation is unique and calls for a different approach. By treating people with respect and recognizing their individual achievements and skills, we've built a strong, loyal team that really brings its best to the office every day.

▶ If your kids want to join the family business, will you start them at the bottom?

Well, by the time the kids are old enough to join the family business there's a good chance the family business will be the New York Jets.

Regardless, I guarantee they will start at rock bottom if they haven't had a chance to go out and live a little first, and if they have, then I'll put them in the place that will benefit most from their education or skill set, just like I'd do for any other hire. More important, I won't let them ascend to be No. 1 unless they deserve to ascend to No. 1. That's something I've been firm about at VaynerMedia. We have friends and family in both businesses, and they're all playing at different levels. No one gets put in a power position unless they've earned it.

Who knows, maybe I'm underestimating how much my enormous love for my kids will color my objectivity and judgment when it comes to deciding what they're qualified to do, but I'd like to think my huge respect for American meritocracy and capitalism will override my paternal feelings. In addition, when you are building an organization the people who grow it with you become family. By the time my kids are ready to be in the business there could be fifty people who have been working here with me for twentyfive years, and at that point my love for them will be extreme. Not as extreme as the love I feel for my kids, of course, but damn close. If my kids come on board, they will have to respect that and deal with it.

▶ I'm in sales for a third-generation residential construction company and getting my "at bat." How do I increase business but keep old minds happy?

I was extremely fortunate because my dad gave me plenty of room when I was at Wine Library to try out new things and test ideas. And since those ideas allowed me to make a huge and immediate impact, I had a lot of "air cover" to do my thing. So I never lived this problem. But I feel like I'm living it now at VaynerMedia. I'm working with clients who are strongly grounded in the old ways of B2B. They can be so skeptical, so hesitant. And I've found that when dealing with these kinds of people, you have to get a little real, even a little harsh. I have no problem telling them aggressively and with conviction that clinging to romantic notions and tradition is the quickest way to go out of business.

You're going to have to do your version of the same thing. Too many young people in your position spend all their energy trying to make their dads and grandpas and great-grandpas happy, tiptoeing around them and trying not to piss them off. But how can the business adapt to the new year and the new era when everyone is still doing what their grandpa or grandma did? For your business to stay relevant, you have to change. You don't have a choice.

But old minds are tough to move. You're probably going to have to try several angles to see which one will get them to accept your new ideas. Some might respond well to kindness and sugar; others will only hear you if you go extremely rogue and aggressive. You might need to be stunningly compassionate or massively disrespectful. Try every option until something works. You really don't have any other choice.

I get it. No one wants to ruin Thanksgiving forever. And it would be a real blow if Grandpa fired you. But remember, you don't need to be rude, or yell or fight. You do, however, have to be blunt and stand your ground. Bring backup. See if you can get anyone else in the business on your side before making your final stand. Bring incontrovertible evidence. Your grandpa or dad may still dig in his heels, but if he's a good businessman—and you have to assume he is to have kept things going this long—he'll give your idea a second look.

Most important, should Grandpa back down and give you the keys to run this show, you'd better execute. Oh man, you'd better execute. Because if you don't you will be forever in his eyes the naïve kid in the family.

If you want to move mountains, you've got to come with thunder.

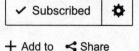
# CHAPTER 5
# PARENTING

---

**IN THIS CHAPTER I TALK ABOUT BUILDING
CONFIDENCE IN KIDS AND COLLEAGUES, WHY I
DON'T CARE IF YOU'RE RICH OR POOR, AND WHY
PARENTS SHOULDN'T BE AFRAID OF SOCIAL
MEDIA.**

---

Parenting, like family business, is an intensely personal topic. How we parent depends so much on things that are unique to us, from our financial situation to our partners to our family dynamics. So I'm petrified to give parenting advice, and yet I can't shy away from it because I feel so strongly that the way we are parented affects everything we do in life, including what kind of entrepreneur we might become.

I often say that I was perfectly parented. I truly believe that the way I was raised has everything to do with how I achieved my success. I know how it feels to be the kid who marches to his own drum, and I'm incredibly fortunate that I was born to parents who not only let me, but also encouraged me to do more of it. I observed how they instilled in me qualities that make me the man as well as the businessman I am today, and I'm passionate about their execution and would love to see it replicated everywhere. I feel like I have something valuable to say to anyone raising a potential entrepreneur or interested in helping shape and guide the next generation of industry leaders.

You should only take the advice of entrepreneurs or businesspeople who have actually built businesses, not people who have just talked about it. So the best people to turn to for parenting advice are probably people who have seen a few more cycles than I have, with grown kids. However, I work with a lot of young people who tell me their stories, and I know the pressures and concerns they and their parents have had as they started their entrepreneurial journeys. I've spoken to a lot of parents about what I do and the world I do it in. I have a perspective that could ease a lot of people's concerns about what the future holds for our kids. I realize it's all just one man's point of view, but from where I'm sitting, it's all looking good.

---

▶ What's the number-one lesson you've learned since becoming a father?

---

I feel like I've been practicing to be a father my whole life. Believe it or not, I am filled with nurturing DNA. My brother, AJ, is eleven years younger than I am, so when I was nineteen he was only eight. My dad was old-school and worked all the time, so I had a lot of chances to be there for my brother in a way that most big brothers might not get very often.

I suspect I'm closer to my parents and siblings than most people are to theirs, so I can't say that fatherhood taught me the meaning of unconditional love. Which is why I'm so utterly stunned at the depth of my feelings for my two kids. Their pain literally is my pain. The other day Misha told me that someone at school called her a chatterbox and it hurt her feelings. She's so much like me. My first-grade music teacher called me a motormouth, so I knew how she felt. But it was crazy how hard it was for me to see her so sad, and we haven't even come close to the zits zone or bullying zone or awkward-teen zone.

I guess the lesson I've learned is that the love we feel for our kids really is something bigger and more powerful than anything in the world. And that DNA is no joke.

---

▶ How exactly did your mother instill that self-confidence in you?

---

I was born with some, but she brainwashed me into thinking that the ordinary things I was doing right were extraordinary. Like, down to getting a good haircut and picking up a ball. For real. I believed her, so when I went out on my own to take on the world, I did it fearlessly.

How did she keep me from turning into a spoiled, self-centered brat? Because when I did something wrong, she treated that as an extraordinary thing, too. Except instead of loading me with praise, my mom would drill me with her look, her words, and the occasional "umph." Anyone raised in the old-school European way knows what I'm talking about.

I intend to pass the same can-do encouragement I received from my mother to my daughter. Right now I tell her that her twirl is the best goddamn twirl I've ever seen, and I'll spend the rest of my life applauding her efforts. I'll do the same for my little man, Xander, who gets praised for the silliest feats. And I'll do the same for my employees. I know the people I work with every day feel better about themselves than they did before they knew me. We'll hire new senior staff and after a few days they'll tell me they're flabbergasted by the confidence of the youngsters working here. That's by design. Pumping everyone full of confidence makes for a more creative, risk-taking environment. I don't do it by praising my staff daily. Rather, I instill it in my leaders and encourage them to let it trickle down.

---

▶ *Shark Tank*'s Barbara Corcoran doesn't invest in "rich kids'" businesses. How do you feel about entrepreneurs from privilege?

---

For a long time I held the same prejudices about rich kids as a lot of people do, that is, I assumed that because of their wealth they're not hungry and they've been handed their successes. But I've come to realize that it's not always true. I have plenty of good friends who grew up wealthy but are hungry and fiery and make things happen. So in the end, whether I'm deciding whether to invest in you or hire you, I'm not going to care if you were born rich. I only care if you were raised lazy.

Everything trickles from the top. That's why when I'm considering investing in people who come from a super-privileged background, I spend a lot of time trying to find out more about how they were raised. Did their parents spoil them or did they make them work for what they wanted? Did they teach them the value of having money? Did they talk to them about how money factors into our country's discussions about class, education, and politics, or how the goods we take for granted are often considered luxuries in other parts of the world? Those are the things that tell me whether it will be a good idea to invest in their business. Because if they were raised right there's a good chance they have a strong work ethic, and that they will apply what they learned at home to their own businesses, thus setting a proper tone and creating a robust culture. And those are the kinds of businesses I think will give me the best ROI.

There's nothing wrong with being born rich, or being rich at all, unless you act like being rich matters in the grand scheme of things, like it somehow makes you better or more deserving than the rest of the world. I'm grateful for the perspective my humble beginnings have given me. My kids are being raised in a completely different environment, but if they act like "bad rich kids" I will humble them and make them cry. If they grow up soft and spoiled, that will be on me. But they won't. They will know what it means to work and sweat to get what they want, because Lizzie and I are committed to making sure of it.

---

▶ I'm curious to know your thoughts on tech consumption by young children.

---

If you were to tell a caveman what modern-day humans would be like, he'd have been horrified. But that's evolution. Our kids will be different from us, and that's not bad.

We've got to stop acting as though tech is an intruder in our children's lives. Tech *is* their lives. Worrying that tech will rob them of the pleasures of childhood is akin to previous generations worrying their kids will be soft because they have indoor plumbing, or that rock and roll will make them degenerates, or that their brains will rot from too much TV. Every generation fears for the next one, but we don't have to. Our kids will be less informationally smart but they will be interesting characters and they will do great things.

But if you believe that tech should have a limited place in your child's life, have at it. Here's the great thing about being a parent: You can do whatever you want. If you don't want your kids watching a lot of videos on YouTube, limit their use of the iPad. If you want to set up a rule that electronics are shut off after 8 P.M., go for it. If you think it's best to institute a policy of one half hour of sports or exercise or outdoor time for every half hour of screen time, that's your prerogative. Your kids, your house, your rules. I'm not restricting my kids' screen time, because I believe in preparing them for the world they're going to live in. I suspect the kids that do grow up with severe restrictions will go bananas once they're let loose on their own and have a hard time learning to discipline themselves. I think mine won't think unlimited time for games or texting is anything unusual, and will therefore have learned to balance their time well.

---

▶ In the future, how are you going to treat social media with your children?

---

It's hard to find pictures of Lizzie on the Internet and there are even fewer of the kids. I'm well aware of the dark side to social media, and that kids need to be taught to use it wisely and well. Like every parent who loves his children, I want to protect them from bullying and teasing or getting exposed to things too early. It's a risk that's compounded by the fact that I'm raising my children in Manhattan, where kids grow up fast and seven-year-olds act like seventeen-year-olds.

I'm a counterpuncher; I react to what I see. It's too soon to tell where social media will be by the time my children are ready to participate in it, so there's really no way I can predict what kinds of limitations or rules, if any, we will need to put into place one day. In the meantime, my wife and I have spent a lot of time on mission statements and being clear they understand our expectations of them. I can't control how the outside world evolves, but the core pillars of good parenting haven't changed since the beginning of time. I believe in old-school values, so I'm working to instill good core fundamentals, like good manners and strong self-esteem. Those two things will serve my kids well whether they're communicating and socializing online or off. If my kids start posting videos one day, my hope is they'll be comfortable enough in their own skins that they won't care how their hair looks or whether the lighting is quite right. They'll just be who they are and expect the world to love them for it.

---

▶ I'm speaking to parents at a public school event on parenting in a social media world. What would you teach them?

---

Parents always get really upset with me because they feel I'm propagating a medium that's distracting their kids and dulling their brains. Meanwhile, many of them are the same parents that immediately throw an iPad at their kid the minute he cries or gets bored at a restaurant. I'm not the problem, people.

I like to tell parents that it has never been a better time to be a parent because all the social networking tools will allow us to spy on our teenagers like never before. Fearing tech and limiting their children's time on it is not preparing them to live in the future. I would tell the parents at your event to stop playing defense and start playing offense and get pumped about all the opportunities and new discoveries coming this way for the new generation.

# CHAPTER 6
# HUSTLE

## IN THIS CHAPTER I TALK ABOUT THE VALUE OF KEEPING YOUR MOUTH SHUT, MY FORMULA FOR GOOD HEALTH, AND HOW TO MAKE TIME WHEN YOU DON'T HAVE ANY LEFT.

Here's a question that no one has yet asked me: What is the one tangible thing people can do to change the direction of their lives?

Hustle.

Anyone who follows sports, and especially drafts, knows that a less gifted competitor can outplay even the most naturally talented athlete if that competitor has more hustle. Similarly, it's hustle, not talent, that is the differentiator between entrepreneurs who succeed and those who don't. I have never seen anyone increase his or her natural talent, but I have seen people transform themselves by increasing their hustle. Of course, if you're born with a healthy dose of it woven into your DNA, you've got a terrific advantage. But the great thing about hustle is that if you're not born with it, you can get it. It's the most tangible, most easy-to-get entrepreneurial quality because you're in complete control of it. If you're not self-aware, you're somewhat dependent on other people being honest enough that you become cognizant of your strengths and weaknesses. I'm not even sure it's possible to teach yourself to be more intuitive. But if you want to turn up the hustle, you just have to spend more time doing whatever it is that takes you where you want to go. You just have to be willing to do more than the competition. And you have to do it every single day. It's like career calisthenics, something people can directly apply to their work lives and see results. It doesn't guarantee you will succeed—plenty of hardworking people don't—but it will guarantee that you won't ever torture yourself with thoughts of "Should've, would've, could've." Because you'll know without a doubt that you put your heart and soul and sweat all in.

I'm self-aware enough to know I have a lot of talent, but it's my work ethic—my hustle—that has been a substantial backbone to my success. I will outwork anyone. How about you? You can be a phenomenal content creator, but if you lack passion or a willingness to sweat there is someone else out there who is going to make more opportunities for herself and more money than you. Don't let that happen. Put down Clash of Clans. Binge-watch *Game of Thrones* or *Walking Dead* next year. And get to work.

---

▶ How do you define hustle?

---

It's maximizing the energy you put into what you are passionate about.

It's squeezing every last bit of juice out of your day.

It's putting all your effort into achieving the goal at hand.

It's making every minute count. Every. Single. Minute.

I wish I could have hustled like I do now in the early days of my career. When I was twenty-six, no one, not me, not society, certainly not the wine world, was into email yet. I left around 7:30 or 8:30 P.M. and the store closed at 9 P.M. I had time to play Monopoly on GameCube. I lived in an apartment with a girlfriend and my best friend lived above me. I didn't go out to meetings. I lived in New Jersey and didn't have that New York City hustle down yet.

Since then I've made up for lost time. It's become clear to me that it's much better to be a businessperson than an athlete because as a businessperson you have plenty of time to hit your prime. My hustle today is at an all-time high because it can be. Some people complain about living in a world that makes it possible to work at such intense levels, but every entrepreneur worth his or her salt is grateful as hell for the possibilities tech and the Internet offer us to keep hustling when everyone else is chilling. For some, their willingness to hustle more than the other guy or gal is their greatest competitive advantage.

A lot of new entrepreneurs tell me they're hustling, and then they'll ask me if I liked the last episode of *Ballers*. They're trying to get a business off the ground and they've got time to watch TV? It's like wanting to lose weight and sneaking away to scarf down a Big Mac. It's just not going to work. I'm twenty years into my career with two businesses under my belt and the only time I take to watch TV is when the Jets are on. There is so much hustle in my day I don't even have a second to spare to "hang out" and catch up with the people around me when I'm at work. It may not be ideal for most, but I love it because it allows me to get the things done that I seek to accomplish.

You want to increase engagement around your content? Raise revenue? Gain brand awareness? Become an influencer? Sell more? Then try the following:

**Pounce on every opportunity.**
**Create great content and get it out there.**
**Work toward gaining exposure.**

**Keep an eye open to new environments and conversations.**
**Increase the value you can offer others.**
**Biz dev.**
**Wake up before everybody else and work into the night.**
**Hustle until there's not a single drop of juice left.**

---

▶ Is hustle something that can be taught?

---

I don't know if it can be taught so much as it can be inspired.

Everyone has individual work ethics that affect their job performance, and ultimately, their success in life. This isn't to say that unsuccessful people don't have strong work ethics; any number of things in life can happen to make someone's life turn out the way it does. But while we all start out with a baseline work ethic, how much we choose to push ourselves is fundamentally affected by whom we're working for.

If you work for yourself, it should be really easy to give yourself that high-grade hustle since you're pumped to be running your own show and doing what you love. If you work for someone else, your attitude and effort are likely going to depend on how inspired you are by your leader. That's why I try so hard to instill a strong sense of trust and safety (as well as very high standards) in our company culture, so that the people that work for me feel inspired to go all-in and deliver. No one wants to let a good leader down. And in a strong merit-based workplace, they'll also strive to take advantage of the opportunity to grow and rise through the ranks.

Look at your level of hustle and evaluate it. Ask yourself, Am I working as hard as I could? Am I doing great work? If you work for yourself and the answer is no, think long and hard about the business you have started or the consulting work you're doing. Is it a good fit? Are you playing to your strengths? Would you be more motivated and feel more confident if you worked with a partner? If you're working for someone else, and you feel like you're not living up to your potential, please consider finding a new place to work. If you want to succeed, you've got to surround yourself with the right kind of people. Go where you are motivated to take risks. Be with people who allow you to make your best work. Your DNA matters, but make sure your circumstances are allowing you to win.

---

▶ What's your number one piece of advice for marketing a lean, local, city-based social start-up? It's still undeveloped.

---

I hated this question. The only reason I answered it was that the query came from someone who tweeted he wouldn't eat unless I did. Obviously getting some feedback meant a lot to this person. My scornful response probably wasn't what he was going for, though. I mean, really? The product wasn't even developed yet and he was worrying about marketing? The thing is, I know he's not the only one. So let me just say this: STOP it. You cannot properly market something if you don't even know whether it's any good. You've got to develop it, feel it, taste it, put it out in the wild, and reverse-engineer it so you know it's serviceable and valuable to consumers.

Now, once you have a product, there could be tons of things you could do to promote a local business—Facebook ads, tweets, geolocation, mobile ads, Google AdWords—the options are tremendous. And who knows, you might not need to pull out all the stops. After all, great products don't need that much marketing. Marketing, however, won't fix a crap product or app or service.

▶ What is your advice for small business owners with limited budgets? Local listings, SEO, writing content, social media?

I loved this question as much as I hated the last one. And here's the answer: Work more. Whatever it is you're doing, add a few more hours of hustle. It's the greatest way to shore up the gap between you and a bigger competitor. I promise you Goliath will never work as hard as you.

This is an issue I had to grapple with myself when I started working in my father's business, Wine Library. I didn't have the base that I have now, of course. No one gave a crap about us. So I went out and pounded the pavement, walking into any business that might be relevant to my community and passing out flyers and coupons one by one to gain more exposure. And then we made sure to have such amazing customer service when people walked in the door that they couldn't wait to return.

What could a start-up do today to get that kind of exposure? The answer is going to be different depending on your business. If you're e-commerce, Facebook ads for sure—it has one of the best ROI going right now. Google AdWords is a strong contender and banner retargeting would work well for you, too. If you're trying to drive retail into a store, start spending time on Yelp and Foursquare's Swarm, and yes, local TV and radio. Maybe it would be worth your while to go to the barber and ask if you can put a flyer in the window. Make cold calls. Network. Bizdev. Barter with local businesses. Attend Chamber of Commerce events. Get creative! Fight, attack, talk, ask friends for help . . . This is your life!

▶ What would you do if you were starting over and trying to get the
name GaryVee out there today?

I would do exactly what I did back then—*I'd keep my mouth shut.*

Go ahead and google it. You won't find a single piece of content
from me that predates *WLTV.* For the first eight years of my career,
1998–2006, from the time I was twenty-two to the time I was
thirty, I did nothing to build the Gary Vaynerchuk brand.

So what was I doing?

I was *working.* I was learning, practicing, questioning, research-
ing, and experimenting. I was building the expertise and experience that would allow me to position myself as an authority, not
just in the wine world but in the business world as well. Today
I can say I built two $50 million businesses in five-year periods,
and showed a talent for investing in companies early and making
a lot of money. I can rattle off an educated answer to almost any
question about wine or Internet business you can throw at me. You
think I came by all that knowledge overnight? I got in the trenches
and lived my business and did the work that allowed me to build
the Gary Vaynerchuk brand. I created reasons for people to think I
was worth paying attention to and even worth spending money on
to hear me speak at events or read my books.

I'm stunned at how many people think you can just hop onto
YouTube and build a personal brand without actually having anything to show for it. You have to know something in order to be a
brand. You want to be sought after as an expert? What have you
done to make people want to hear you speak? Have you accomplished anything? Have you proven yourself in any way?

No? Then shut up and get to work.

People have tried to argue with me that you don't have to be a
practitioner to have something valuable to contribute on a subject.
For example, they'll point to football coaches who never played pro

ball as proof that you don't have to be a great player to be a great coach. And to that I say: seriously? Have you studied these football coaches' backgrounds? Ignoring the fact that coaching is an entirely different skill set from playing, no football coach comes out of nowhere at twenty-three and wins Super Bowls. They've been ball boys since they were seven. They're the sons and daughters of coaches. They've lived and breathed their sport their whole lives.

Don't ever think you can hack expertise and branding by relying on social media and modern tech. There is no substitute for honest hard work. You have to execute and accomplish something before earning the privilege of being a personal brand.

---

▶ When you have a billion-dollar potential business plan without financial resources and inventory, where do you start with funding?

---

I don't think you should. Not yet anyway. You know why?

Because ideas are shit without execution.

Do you know how many emails I receive from people swearing they have a billion-dollar idea? Everybody's got ideas. Hell, I have unlimited ideas.

There are people out there who might finance a venture based on ideas alone. It's happened. But in general, those ideas don't go anywhere because that's all they were—ideas. This is why so many businesses are starting to fail in the tech space, and I am sure by the time you are reading this book many more tech companies funded in 2010–14 will be done and finished. Passion is great and creativity is awesome, but practicality matters more than the current business world values. You've got to put the work in before approaching anyone for financial backing. That's what all the entrepreneurs we look up to did. They didn't pat themselves on the back just for having a great idea. They hustled and made it come to life first. They made sure their idea actually did what they believed it could.

---

▶ Do you respond to posts, tweets, and messages yourself, or do you get your staff to do it?

---

The thing I might be most proud of is that every tweet I've ever sent out has come from my two fingers. I can't write for shit so I collaborate with a professional writer on my books, and Steve and India usually massage my blog posts and articles, adding sprinkles and turning them into English based on answers from my show or interviews, or interviewing me for them. But all the base material you'll ever read or hear is mine, and if I ever talk to you on Twitter, Instagram, or Facebook, it's really me.

---

▶ Do you work seven days a week?

---

Early on in my relationship with my wife (I think it was the second date), I told her that if time went on and I still didn't have my New York Jets, I was going to be working harder and be a lot busier than I already was. Lucky for me, she married me anyway. But believe me, I never take her understanding and acceptance for granted. Today I'm typically and happily consumed with work Monday through Friday, and my calendar is fully booked from 6 A.M. to 11 P.M. But once I'm home on Friday night, that's it. I turn everything off for the weekend and devote my time to my wife and kids.

That's my version of work-life balance. Will it always be? No. Lizzie and I are constantly talking about what's working and what isn't, and I'm aware that as the children get older there are going to be days when I have to run to the school at 5 P.M. to watch a recital or go to a baseball or football practice (you know which one I'd prefer). You have to adjust as life evolves.

I think a lot of people make the mistake of assuming that if you believe in hustle, you can't ever take a step back. That's too narrow a definition. Hustle means adjusting to business opportunities as they come and adjusting to life as it changes. If your north star is family, then there's no shame in revolving your hustle around that. It's about quality versus quantity, being fully engaged while you're working, not necessarily working every day of the week. Instead of 365 days of complete insanity, you can have 265 days of really hard work with 100 days of rest and rejuvenation. Hustle is not just working obnoxiously hard—it's also working obnoxiously smart.

And when I rest, boy, do I rest. I couldn't care less about traveling the world when I'm on vacation—I just want to lie on a beach in peace. So now you know that if you bump into me on the street or at a function, by all means come by and say hi, but if you happen to catch me on the beach with my eyes closed, don't bother me. I'm resting.

---

▶ How do you avoid procrastination so well?

---

I would be an obnoxious procrastinator if I weren't so busy and I have no choice but to get as much done in every minute as I can. What some people might call procrastinating I call reprioritizing. I'm in constant audit mode adjusting to real life all the time. Something might be super-important one day only to get demoted the next when I open my inbox in the morning. Trying to keep track of what's most important and when can drive my assistant crazy. He'll have worked out a whole schedule for me based on what I told him was most important to me and by the end of one three-hour flight he'll get an email from me adding another fifteen things that force him to completely dismantle it. Apparently he has figured out that if I tell him something is "tippy top" that's the thing to put ahead of everything else.

You might think that means that I'm only half paying attention to everything, but you'd be wrong. I live in the moment, and my pants are on fire for whatever it is I'm paying attention to at that time. As long as you're treating something every day as a tippy-top item and executing on it, you're moving the needle.

---

▶ Are you a morning person?

---

I am not. Believe it or not I make it a point to get six to seven hours of sleep per night, and I sleep like a brick. It takes a lot to wake me up. I mean *a lot*. I'm rising with a little more energy since I started working out and eating right, but there was a time when someone could have broken into my home, stabbed me in the leg with a knife, and stolen everything I own and I wouldn't have noticed until the next morning.

The thing is, though, I've never really understood why it would be an advantage to be a morning person, or why morning is valued more than other parts of the day. If you do your best work first thing in the morning, great. But some people work best at 3 A.M., 5 P.M., or 10 P.M. There is no right time to hustle, as long as you *are* hustling.

You don't want to exhaust yourself, or collapse, or make yourself crazy. Just work as hard as you can when you are working, and rest when it's time. Because guess what? *It's not about how much you sleep. It's what you do while you're awake.*

▶ How do you deal with burnout?

It doesn't happen to me very often that I decide I want to check out and bury my head under the covers. I think the last time was when the state of Texas singled out Wine Library and restricted our shipping while allowing many other stores to ship. We lost about $4 million in revenue. I think the day I realized we'd lost that fight I went to sleep at 6 P.M.

If I'm feeling burned out or stressed by work, it means that I'm focusing too much on business instead of the big picture. So when I feel myself start to get that way, I just try to imagine how it would feel if my mom died (I know it's dark but it's the truth). That's all it takes to put the whole world back into perspective and move on.

So in a nutshell, my solution to burnout is rest and recalibration.

▶ What are your practical #HustleHacks when it comes to diet, sleep, and your daily routine? How do you maintain energy and brainpower while hustling nonstop?

The reason I can hustle the way I do is that I love it. I love taking my pouting selfies and traveling at 6 A.M. to a random airport. The day I answered this question on the show I woke up at 5:15 to play basketball after getting back into town at midnight because I love it. If I'd been waking up to meet Muscle Mike, my trainer, to work out I'd have probably been grumpier. Passion is an unmatched fuel. Add being happy to that and you have a wonderful formula for good health.

▶ You've said you watch us fans of the show and can tell if people
are hustling. How? Engagement, frequency, or gut?

Mark my words, if you tell me you're hustling, I will go to your
Instagram or Twitter account and take a look at your work. I will
click the posts and hit the profile where it says "view all with re-
plies," and I'll study the engagement rates. I love it when I see one
engagement after another with just some retweets. Then I'll hit the
URL on the account. I'll figure out what the business is and then
analyze the profiles and the pictures. I usually see too many people
in the right-hook business, but boy does it make me smile when I
see people jabbing the shit out of things. Then I'll worry. Are they
doing the right mix? Are there too few right hooks? Are they being
responsive enough? I can spend ten minutes on this, which in my
world is insanity. I've got unanswered emails because I'm spending
time on your Twitter accounts. But I believe in karma, and I believe
that the reason I can give you the answers you need is that I know
you better than you think I do.

▶ We spend so much time pouring our creativity into projects for
our clients that when it's time to shift gears and focus on our
own brand, we're exhausted. How do you keep the fire burning for
both?

You need to work harder and faster.

Working harder is easy. Drop the hour you're watching *Scan-
dal* and voila, you've got more time to hustle. Working faster,
however, is a little trickier. It takes practice. Train yourself to do
a little bit more in each hour than you normally would. Maybe
you save checking your emails until lunch. Maybe you turn off

your phone. Maybe you work odd hours. Every day add something more and get it all done. The first few days you may not finish what you started out to do, but keep challenging yourself and you'll get there. It's like training for a marathon. It takes time, but once you've been at this for a while you'll see that you can accomplish much more in one day than you ever thought you could.

Don't kid yourself. Most people say they're working a full eight hours a day, but very few really are. When someone tells me they've got no more time to give, I'll go through their Twitter and check them out. Usually I'll find fifteen minutes here and there where they watched a YouTube video, or took a quiz about God knows what. And you're probably thinking, So what? We're not machines. Aren't we allowed to goof off for just a few minutes? Sure. But then don't complain that you're not getting everything done.

I do not have one spare second during the workday. My team fights for minutes on my calendar. Even seconds. It's basically an inside joke at this point.

I used to think I was the biggest workaholic who ever lived. When I was twenty-two to about thirty, I really thought I was all in. But I wasn't, because I had enough time to bullshit about baseball with friends. I actually had free time. It wasn't until I started working more hours and dramatically faster that my career really started to explode. It's the context of those first eight years of my career that gives me the audacity you see in this chapter. I just know the difference between what hard work looked like then, and what running a business and investing in and closely monitoring 150-plus companies looks like now. You have the time if you are good at making it.

So that's the answer to keeping that fire burning when you're balancing your own stuff with your clients'. Work hard and work fast. Be the machine.

▶ I'd love to hear more on *how* to hustle faster!

Take short meetings. Stop focusing on dumb shit. Don't be afraid to break things. Don't be romantic. Don't take the time to breathe. Don't aim for perfect.

And whatever you do, keep moving. Reread this a few times . . .

▶ Do you ever get sick, and if so, how do you still hustle through it?

The old me got sick sometimes, but since I married LizzieVee eleven years ago I think I've only been ill once. She deserves a big shout-out for getting me to wash my hands. Honestly, I think for some people like me it's a question of mind over matter. I mean, I take more than one hundred flights per year. You'd think a bug would eventually get me. But it hasn't, and I think a large part of the reason why is that the brain is a powerful organ, and I am so focused and so determined not to get sick, that I just don't. It helps, too, that I've started exercising and eating right, but that's such a recent event I really do think I outwilled many colds.

But let's say I did get sick. Would I drag my sorry ass into the office, possibly infecting all my colleagues because I'm afraid of what will happen if I'm not there? Absolutely not. And I don't want anyone else coming in when they're sick, either. When the #vayner-plague hits us (search Twitter, it's a real thing) I want people to stay home, take care of themselves, and get better. In some businesses there's a real stigma around staying home when you're sick, like it means you're weak or unmotivated. (I have to admit early in my career I saw it that way, but I have evolved.) Coming in when you're sick doesn't show dedication, it's selfish. And kind of gross. And not fun for your coworkers or for you.

That doesn't mean I want my sick employees working from home if they feel like they're dying, either. You get on a call with them and they can't get their point across because they're coughing up a lung. How is that helpful to anyone?

When you're hustling, hustle with all you've got. When you're sick, stop. Let it happen. Your body is trying to tell you something. Listen to it. The work isn't going anywhere, and you can make up for lost time. Get better so that when you can come back to work, you come back with fire.

---

▶ What's the biggest "but" you hear from others that holds them back? What is your "but" and how do you get off of it?

---

Oh my God, the excuses. When you start a sentence with "I want to . . ." then end up with "but" midway through, you're making an excuse. You can probably guess a few of the most common. You may have even used one or two in your life: "I didn't have any money," "I didn't have a chance," "I grew up in a poor neighborhood," "I didn't have a mentor." People are loaded with "buts"; that's why the majority of people live pretty ordinary lives. *But* is not a word to use when you talk about your aspirations. If you are serious about reaching your dreams, nothing will get in the way.

I'm not saying that obstacles to success don't exist. You could be born under a dictatorship or other repressive regime. A female entrepreneur in the Middle East objectively does not have as much of a chance of succeeding as a woman in New York City. And any white male born in a semi-affluent environment is bound to have a leg up on minorities in poor communities. Adversity, discrimination, sexism—it's all real. And for many, certain prejudices, injustices, and strokes of plain bad luck are serious enough to deter them from pressing forward. But then there's another group, a smaller group, who when faced with these challenges choose to reject them and forge ahead anyway. If anything, coming from less or from behind can be a huge advantage because you will never, ever assume anything will come to you easily. That breeds a lot of courage and perseverance. A lot of people born to privilege just don't have the hustle because they never needed it.

Don't ever let your circumstances determine your outcome. You are bigger and better than that. You can always control your own destiny. Use what you've got, find what you don't, and make your dreams come true.

What's my "but"? I want to buy the New York Jets, but I love the climb and think about my legacy so much I sometimes leave money on the table that I'll probably need to accomplish that dream. You know one "but" you won't hear from me, however? The one that shifts the blame for anything that goes wrong at VaynerMedia away from me. I'll never make excuses. I love taking that blame, because once I do we can work toward coming up with solutions instead of talking endlessly about the problem. Stop saying "but" and you'll be forced to move forward; there will be nothing standing in your way anymore.

---

▶ Is it possible to hustle the way you do anywhere outside the United States?

---

I thought this question was ludicrous. Entrepreneurialism is glorified in this country and the environment supports it, but you're out of your mind if you think the country where you're born makes or breaks your ability to build a business and thrive. My parents were raised in the Soviet Union and steeped in communism from the day they were born, and it only increased their hustle and drive. *Your success is not predicated on your zip code.* You may have a harder road to travel than you would if you lived in the United States, but entrepreneurial success stories come out of every corner of the globe.

---

▶ Isn't working long hours an old-school mind-set? Why not focus on building wealth via passive income?

---

Why not do both? I do. I make a lot of money investing in early-stage start-ups that can sell for one hundred times their original valuation. I didn't do anything, and yet some years I probably make more in passive income than hustle income. So, yes, you could focus on building wealth through passive income, but I assure you that it's not nearly as easy as it seems. Of all the people who have tried to create systems and automate their cash, there has been a very, very small percentage who wound up taking early retirement and lounging on the beach while they collected money from the Internet. The few people who can actually live luxuriously off their passive income put in a boatload of hard work and time getting to the point where they could earn it.

I think there are almost zero people in the world who have earned substantial success without working hard at it. Of course, you might do just fine if your goal is to earn $60K. But those people lying on the beach smoking weed in Jamaica after earning millions of dollars in passive income by doing practically nothing? I don't believe they exist. Show me one, and I'll show you someone who's making his or her money by selling you on the dream of that lifestyle.

---

▶ What athlete, past or present, embodies hustle for you?

---

Wayne Chrebet, the absolute bottom-rung guy on the wide receiver depth chart when he joined the Jets as a walk-on during a practice in 1995. The only reason he got there is that his dad pulled together some VHS tapes and sent them to the head coach. The Jets sucked bad in those years so the coach was willing to take anyone. Not much was expected of Wayne—he's a short white dude who until he joined the Jets had an unimpressive record—and yet his number was just retired last year. He showed huge tenacity, defying his critics and playing through massive concussions. I respect him enormously.

---

▶ How do I get a job working for you?

---

I'm always flattered by this question, but the answer is kind of blunt.

Do something first.

Show me your value. DRock did it when he cold-called me three times and convinced me to let him create the video that became "Clouds and Dirt." Kevin Rose, the founder of Digg, wanted to invest in Square, and CEO Jack Dorsey wouldn't let him, so Kevin made a video explaining the product and offering his insights around Square. After it had received around a hundred thousand views, Jack noticed, and suddenly realized that, what do you know, he could make a little room for Kevin's investment. Now Square is worth billions. Kevin got in on it because he showed Jack what he could do.

What can you do?

---

▶ How do you balance speed/hustle with patience?

---

I bridge the two. Look, I know that I often say things that contradict each other, but that's usually because both statements are true. Like these two: Speed and hustle are massively important. So is patience.

A lot of people pride themselves on being fast and impatient; I see them as the bad version of me. They do everything for their own gain. They're takers. But I think impatient and fast leads to mistakes, causing people to rush outcomes and leave money on the table.

You can be both fast and patient and win. I'm massively patient for the long game, but I'm fast in the real-time world of execution. The two traits can produce some friction for sure, but that's how pearls are formed.

▶ How can you claim "family first" but work nineteen hours a day? How can you be a good dad/hubby and rarely be home?

I get asked versions of this question a lot, and it stems from the way I choose to storytell my life. I play to the extremes. I'm 1,000 percent in while I'm at work, and I'm 1,000 percent in while I'm at home. I go to the kindergarten plays and the other school events that mean something to my children. I take seven weeks of vacation, which is probably five more weeks than most people. I don't play golf or really have any hobbies that take me away from home on the weekends. Plenty of my friends bust my chops and say they spend more time with their family than I do, but when I've audited a few for sport I've been interested to find out how much of that time is spent playing video games, on the phone, or just doing their own thing. Just because you are physically at home doesn't mean you are "home."

In other words, just as I make sure that every minute counts at work, I make sure that every minute counts at home. And as the kids grow older and they need me more, my schedule might change. I may someday have to commit to being home every night by 5:30. I'll admit it might be hard for me, but I'll get over it. There are plenty of other hours in the day when my children don't need me when I can get shit done.

Some people make their kids a part of their ventures, blogging about their lives together or using their pictures and time together as fodder for content. That's fine for them. I would never presume to tell someone else how to raise his or her family. My wife and I have decided that our kids are not part of my business life, which means I can't talk much about my life at home. But I feel great about the time we spend together, and they seem pretty happy, too. The bottom line? Effort!

# CHAPTER 7
# CONTENT AND CONTEXT

---

IN THIS CHAPTER I TALK ABOUT THINKING

LIKE A SUPERMARKET, THE TRUTH ABOUT

AUTOMATING, BUILDING TRUST ON TWITTER,

AND BARTERING YOUR WAY TO THE NEXT BIG

LEVEL.

---

People buy with their hearts, not their heads, and the way to every consumer's heart is through a good story.

The Greeks recited their stories, the medieval bards sang theirs, and then the printing press dominated for more than five hundred years. Less than a century ago we started putting a lot of stories on radio and television. Today we tweet and blog and Vine. But even as the platforms and distribution channels change, the rules of good storytelling have remained the same for businesses since the beginning of commerce: The quality of a brand's storytelling is directly proportional to the quality of its content. If it's not good, no one will pay attention.

What defines quality content nowadays?

**It appeals to the heart.**
**It's shareable.**
**It's native to the platform on which it appears.**
**It breaks through the noise.**

I find that last one ironic. Not very long ago it was only big brands that had the muscle to blast their story all over the radio, newspapers, magazines, and TV. Today's marketer, however, doesn't have to invest in a printing press, or a satellite, or buy expensive advertising. You don't even necessarily need a sales team in order to distribute your story anymore. You're so lucky to have access to the Internet and be able to use its tools to put out your content. Unfortunately, everyone else has them, too. That low bar to entry means that the field is ridiculously crowded, and it's getting harder and harder to get noticed.

Which is why it's so vitally important that everyone from big organizations to solopreneurs to small companies start thinking and acting like media companies. Sure, you're selling liquor, or tech, or original art, but the very survival of your company will depend on distributing your story through your content as often as possible to as many people as possible. And not just any content, but content that brings value to your current customers while attracting new customers as well. Netflix gets it. That's why they started making their own TV series. So does Starbucks, which is developing original documentaries that tie into themes relevant to the socially conscious brand. Red Bull, too, is producing original videos, articles, and news covering sports, lifestyle, and culture. If you're not putting out good content on a regular basis, you will be drowned out by all the companies who are. You will be Blockbuster video. You will be Borders. You will be the carriage driver who bought a lot of horses just as the first Model T drove off the lot.

This advice goes for individuals, too. Like it or not, unless you're living completely off the grid you've got an online identity, and everyone, from dates to schools to employers, will rely on the Internet to see what they can learn about you before ever meeting you. It's in your best interest to shape what they see. If you're not producing content, you don't exist.

It takes far more time than money, so for a while you may have to allocate your time differently than you might have been taught back in b-school. Staffing, strategizing, and selling are all important, but if you must, take a few hours away from those operations every day and put that time toward creating content. That's how you scale the unscalable.

You don't have to have a billion dollars like Starbucks or Red Bull to become your own media company. All you have to do is put the time in and be aware of emerging social networks. That's how I got my start. I didn't have millions of dollars to get Wine Library's story out there. I distributed my content on these weird new platforms called Twitter and Facebook and YouTube. They were free and easy to use, and no one else there was doing what I was doing, which meant my content got noticed. Now you've got Instagram and Snapchat, Medium and Meerkat, and many, many more. Mold your content so it feels native to these platforms and creates context, scratching the emotional itch that drew your consumer to the platform in the first place. Meanwhile, keep your eyes open to the new up-and-comers. Take advantage of the platforms no one is using yet. Make them work for you. People and brands are using content and context to become stars on them every day.

---

▶ Can anyone create good micro-content? How can you make sure your team consistently creates good content?

---

Of course anyone can create good content. It's all about having respect.

First, respect the platforms. A forty-year-old woman is looking for something different on Facebook than on Pinterest. On the
former she's keeping up with her friends and family, and on the
latter she's probably shopping, doing research, collecting ideas, and
searching for inspiration. So you have to strategize around that and
adapt your storytelling accordingly. On Pinterest, you'd create gorgeous photographs or supercool infographics she might want to add
to her board, but on Facebook, you'd write a zingy, funny status
update or a short article about something in the cultural zeitgeist
that she might be compelled to like or even share. Medium and
LinkedIn have a similar intellectual vibe and sometimes share their
audience, but even then if you have the time it's great if you can add
something unique to each piece you post. Feel free to repurpose
material across platforms, including what you post on your blog—
just don't make it look or feel like recycled material. Content is
never one-size-fits-all.

Second, respect your audience. That means putting out content the forty-year-old woman would like, not the content you
would like. In other words, not the right hooks you're itching
to throw to get this forty-year-old woman to buy your product
or service. At least, not at first. And not often. If I want to sell
wine, I can get much closer to my consumer with content that
intrigues and amuses like "Five Bottles Under $10 That Help You
Get Through the Day When You Have 8-Year-Old Kids," than
with "Five Reasons My Wine Is the Best!" By putting out content my audience wants to read or see or watch, I'm drawing her
in, gaining her trust, and making my brand a destination. That's
going to be a lot more valuable in the long run than a forgettable
one-off sales pitch.

Good content should rarely be about what you want. Instead
think about what your audience wants, and give them lots and lots
of it.

Now, the second part of this question is interesting. What if you're no longer directly responsible for making your company's content? What if you've grown enough where you have to trust your team to do it for you?

That's a tough one. You've brought your brand or business to success by infusing it with your essence and your spirit, and now somehow you have to teach others to basically be you. I think it's done through osmosis. Start at the very beginning, when you hire your first employee. Hire people who want to learn, and stick close to them. Talk to them, allow them to be a part of your thinking, involve them in the process. You basically want to pour your point of view, ideas, and values into the water of your organization, and give your team lots of chances to drink. If they've properly absorbed the essence of your brand, and they know how to respect platforms and consumers, they should start creating exactly the kind of content you would on your own.

---

▶ If you owned a hockey team, what would you do with Snapchat?

---

I'd recognize that Snapchat skews young and puts out content that kids ages 13–35 care about. I'd draw on the pictures, run contests, and come up with ideas that really engage that demographic and make them believe that I hear them and am grateful for their attention. I wouldn't even bother to try to reach my 40–60-year-old season ticket holders, because they're not there yet, though by 2018 my feeling is they will be. Snapchat is a gold mine of opportunity for any team that wants to create real relationships and build loyalty with its young fans.

DR. THIAGO MORAES

FOUNDER OF GALLOPER AND VACOVET

tmequine.com

▶ What are your thoughts about the new TLD extensions market? We've seen some new extensions sold for good money, like dui.attorney. Is this going to take off as people expect? Is this something that VaynerMedia would bet on?

The new TLD (top-level domains) extension game is really intriguing to me. I think it will basically play out along the lines of supply and demand. The fact is that .com addresses have enormous value because back in the early days of the Internet, .com was really the only market (along with .net and .org). So if you wanted to own the word *car*, or *wine*, or *tennis*, .com became the one place where you could really do that for real. There was only one cars.com, and thousands of people competed for it. As the new TLDs become more accepted by the market, the value of .com domains will crash. I think they're opening Pandora's box, which will make this interesting to watch. On the other hand, I've also got a hunch that people are lazy. It's tough to teach people new behaviors, so it's safe to assume that .com domains will retain most of their value for quite some time.

▶ Everyone visiting my site will be there for custom music. Should I delay them with content?

Your question itself reveals your problem. You want to delay people with content? That's messed up. It means your strategy is to find value that suits you, not content that brings your customers any value. The last thing people want is to be delayed. They do, however, want to be intrigued. So give them something that will make them glad they stopped for an extra ten seconds or four minutes. Maybe post behind-the-scenes videos of you composing your music, or a short blurb of you greeting people and sharing your thoughts for the day. Make it personal, and make it one of the reasons people come to your site. Few people come to the bar just because there's a dartboard, but it sure makes the place a lot more fun.

If you are trying to sell ads and trying to encourage viewers to spend more time on your site so that you can leverage that to advertisers, you have to do it organically, not by making it hard for consumers to get what they came for. Think like a supermarket. Supermarkets know you came for essentials so they put the milk and eggs far away from the entrance so that you have to travel the whole store to get what you came for. Along the way they try to show you endcaps and displays of items to raise your bill, but they don't block the milk from you or make you go downstairs.

▶ What's the best way to grow a following or community from nothing?

Put out quality content every day and engage around it.

It really is that simple and that difficult. No one becomes a sensation by accident. The talent to put out content is only one piece of the equation. One percent of the magic. One percent of people who make it big in social media might do it on content creation talent alone, but the rest of us have to work our butts off to bring our community in to see what we're creating. You can have a terrific idea for a YouTube show, but if you don't get that content out you'll have nothing around which to build your community. And if you don't put in the work to engage, rarely will anyone see your content. The two almost always work together, especially in the beginning.

It's hard to put out content every day, and even harder when you've got high standards. But you've got to try. Eventually scale can take over and pure momentum kicks in and you can ride the wave of all that work, but that work really never ends if you want the amazing upside of fame, money, or accolades. Whether you're putting out pictures on Pinterest, drawings on Snapchat, photos on Instagram, a video, or a written blog, you need to focus on getting as close to that daily goal as possible. BuzzFeed puts out a ton of content all day, every day, ranging on a variety of topics. Seth Godin, on the other hand, puts out his best effort once a day. Either scenario will work so long as the content is high quality. If you can't keep that up, six days is better than five, five is better than four, and four is better than three. And if you can only come up with enough ideas or energy to put out content once or twice a week, well then, that's what it is, though it limits your chances for the exposure you'll need to play this game.

Give people something to look forward to. Keep yourself on your audience's radar. Create context by responding to comments and otherwise engaging people so they know who you are, that you're paying attention, and that you care. Give them every possible opportunity to share your name with someone who doesn't know you yet and to become part of the conversation. Work hard *and* smart. There's no reason you can't do both.

▶ The company I'm working for has a great story but we're not getting the engagement we hoped we would. Is it worthwhile to promote our Facebook posts, tweets, and LinkedIn posts in order to gain more engagement from our social posts?

Easy: yes. Promoting posts is almost always a good investment if you can afford to target properly. I could go into detail about how to use Twitter and Facebook ads here, but you can find that information in Chapters 9 and 10. Instead, let me ask you a question:

Are you sure your content is as good as you think it is?

Remember, you need to put out content your audience likes, not what you like. There's an easy way to know if your content is valuable: Look at the raw engagement numbers. How many people are sharing? How many people are leaving comments? How many views are your videos getting? If you are provoking a reaction in the people consuming your content, and they're taking time out of their day to share it, that's great news. Pay attention.

Then, look at the big picture. How many people are actually buying? How many books did you sell because you provided free content? On what days do sales spike? Always keep track of what is going out when, and how that affects traffic to your retail site or app.

Let's say your engagement numbers aren't what you'd like them to be, but you're utterly confident your content's quality and subject are hitting the right notes. Is it possible the problem is with your actual storytelling? Is it contextually appropriate for the platform? Are you using the right hashtags? Are you linking properly? Is your content the right length? Are your logos all in the right spots? There are certain storytelling details unique to every platform whose presence or lack thereof can make or break a piece of content. Are you hitting every one of them every time? (If you need a refresher, I discuss each one in detail in *Jab, Jab, Jab, Right Hook*.)

This is why content and engagement can rarely stand alone. The quality of one almost always affects the reach and effectiveness of the other.

---

▶ What's better for content, blogging or vlogging?

---

What are you good at? You can crush anything if you're good at it. I'm not a great writer, but boy can I make a terrific video. So I focus on making videos, and then I delegate the transcription of those videos to someone else to make sure people who like to read their content get what they need.

Since I've started *The #AskGaryVee Show* I've spent a lot of time looking at other videos and have been asked by many to take a look at their version of my show. Many are below average at best. Making compelling videos is clearly not these people's strength. Many of them would do better communicating their ideas through illustrations or cartoons, articles, or podcasts. They need to focus on their strengths, find some other outlet for their content, and put everything they have into it. I bet they'd see an incredible increase in their engagement and reach.

---

▶ I have 39K Instagram followers and I average about 250 likes per photo. I also run the Instagram account for the company I work for, and we have 6K followers and also get 250 likes per photo. What am I doing wrong on my personal account?

---

Logically, two accounts with such vastly different totals of followers should not be getting the same number of likes per photo. When this happens, it's because your company brand is more beloved to its community than you are to yours. We can't know why people like or follow someone else on Instagram, or anywhere else for that matter. Maybe they think you're someone else. Maybe they liked one picture you posted, got bored by the rest, and forgot about you. Very few people actively go back into their accounts and delete the people or brands in whom they've lost interest, because it's not really worth the trouble, and Facebook's algorithms make it so that they can't see what they don't engage with regularly. I think this is a practice that other platforms might replicate in the future.

So how do we restore these followers' interest in you? Look at what you post for yourself and what you post for your company. What's the difference? This particular question came from someone storytelling on Instagram. Instagram is a place where human emotion reigns. The photos on the company site were filled with people; the individual account was filled with pictures of buildings and tunnels. They were good pictures, but they weren't what people on Instagram generally respond to. There was no mix, and there needed to be.

The same analysis needs to be done on any platform where you run more than one account where one is performing well and the other isn't. Try to incorporate what's working in one into the other and see if that helps.

---

▶ Should I post articles on my blog and just mention them on social, or post natively on sites like LinkedIn, Facebook, and Medium? Or both?

---

Most people try to tell new marketers that they need to own their content and keep it on their own site so they can monetize it, usually with low-paying ads. The problem is that when you're only posting on your own site you're at the mercy of the traffic that goes there. For most people that's not a huge number, or at least it's not as many visitors as they'd like. But if you post content on sites where the potential for virality isn't dependent on your popularity but on the quality of your content, you can gain a lot of followers. I have a lot of reach and fans but I still love Medium, because when I post something and I can see that 1,950 people have read it, I'm relatively confident that often as many as 700 have never heard of me before. That's 700 people who now know my name, who might go to my site, or hit me up on Twitter or Facebook, or might share my content on their own sites. And when something like that happens to someone with only 400 followers, it can have an even bigger impact on his or her brand or business. In short, don't worry so much about owning and monetizing your content, especially early on. Get it out whatever way you can, and worry about monetizing the results later.

---

▶ What do you think of the recent Omnicom advice to move 25 percent of ad budgets to online video and the space in general?

---

Online video is at the top of the dog pile when it comes to content, so I'm all for moving traditional media dollars toward it. But I see a lot of people misplacing the money and misplaying that move. If you tell people to spend only 25 percent of their ad budget on online video, they tend to think they only need to spend 15–20 percent of that on the video *production*. The quality. The very stuff itself. That means 80–85 percent allocated for distribution. So the dollars aren't being spent on improving the quality of the video, just on getting more video reach. And the same thing goes for content and distribution as goes for content and engagement—to get the results you want, they have to work together. Allocating more money to online video isn't going to do you any good if the bulk of your money is spent on pounding out hard-core right hooks that nobody likes. To most marketers, online video means pre-rolls on YouTube—the ones that consumers immediately tab out of or ignore while checking their cell phone for the fifteen seconds it plays, and don't actually consume. Or a pop-up video—the kind that takes up thirty seconds of people's time before it allows them to read the article they came for. *You know, horribly intrusive and annoying crap, the stuff that steals time, one of our precious assets.* So when I hear marketers being told to allocate their budgets to online video, I hear them being advised to spend more on stuff that no one wants, which is pointless, and therefore very bad advice.

What would be good advice?

Move 25 percent of your ad budget to creating *really great online videos that bring value to your customer.*

If you're not making a good video, who cares if you distribute it to a million people? Make interesting and engaging content that speaks to the people you are trying to sell to. Figure out the most native ways to distribute it on multiple platforms (including and especially Facebook ads and Snapchat and more and more).

---

▶ Short or long videos? What's the value?

---

Quality trumps everything. Back in 2007, Yahoo and Google separately flew me out to California to figure out why my thirty-minute *Wine Library TV* was doing so well, even though all their research told them that people preferred short online videos. Eight years later many marketing gurus are still spewing that videos have to be short or else no one will watch them. But that's just not true.

I like short and long, so long as it's good. *Avatar* was a three-plus-hour movie. People loved it and sat through it. There are six-second Vines out there that people won't watch to the end. Length has nothing to do with quality or value; it's all about your message and what you do within the constraints of the platform you want to use.

---

▶ How do new and small channels gain a following when people don't engage?

---

During the early days of *Wine Library TV* the only people watching were my mom and a few friends. But the quality of the program was really good and I hustled, so the show broke out. That's all you can do: put out great content, engage with your tiny audience, and go out and try to get exposure for your content by collaborating or getting press or guest posting on someone else's platform. If you're watching *The #AskGaryVee Show* today it may seem like perhaps I'm not engaging with my audience with quite the 24/7 mentality I tell others to, and it's true the engagement is not where *WLTV* was. But still, every day and after every episode is posted I spend thirty to ninety minutes reading and engaging with my audience, and not a day goes by that I don't see four to five comments of appreciation. At this point I'm capitalizing on ten years of a well-executed engagement around my content. Hopefully one day you will be able to do the same.

There's one more thing you might do if you're struggling to get fans: Ask yourself if you have enough business development chops. If you really think you have unique content that's just not tapping into the right audience or gaining visibility (a romantic notion at worst, an audacious one at best), then maybe you need to partner up with someone who can do "biz dev" better than you. It's worth a shot, because the alternative is that you're delusional and your stuff is really just average.

▶ Gary, what would you say to the current pro athlete, retired athlete, or even an up-and-coming athlete who is getting scholarship offers, who wants to brand themselves? Should an athlete have an official website? If businesses are now considered media companies, should athletes be thinking along these same lines?

Yes.

The day an athlete retires, he or she is dramatically less valuable than the day before. It's been incredible to watch over the past few years how dramatic the depreciation is for an athlete upon retirement, even MVPs and Hall of Famers. So it's imperative to stay in front of your audience at every stage in your athletic career, whether by creating content or just having a destination for your POV. For example, Derek Jeter just wrote his thoughts on Yogi Berra's passing on his own site, *The Player's Tribune*. I think content is important because it leads to other revenue streams available to retired players, like public appearances, speaking engagements, and other opportunities.

For a younger player, it could mean the difference between getting scouted by an NCAA Division 1 school and a Division 2 school because some recruiter might have discovered you based on a video shared out of you making an incredible catch. The days of sending VHS tapes to every school are over. Now you're putting content out on the Internet in the hopes of being discovered in the same way everything else gets discovered.

Finally, it's a tremendous hedge against mainstream media. Players are often misquoted, or their statements are taken out of context. With their own platforms, both on social and on a website, they have a chance to stay on the offense. These kinds of platforms are an extremely healthy way for athletes to keep the media at bay in a world where the media is only interested in selling itself and producing headlines that aren't real stories.

A site and a personal brand are tremendously important in every stage of an athlete's career—pre, during, and post—and bring massive value in allowing players to communicate on their own terms.

---

▶ You say to put quality content out daily. Can I add curated content, and if so, what's the mix?

---

I can pat myself on the back for putting out a tremendous amount of original content, but at the same time one of my biggest weaknesses is my lack of curated content. I should do it more, like Guy Kawasaki. Have you seen how many pieces of curated content he puts out? Hundreds! I'd like to, because it's a smart tactic, but I have the same problem with curating content as I do with offering quotes for books: If I'm going to do it, I have to read it first. And while I make time for many, many things that are important to me, reading isn't one of them. But if I added curated content to my original material, it would bring me even more exposure and create more opportunity. Curating is like DJ'ing the world's content and spinning it in your voice. In a world where context is everything, it's an enormous skill.

Platforms are recognizing that content is more valuable when people are allowed to add their context to it and are building the tools to allow them to do it easily. One of the reasons I invested in Tumblr was that it encouraged reblogging. And I love the potential of Twitter's quote retweet that gives you 250 characters to work with. Your thoughts and opinions about George Clooney's wedding or Apple have real value when you can contextualize it to your audience's world, whether it's music, restaurants, yoga, or pumpkin farming.

---

▶ I work in two different spaces. How do I use social media
 platforms so that I'm not confusing my audience?

---

There are a couple of ways you can handle this. Let's say you're talking business and wine. One strategy, which is probably the easier of the two, is to create two separate accounts on every platform—two profiles on Twitter, two pages on Facebook, two different boards on Pinterest, and so on—dedicated to their respective topic. The other, harder option is to become a Renaissance person, and become so branded in both topics that everyone knows they can come to you for one or the other and get equally good information or entertainment. But even if you do that, you'll still need to target specific audiences with promoted content and Facebook ads to make sure that the right people are seeing what you want them to see. You have to adjust to each platform to ensure your storytelling is always giving your audience what it wants.

---

▶ Is there a way to drive traffic to a website when posting content
 directly to Facebook?

---

Facebook is content awareness gold. Post a link to an article or video and if your post earns enough likes, shares, and comments, you can just step back and allow the awareness to grow organically. But if you want things to move a little faster, or you want to hedge your bets, you can actively drive a crapload of views with Facebook ads. It's absolutely worth the investment.

---

▶ Should I wait until my website is 100 percent built before putting out content or put out content while I'm still building it?

---

Tommy Mottola, the ex-president of Sony, once told me privately that he never let any of his artists go on TV until he was ready to sell something. His thinking was that it would be a wasted opportunity if a fan saw the artist perform and, inspired, ran to the store to buy the CD only to find out it wasn't coming out for another week. In that context it made sense to wait. But what's your objective? To sell, right? If the only place you can get your goal accomplished, whether it's selling a product or getting people to sign up for something or do something, is on your website, then obviously you need to finish the website. But how often is that the case nowadays? How often are we really limited to our sites to do business?

When VaynerMedia was in its early days, our website was garbage by most people's standards. We didn't mention the work we were doing or make any reference to our clients. We looked like we were going out of business. I did that on purpose. We were a new agency, and I was David. And when you're David, you don't play Goliath's game. I needed to make sure that the bigger agencies didn't know how big we were actually getting. This can be an enormously helpful strategy when you're new to the field and you want to stay beneath your competitors' radar. You get creative with your content, curating, adding context, and putting out original pieces that don't necessarily talk about your business but do establish you as an authority and a place for people to convene on a topic.

If you can achieve your business objective outside the website, do it, because not only are you executing, you're also telling your story, which builds up leverage and equity that you can use later to drive people to your website if you want to. Don't ever waste time or opportunity. Sell against the impressions you're getting in social. If you can make your money or do the thing you want to do natively on a platform, do it there. And you know what? Do it there even when your website is 100 percent complete. Use every channel you've got.

---

▶ Should I avoid doing podcasts or videos if I have a foreign accent?

---

I might be a little biased because all of my relatives have Russian accents, so when I hear one it makes me feel comfortable and at home. Are there certain Americans who think accents reflect untrustworthiness and inferiority? Yup. There are idiots everywhere. But there are many, many more people for whom accents don't matter at all. Obviously, because many of the most successful entrepreneurs in this country do have accents. Have you ever heard Sergey Brin speak?

You're never going to please everyone. I don't have an accent but a lot of people don't like the way I speak, either—too much cursing, arrogance, and bravado. But there are pros and cons to everything. What alienates me from one person is probably the very thing that draws someone else with a different sensibility to me. If you think you can skillfully communicate through a video or audio podcast, invest in it and the market will come to you if you're good at it. If you're not, don't do it, because they won't come and it won't be because of your accent. Try it for 180 days and see what happens. See what does and doesn't work (be honest!), adjust, and then decide whether it's worth the effort to continue down this path or try another.

> ▶ If you're not from an English-speaking country, should you produce content in English to reach a higher number of people, or should you produce content in the native language of your country?

Simple: You should be speaking in the language of the people you want to reach. So if you're trying to reach consumers who speak your native tongue, that's what you should use. The only exception might be if English is a second language in your country and 80 or 90 percent of its inhabitants are comfortable with it, too. If English has a bigger stake in the overall market you want to reach, use it exclusively.

That said, maybe you want to reach your native language speakers *and* English speakers. On Facebook you can, so long as you plan your distribution ahead of time by using the targeting capabilities that allow you to segment your audience and decide where your content will go by language and region. You can't target so easily on the other platforms, but some people get around that creatively. I have a former client that used Spanglish on Twitter and Pinterest. It works for them. Why couldn't it work for you?

> ▶ I am growing my business and looking to include partners for content. What's the best way to recruit them? Money? The promise of exposure?

You have to know what will motivate the people you're trying to connect with. If you have a big enough platform to create exposure, people will do it for free. Why do you think DRock offered to make a video for me pro bono? Because he knew it would be good for his exposure. Some experiences have more long-term worth than money. The reason I'm willing to accept other people's free work and hustle is that I know that by giving them a shout-out I can help them. That's what I was thinking when I agreed to let DRock film "Clouds and Dirt"; I figured I'd get a cool video and he'd get something good for his portfolio. It felt like an even trade. But then when I saw the extent of DRock's talent, I realized that he was actually bringing me something way more valuable than a five-minute video. He could amp up my entire video content production. So I swooped in, and this show exists because he could provide the infrastructure.

Tailor your approach to each potential partner by offering him or her the thing they value most. Maybe it's money. Maybe it's your Rolodex. Maybe it's exposure. Study up and make no assumptions.

---

▶ How much time do you spend creating a single piece of content? Do you focus on video because it's more natural for you?

---

I'm a talker, so video has always been my best channel for communicating my thoughts and ideas. It wasn't always easy. I used to have to walk around with a Flip cam and follow this whole convoluted process to get my videos online. Now when I use Twitter's video product, for example, I can work straight through the Twitter app. So technically it's much easier for me to create my video content than it ever has been, and it takes me very little time. If you're seeing more written content from me now, it's because I have a team in place to help me adapt the videos into interesting written pieces.

I don't ever stress over what I'm going to say in a video or how it's going to look. Whatever happens happens. We're living in a culture where fourteen-year-old girls are taking forty minutes to take a picture because they keep futzing with the lighting, and then if the picture doesn't get enough likes they take it down. I couldn't care less about lighting or the angles; I know I'm pretty. What I do care about is substance, and that's where all my effort goes.

> ▶ You've talked before about "recycling" a tweet, but what about other content such as a blog post? How often do you pull a piece from the archives to dust it off and republish?

I haven't recycled a lot, though it's something I might consider doing more now that I have a team to help me adapt pieces of content. In fact, they are constantly on the lookout for nuggets from *The #AskGaryVee Show* that can be turned into articles, infographics, animated GIFs, and short movies. I do think it's valuable for people to look back on their own content (though I admit I rarely do it). It can be interesting to revisit your position and put out a 2.0 version of a piece that resonated well with your audience.

What might be more valuable to you than recycling an old piece, however, would be to focus on putting out content across multiple platforms in a very jab-jab-jab-right-hook way. At the time I was writing this book I had started repurposing more and more across different platforms with tweaks to titles and pictures and I was seeing the value.

> ▶ I spend ten to fifteen hours on image posts I make for my company on social media. They are hand-drawn lettering posts as well as computer drawn. I get way more likes on my hand-drawn posts than the computer-drawn ones. But lettering takes a long time to do, and I don't think I can keep up a daily social media content output. What should I do?

I suspect a lot of artists have had similar dilemmas. Quality and artistic integrity is imperative, but you can't let yourself get paralyzed by perfectionism. Whenever your effort is disproportionate to the value you get in return for doing work, you have to make an adjustment. How many times have you been absolutely sure you were going to miss a deadline, and then miraculously pulled it off? It's amazing how fast and efficiently we can work when we force ourselves.

Content creates opportunity, and if you can't produce the content at the rate your audience wants it or that benefits you, your business won't survive. So get faster. Experiment. See what you can accomplish in two hours. Even if you hate the results or you see less engagement than usual, do this several times in a row. First of all, practice will help you get more efficient. Second, you might be surprised at how much your audience still likes what you produce.

---

▶ Is it wrong to have my Pinterest account tied to my Twitter account so when I post to Pinterest it autoposts to Twitter?

---

Yes, it is wrong. Why do you tweet? To get your message out. What's the best way to get your message out? To make native content. Why on earth would you use Twitter as a Pinterest distributor when you could just tell your story directly on Twitter? Maybe autoposting on Twitter from Instagram is efficient, but it's not particularly compelling.

---

▶ How can I take my website to the next level by making it go viral and increasing sales and visibility?

---

Content, content, content. It's the gateway drug to subscriptions, sales, and everything else. If you're just starting out, obviously you just have to hustle and put out as much quality content as you can. But what if you've been at this awhile, seen some success, made a name for yourself, and want to go even bigger? The way to do that on a big scale without spending too much money is to use your brand equity to your advantage. Find people who can bring you value who could benefit from exposure in your industry, and offer them the chance to create content for your site. You could offer some payment, but you'd be surprised at how many young people or retirees who love talking about your industry or topic would do this kind of work for very little, and maybe even for free, because they believe your brand equity is worth as much to them in the long run as money. Choose carefully—make sure the people you approach will bring you as much value as you can bring them. And then work together so you all benefit. Your team's enthusiasm and the content's quality will shine when everyone feels they have a stake in a project's success.

---

▶ I posted a video on Facebook that got 2,700 views and 35 shares in one day. It took one year for me to get the same number of views on YouTube. Should I focus on creating videos for Facebook exclusively?

---

*One fan can be more valuable than 2,000 if it's the right fan. For that reason, I would never tell anyone to abandon a platform entirely.* Who knows, one of those YouTube viewers may be incredibly influential in your industry. There's no reason why you can't put video on both YouTube and Facebook at the same time. The content could be similar, with small edits made to make sure each is native and that the calls to action resonate with their respective audience. That said, I am very optimistic about Facebook's shareability, which has enormous upside to many just starting out.

▶ Since you're such a fan of Facebook videos, do you plan on
embedding them on your website instead of your YouTube videos,
and is it more beneficial to do so if you are not monetizing?

There's a lot of debate over the value of Facebook videos versus You-
Tube videos because of the difference in the way the two platforms
measure views, or as YouTube calls it now, "watch time." But I care
less about a hundred thousand views on YouTube than I do about
taking advantage of the virality possible through Facebook. When
you're not monetizing, virality is everything, and Facebook gives
your fans an easy way to share your content and get new people to
see it. Facebook gives you a chance to make a good first impression, and I think it's a better place to find new fans than YouTube.
That doesn't mean that YouTube isn't a powerful platform and that
you should dismiss the value of subscriptions. But not tasting what
Facebook could be bringing to you is a mistake. At the time of this
writing the embed product isn't there yet for Facebook—it's still
clunky—but if it does get there that's the future.

▶ You say you don't consume much media, but isn't it kind of
necessary in order to put out relevant, current content?

The reason I produce so much relevant good content is that I listen
to my community. I don't need to watch other shows or pay attention to other thought leaders to know what people are struggling
with or talking about. I can see it every day, right there on my
phone. And because I listen well, I'm able to create content that
speaks to my community's needs. The fact that my content spreads
to and speaks to the needs of people beyond my community proves
that I know my craft. So I guess you can say the people I inter-

act with and who consume my type of content are the "content" I consume. What's great about this is that many of these people have plenty of other interests and expertise, in areas ranging from science to music and everything in between, which allows me to get plenty of other "content," too.

---

▶ Is Pinterest really such a good marketing tool, and how could a small business like a restaurant use it well?

---

Pinterest was once just a place mainly for sharing, but in the last year or so as people have become increasingly visually oriented online, it has become the new must-have search engine. Many people are using Pinterest as a search engine in visual form, and that's a bigger deal than most realize. Men are starting to use Pinterest a lot more, too. I think Google should be shaking in its pants.

Now, as to how a small business should use Pinterest. Think visual. Infographics do really well there. If you're a restaurant, share beautiful pictures of your food, or behind-the-scenes shots in your kitchen or office. Take photos of the street where you're located, or your neighbors and fellow business owners. Give us a sense that you're invested in your immediate community as well as the online one. Act like a media company and put out content that's interesting and valuable, not necessarily to you, but to your customers. Think more like Food Network or Zagat and less like a single restaurant.

---

▶ What kinds of headlines attract you on social media?

---

Usually things that scare me, like "Jets running back in trouble." I couldn't tell you specifically what kinds of headlines really attract me. All I know is that if I click on one, the person who wrote it is doing his or her job well.

We all need to accept that the "BuzzFeedification" of media is in play. When the *New York Times* uses slang and headlines an article with "Five Ways to . . ." you know the trend has gone mainstream. And so whether you're raising money for charity or selling boots, you need to get good at writing this kind of attention-grabbing copy. Because if you can't, you're in trouble. Of course, as many more of us create these headlines the consumer will become accustomed to them, and then there will be a new thing that will stand out. You should always be testing to see if you can be first to figure out what those things may be.

---

▶ I know you're not big on automation, but it's a reality. How do you decide what and when to automate, and what's your take on marketing automation software? You're an advisor to HubSpot. Thoughts on that space?

---

Let me be clear: You should never automate your content to pretend you're generating the content right then and there—in other words, to help you fake a human interaction. Ever. Especially tweets, for reasons you'll read about below.

That does not mean you should never ever automate, though.

Automation is extremely useful when you want to confirm receipt of an online order, a registration or subscription, or email correspondence from a customer. It reassures people that their emails or orders aren't disappearing into the ether. It offers peace of mind, and that's good customer service.

There. Now you know when you can automate. In almost all other cases, don't. Here's why:

**1.** It makes you look insincere.

Automation should not be used to replace human interaction. Even in the case of an automated confirmation email, you should never sign off with your own name. You can sign your company name, or even as "The Team at Insert-Your-Company-Name-Here," but unless you actually hand-type your customer's name and hit the send button, that email is not really from you, and you shouldn't pretend it is.

Think about how much it means to get a personal reply from someone in today's world. The importance social media users place on a tweet or favorite from someone they admire, whether it's an individual or a company, is huge. Let's say you arrange for anyone who follows you on Twitter to receive a direct message that says, "Thanks for the follow @whoeveryouare!" Now you've led Whoeveryouare to believe that you're actually engaging. But you're not. And that's not only dishonest, it's spammy. Same if you automate a follow on Facebook. I mean really, does it take that much time to say a quick "thank you" in person?

This idea that automating human behavior is acceptable in the interest of saving time in a busy world goes completely against all the authenticity and transparency that make the social media age so unique and wonderful. Bottom line: I actually adore automation as long as its intent isn't to trick someone into thinking it was done by a human being in the moment.

**2.** It puts you at the mercy of others.

Look at the New England Patriots who were so excited about reaching one million Twitter followers they decided to send an automated response to every fan who retweeted their celebratory tweet and designed a custom jersey graphic featuring the fan's user name. Unfortunately, one of its fans had a horrible user name that I will not repeat here because I know better than to mindlessly repeat such an ugly thing. Because I'm human. But the computer didn't know better, because it's not. And so it created a jersey bearing the offensive Twitter handle and tweeted it, leaving the Patriots to grovel for forgiveness when the Internet went crazy on them.

How about all the people who were automating their tweets during the Boston Marathon bombing? I saw my own friends posting right hooks just as my feeds were filling up with horrific, bloody images, and I was frantically DM'ing them to warn them to stop because they could potentially ruin their brand. After all, what does it say about you if you're tweeting or posting "Our new line is in, what a great day!" in the middle of a national tragedy? It says at best that you're not paying attention, and at worst that you don't care. In a world where everything is real time, automation is dangerous. You cannot let mainstream media pick up on that kind of mistake, because that mistake could be the end of your career. That, to me, is not worth the upside of automation.

**3.** It makes you look like an asshole.

You know that guy who shows up at a conference and barely says hello before sticking his business card in your hand and moving on to the next person? Don't be that guy. No one likes that guy. These social networks are supposed to be social. If all you're doing is taking without giving, or thanking, or caring, eventually people are going to turn their backs on you.

Now, if you are bound and determined to automate, there is one thing you can do that will make it acceptable in my eyes: humanize it. Let's say people are engaging with your automated tweet. Great. But don't leave it at that. As soon as you can, come back in person and engage again. Make sure your follower knows that this time it really is you, and that you appreciate the time they spent on your feed or page. Work on building that real relationship. That's something no robot will ever be able to do better than you. And if that sounds sentimental, believe me, it's not. It's practical, because building real relationships sells shit.

Automation robs you of the ability to create real context around your content.

It is completely contrary to everything upon which many have built their careers, and against everything the social media age could potentially represent: authenticity, transparency, honesty, and caring. The bottom line on this subject is that there has to be a balance. It's an art *and* a science. Too many are too all in on the science and a few are way too heavy on the art and do too many things that aren't scalable. I am clearly comfortable with the artsy hippy mentality but that's because social media specifically offers the opportunity to overindex for those who actually put in the engagement work.

---

▶ How do you think overly edited photos and text overlays affect the authenticity of Instagram posts?

---

It depends on what you're trying to accomplish. If you're a photographer, you shouldn't edit because you want your art to shine. But if your goal is just to inspire people, a quote over a photo can be a powerful thing. At the end of the day, the audience will find your content, and if they like it, they'll let you know. If they don't, they'll let you know that, too, even if it's just with their silence as they quietly unfollow you. It's more likely that they'll like your work if you like your work, so don't ever try to be someone you're not or follow a trend. Do your thing with passion and commitment. Creative is judged by the target audience, not by some Jets fan who thinks he is a know-it-all on this stuff (yeah, that's me sticking it to me).

▶ What advice would you give people who want to grow their companies but don't have your personality and have a hard time meeting people?

Become the flower and let the bees come to you. You know, I'm a big fan of betting on your strengths versus working on your weaknesses. If you're introverted and networking doesn't come naturally to you, don't force yourself to be all rah-rah and attend conferences where you have to shake people's hands. Instead, put out good content and let your work speak for itself. In addition, email and engage with other influential people in your industry and try to let them see how it would be valuable to let you post your content on their blogs or sites. That doesn't take any networking, just good old-fashioned hustle and talent.

▶ What's the best way for a real estate agent to gain buyers' trust on Twitter?

Listen, engage, create content.

Listening is easy. So easy it only took me—me, with absolutely zero experience in selling real estate—a whole fifteen minutes to use the Twitter Search function to find thirteen tweets from people interested in finding a new home. If I can do it, any real estate agent can.

Engaging should be easy, too. Find people who are talking about apartment or house hunting, or planning a move to your area, and then answer them! How can I help? Where are you looking? What's your price range? I know this works because a Realtor named Jason Grant tweeted that he tried my advice and got a lead. And it makes sense. If you were at a cocktail party and you met someone looking for a home, wouldn't you give her your card and assure her you'd love to help? You can do that every single day!

Finally, like successful people do in every industry, put out that content. Think about how many real estate–themed shows have been on TV in the past two decades. It wasn't just the people in the market for a home pushing those shows up in the ratings; it was all the viewers wishing they could have a new home, and design lovers, and architecture lovers—many of whom, someday, may in fact need to move. So make content they want to watch as much as they want to watch *Property Brothers.*

Review the neighborhoods where you sell. Interview the principal of the local school, the local wine merchant, the sub shop, and the neighbors. Tell stories that make people feel warm and fuzzy about moving to your part of the country, and back up those stories with good data that reassures people you're practical and looking out for their best interests.

This kind of content creation and engagement can be done. As far back as 2009, when I published *Crush It*, I got a video from a guy who had attached a Flip cam to his car so the world could accompany him on drives through neighborhoods and hear his thoughts. It was a fresh and creative move and he was making a huge impact. And amazingly, so few people are doing this kind of thing well that there is still plenty of room for real estate agents to make their mark this way.

---

▶ Do you think brands need to be represented across all social platforms or just the most popular ones?

---

Neither. No brand should be on any platform where it doesn't know how to communicate, nor should they go there if no audience exists. If you sell adult diapers, I'd argue that Snapchat is not going to kill it for you even if it's popular. If you sell selfie sticks that are only marketed to fifteen-year-old girls, Facebook is probably not the best place for you. If you're trying to reach sixty-year-old gray-haired execs, consider LinkedIn. Twenty-five to forty-five-year-old women? Get on Instagram, Facebook, and Pinterest for sure. Twenty-eight-year-old dudes? Pinterest, not so much.

It's not the size of the platform that matters; it's whom you're trying to reach. Figure out whom you're trying to sell to, and story-tell on the platforms they love.

# CHAPTER 8
# JABS AND RIGHT HOOKS

---

## IN THIS CHAPTER, I TALK ABOUT THE NUMBER-ONE RULE FOR SALESPEOPLE, THE POWER OF THE ASK, AND HOW TO AMPLIFY YOUR AUDIENCE'S WORD OF MOUTH.

---

What more could I possibly say about this?

Jab: the content you put out that entertains, distracts, attracts, informs, or otherwise engages and builds a relationship between you and your audience. It builds your brand, raises people's awareness of who you are and what you represent, and opens people up to receiving a right hook when the time is right.

Right hook: the content you put out that brings in the sale. The one that offers the 10 percent off, or announces the new line, or merely says, "Buy my stuff."

It sounds so simple, but to make jabs and right hooks land with enough impact requires finesse, good improv skills, and a deep understanding of the psychology behind every platform you use. A jab on Pinterest will look completely different from one thrown on Twitter. A right hook on Instagram won't work if it's just something you recycled from Facebook. Each platform speaks to its users in a different way, and you have to learn the language. A short scan on any platform shows me that most people still aren't fluent.

Want more details? Read my third book, *Jab, Jab, Jab, Right Hook*.

The end.

---

▶ What's the best advice you can give salespeople in the social media/digital world age?

---

Don't skip this one if you don't think of yourself as a salesperson, because if you're running a business or trying to make money of any kind, you're in sales, and here's the cardinal rule everyone in sales needs to follow: Don't close too early.

Most people don't jab—bring value—enough before pulling back for that right hook—going in for the sale. They're less concerned with providing value than with making the sale, and it backfires every time. Why did I decide to do *The #AskGaryVee Show*? Did I miss the limelight? I already get plenty of media attention, so that wasn't it. It was because I knew that a lot of entrepreneurs, managers, and marketers were still out there looking for guidance and inspiration, and I realized there was a format I could use to reach them that I hadn't tried yet. I thought it might not only be helpful, but fun, too. You want to be tactical, but you have to practice the religion of providing value first. How many people put out stories, give free stuff, or engage with people? Probably quite a lot. Now, how many do that without any expectations in return? Very, very few. Be one of those few. When you have no expectations people can sense it, and funny enough, the absence of pressure or obligation actually makes them *want* to reciprocate.

That's the best advice I can offer. But I have other advice, too:

1.  Sweep the leg, like in *The Karate Kid* (the original with Ralph Macchio and Pat Morita, not the newer one with Jaden Smith and Jackie Chan). That's literally how I think about it when I'm gearing up for a right hook. You have to go in for the kill. With what? Honesty. Don't bashfully tread around the question. Don't try to be cute.

    Just. Freaking. Ask.

    If I were the CEO of Toyota (and I'm being very serious here), my Super Bowl ad would sound something like this: "Hey. I'm Gary Vaynerchuk and I'm the CEO of Toyota. I want you to buy my cars. What do I have to do to make that happen? Let us know." To me, *that* is a good Super Bowl commercial. Forget the pony. Forget the eagle and the cute dog. All of that distracts us from the main question, which is: What can I do to get *your* business? In addition, it would be so radically different in style and tone from the other commercials it would likely get a huge reaction.

2.  Learn about Facebook ads because the segmentation is incredible. Turn to Chapter 10 to learn more about them.

3.  Use Twitter Search to act as your bionic ears. Let's say you're biking across Canada for Pencils of Promise and documenting daily videos on YouTube, like one fan I spoke with on the show. If you want donations but you don't want to throw out an endless stream of right hooks, you could go into Twitter Search and search for people talking about Pencils of Promise, then jump into their conversation. But don't try to bring the attention back to you, like, "You hiked the Appalachian Trail and raised $20K? Well, here's what I did!" On Twitter, you jab by listening. You jump in and your only response to their accomplishment is "Hey, that's phenomenal." And just by interacting, just by showing interest and paying attention, you'll probably spur that person to look at your profile and see your other tweets, the ones that do tell the world what you're

up to. So you jabbed by listening, and then you jabbed with content that led someone to become aware that you're seeking donations on behalf of Pencils of Promise. Congrats—your double jab just led to a right hook, and all you had to do was be nice.

4. Create serendipity. If you're doing something noble, like biking across Canada for Pencils of Promise, or, like another fan, visiting all fifty-nine national parks in honor of the hundredth anniversary of the National Park Service, tell the world about it. Share pictures through Instagram and livestream on Meerkat to create opportunities for discovery, exposure, and business development through your content.

5. LinkedIn allows you to search people by their titles, so now you can hit up every person who's a CEO of a financial services company if that's your target buyer.

---

▶ What's the best way to make a right hook seem like a jab?

---

Don't.

Let me say it again.

DON'T!

Ninety-nine percent of salespeople and businesses try to make right hooks feel like jabs, and they fail because people don't respond well when they feel they're being conned. Be honest. If you're going to do something nice for your customer, do it because you want to, not because it will get you something. I get nothing from doing *The #AskGaryVee Show* other than the pleasure of sharing the God-given wisdom and work experience I've acquired over the years. I want zero in return. Believe me, though, you'll know when I do want something. Months from now, you'll know because whether it's a book, a seminar, or a rare toy, I will clearly say, "Buy this rare toy now! It's $9.99!" I'm sure I talked about this book before it went on sale. Maybe you're reading this now because you watched more than two hundred episodes for free and felt compelled to buy a copy. Or maybe once you consumed the content, you realized it really had value and was worth the cost of a hundred copies that you could distribute to your employees, team members, or community.

There is no disguising the sale. Give when it's time to give. Go all in with authenticity and generosity. On the flip side, don't hesitate to ask for a sale. You're not Mother Teresa. Sell when you need to sell; just be clear about it. So the answer is simple: There is no version of making jabs and right hooks seem like one and the same. Your jabs should be clear, and your right hooks should be even clearer.

---

▶ I've been doing a lot of jabbing but I don't feel like I'm hitting much of anything. Any advice?

---

There are boxers who know how to jab but whose right hooks just aren't powerful enough to knock an opponent out, even when they land perfectly, and even when the opponent isn't expecting it. You just may not be good at closing. Maybe you need to find someone who is a better salesperson than you to complement your strengths. Find a partner who's got a powerful right hook who can bring all of your amazing jabs home.

Another possibility is that what you are offering for sale also isn't worth the jabs you've thrown. For example, the price of this book is well worth the hundreds of pieces of free content I put out. But maybe you offered minimal value in your jabs and are asking for a $20,000 commitment on your hook. That's probably not going to work. They need to line up.

---

▶ As we go from concept to final product, how can we empower our readers to spread the word?

---

What you're really asking is, now that you've amassed an audience by giving them free stuff, how do you sell them something—a book, a workshop, a T-shirt, an expensive barbecue grill, whatever—and get them to spread the word so their friends buy, too? That's the ask. There are only two ways to do it and convert:

**1.** Make a good product. Write an amazing book, develop a life-changing workshop, or build a better grill. Make whatever it is worth more than the money you're asking for it. The best way to convert is to make something so great, consumers value your product or service more than they paid for it. That's the kind of thing people talk about.

**2.** Be up front about what you want from your consumer. You want them to go to your website, share your video, buy your book, or attend your workshop? Don't hedge your right hook. Ask for it. If you've been jabbing well with native content until that moment, your right hook should land squarely in the heart of the consumer and convert the sale.

---

▶ Instagram is good for jabs, but how do you use it for right hooks?

---

I can answer this question because I believe in getting in early and always trying new things. The first couple of years I was on Instagram, I used it exclusively for jabs, like selfies and sneaker shots. But Instagram was begging to be hacked for right hooks, so I did. I've been throwing right hooks there ever since starting *The #Ask-GaryVee Show*.

At one point in time I was posting fifteen-second versions of *#AskGaryVee* episodes. The captions on these videos just said: "Go into my profile." Why? Because I changed the URL in my profile so that it linked to the current episode of the show. At this time, changing your URL is the only way to actually drive people outside of Instagram so they can buy. And that is how you throw a right hook on the platform.

1. Put up a piece of creative.
2. Drive people to your profile in the copy.
3. Link out in your profile and convert your right hook.

I hope you'll test out this right hook tactic. It's worth a shot. If it doesn't work, just keep jabbing on Instagram (the clickable ads are very good alternatives if you want to spend the dollars) and keep throwing your right hooks on Facebook and Twitter, where they're easier. Bam.

**BOOK WINNER!**

JASON FARRIS
@FRESYES
Fresyes.com

▶ I've been putting out jabs based on my expertise (real estate), but I've never really brought up the fact that I have a business to promote. How do I make the transition and establish that I have a product to right-hook for?

When I looked at this question, my first thought was that the answer was actually stunningly easy. My second thought was that it was massively complicated for the people who were actually struggling with it. There's no doubt you could have made this easier for yourself. A lot of people will share content about subjects they're passionate about, say comic books and video games, and in the process of sharing almost accidentally develop and establish a business. It happens, and it's great! I did things a little differently. It was super-easy for me to transition my wine and social media expertise into sales because I was straightforward about my business involvement from day one. I ran a wine store. I run a social media agency. It's always been a part of my identity.

But you did neither. You build up equity purely using your content, and you weren't open about your business interests in your subject matter and expertise. So here is what you do: You attack the problem with a signature piece of content. A manifesto, if you will. Whether it's a five-minute video, or a long-form piece of written content, it needs to be a straightforward explanation of the situation at hand.

For example, you could say: "I've been putting out a lot of content, but all along I've been selling homes. I'd like to start interacting with more of you and seeing if I can help you more directly, so you might see more content from me featuring specific homes, or other business opportunities. If you have any concerns, go ahead and leave some comments."

You could also try something like this: "My passion has become something I want to do full-time. As of recently, I've started selling some of my comics on eBay, so you might see some of those offers on this page. I just want to be transparent and let everybody know that I'm not in the bait-and-switch game."

That's it. Just the simple truth laid out in one signature piece of content that you can point back to in the future.

> ▶ Is there ever such a thing as too much jabbing? Is there ever a time when you withhold content or refrain from engaging in order to build up some mystique?

Great question. Actually, it's two questions.

1. Yes, there's a time where there's too much jabbing. In fact, I wrote the book *Jab, Jab, Jab, Right Hook* because I realized that jabbing was all the early social media practitioners were doing. Marketers had gotten so obsessed with creating perfect jabs they had neglected to create a slamming right hook. They were swinging all the time, but they were missing their mark.

2. Is there ever a time when you shouldn't be in the jabbing business at all? Absolutely. You know who isn't?

Apple.

Apple is in the right-hook business. Look at their social media engagement. It won't take you long because there isn't much. Look at Apple's simple strategy: Make the best crap in the business. And then they did, and then they dominated. No jabs or engaging with consumers on a one-to-one level on social media. They were just the best with the best product, and they knew how to market it.

Some brands want to make themselves more exclusive by not jabbing, but it won't work for everyone. You really have to be the best at what you do. But for those who can pull it off, you can make your brand a rare, valuable commodity.

I could try it. What if I announced that starting now all my content, from the articles on my website to *The #AskGaryVee Show*, would be behind a paywall, and you'd have to pay four dollars to access each episode or batches of articles. How many people would actually pay? Here's what I know: Ninety percent of you would not pay a dime.

If 10 percent of you did, that might make for a better ROI than my current strategy of giving everything away for free. The thing is, though, I like the jab business. I like building up the equity and the awareness. I like it when people pass on my videos and articles and allow other people to discover me. Because that's what makes me run. I like people. I love the climb of building a brand and I know that when I sell, I sell quality and people will buy. If I didn't, I would go the other way. A paywall. Playing hard-to-get. Secret events that cost a lot of money to attend. A private island where I charge you money to visit me. But that's not for me right now! Nope. I'm here for my fans and consumers on the open Web 24/7. It's what feels natural and I enjoy it.

What makes you run? What if that paywall gets *you* a better ROI? You have to analyze your process and figure out what has historically worked best for you, *even if it goes 100 percent against the advice I or anyone else offers.* It is very possible that you will need to try a few different combinations of jabbing and right-hooking before you hit your stride. Some jabs with some right hooks. No jabs and all right hooks. All jabs. Always keep trying new things. Get to know your own DNA and your community's appetite, and run with it.

▶ If my right hook is "Watch my Web series!" what are some good jabs to set that up?

Your content itself is the jab. You want to put out teasers, snippets from your series or short original clips in the form of native content (content that is contextual to the platform, like Facebook or Instagram) that thematically ladder back to what you're doing on your website. Your jabs need to be just that—jabs. Don't put out a post like "My biggest idea ever is . . . go to my website to find out!"

That's lame. Put out great content—jabs that provide value—where your audience spends its time, and your website will get traffic as a by-product. And it's not as though you won't be able to throw right hooks in those social platforms, too.

I started posting long written posts on my Facebook page in the summer of 2015 and the response was overwhelmingly positive. People appreciated that I was creating a seamless experience and saving them time. It's not that your fans don't want to go to your website, it's that they'd rather be in all these other places. So get your butt over there.

---

▶ How do your right hooks differ for a free service versus a paid one?

---

Aside from the conversion numbers they won't look very different. Of course people will watch, read, or try something for free more often than if you charge for it. I would suggest, however, that if you are sending a right hook to someplace where you are charging, include that information in your Facebook or Twitter post. I have seen that letting your consumer know what to expect clearly helps conversion.

---

▶ Many of your jabs and right hooks reach your B2C audience (wine and books), but how does it impact B2B?

---

My right hooks are not often made for B2B, so you'll rarely if ever see me tweet, "Hey, do your business at VaynerMedia!" But my jabs are. The more I make content where I try to provide thought leadership and make accurate predictions, the more likely people who see it are going to consider they might need someone like me for their business. My content has been a gateway drug to RFPs and business inquiries and we have clearly benefited as an agency.

It's admittedly harder to generate a lot of B2B content because it's generally more technical or geared to a smaller target audience. You get fewer at bats, so therefore you need to treat each piece of content as something extra special. Coming up with a captivating piece of B2B content, which tends to be more serious and longer form than other kinds, requires even more rigor and effort than the content you put out for your B2C audience.

Here's what you must remember: No matter who your audience is, you're always one great piece of content away from changing your life. Everyone you know started off as an unknown until they did the thing that made them known. Every rock star or rapper was ignored until they wrote or played the song that put him or her on the charts. Every famous investor was a nobody until he or she made the investment that paid off big. Now, not everyone's content can be at the level of a Madonna or a Chris Sacca, but it still has the potential to change your life. So if you love something—music, photography, diet culture, museums—talk to the world about it, even if only one person is listening. Because all you need is for that person to share it for the pipes of social networking to start humming. You're just one piece of content away from making what you want to happen actually happen.

The problem is most people are not good enough to make that kind of content. That's rough, I know. But talent matters. You have to be good enough to be discovered.

Also, you have to be right. When I put out content that says Facebook is going to buy Instagram, and people say I'm an idiot, and then it happens, guess what? I'm not an idiot! And that builds me street cred. The same thing happens if you post content in the form of a white paper on LinkedIn in which your CEO correctly predicts changes or trends in the industrial Internet, the financial markets, the Supreme Court, or tax reform. Now, if I say wearable tech has no chance because it's a fad, I'll be an idiot (because it really is going to be a big deal). That's not content that takes me forward. It's a lot of pressure. But quality will always be the main differentiator between the content that makes things happen and the content that holds you back.

BOOK WINNER!

ROSS WALKER
@ROss_WalkeR

---

▶ My company is strict, I would say almost too strict on working within their brand guidelines. What is the best way to approach and post content on social, in particular jabs, without being perceived as breaching the company's brand guidelines? In other words, should I tell them to chill the F out, it's social media?

---

Tell them to chill out. Over the last five years, I've spent an enormous amount of time with big brands and their guidelines. First of all, those guidelines are 1,000 percent subjective. They're usually predicated on one or two individuals trying to hold on to the power and act as judge and jury. Trying to execute social media content in the same way as print, radio, and TV just isn't practical, not in the volume of content you're putting out, nor in achieving the context necessary to be successful in those environments.

Now, the problem is that when you come with your message of chilling out, they're not just going to sit back and say, "You're right!" Brands (and their human decision makers) are still fighting very hard for their guidelines.

Now, that's not to say that a brand shouldn't have an identity around its IP. What I'm saying is that the flexibility, and the end consumer's interpretation, gives you a lot more breathing room than most people realize.

> ▶ Do you recommend your website's landing page be a jab, like a blog, or a right hook?

It depends on your business. If you're selling something you only have finite time to reach people when they land on your page, so you need a right hook. But if you're selling information or trying to grow brand awareness, or you've been "selly" for a long time, you might need a countermove to soften your right hooks. To really answer this question properly I'd have to audit what your business or organization has been doing for the last twelve to thirty-six months and figure out what you're trying to achieve. Once that was established, we'd then make sure that all your behavior matched. That's why it's so important that you establish a strategy, a religion, or a belief system to guide what you do. You cannot be wishy-washy.

BOOK WINNER!

SOREN AZORIAN
@SORENAZORIAN
appail.com

> ▶ If you could ask one question of your audience to make sure you're on the right track, what would it be?

I'm a very big believer of just going in for the ask. That's basically what my whole last book was about. I'm not afraid to seek feedback from my audience, and nothing trumps just asking them, "What do you think of my show?" or, "What do you think of my service?"

But that's just part one. The secret is in part two, when you ask, "And how is it going compared to a year ago?"

By asking how it's going compared to a year ago, you're not just getting a snapshot of this moment; you're getting context on how your efforts are trending. This is equally important because while things might seem good, they could actually be stagnating or stale, which to me is actually losing equity.

---

▶ What are the most effective things you've done to drive book sales?

---

Here's the first secret to book sales: Sell it about a year or two before anyone even knows you're writing a book. I started selling my next book during the first episode of *#The AskGaryVee Show*, even though I hadn't given a new book any thought yet. Time is my number-one asset. I like time more than money; that's how valuable it is to me. And yet every day I take time to entertain, to make others think, and to provide value to people who think I'm worth their time (thank you). By taking the time to reach out to a whole new audience, I'm creating a new pool of buyers for my next book. At the time this particular question aired, the book I was selling was the book you hold in your hands. My most recent episode as of this printing, however? That's me gearing up for something else.

I'm surprised by how many people haven't figured out the second secret to book sales: People don't want more content as much as they want more access. Authors always want to offer customers special deals like a free e-book for every three books he or she buys. I try to do better than that. One of the biggest things I ever did that sold a lot of all four of my business books was to give myself.

I literally sold the one thing people wanted most from me—my time. If you bought a certain number of books, I'd do a live Q&A on your video blog, come to your school, do a talk, even make a happy-birthday video. Fans want to spend more time with the authors they love and admire. Let them.

Third, use social media to jab and build lots of new fans. Make awesome content that gets attention. Build value up front and create leverage. Engage in one-on-one marketing.

Fourth, scale the unscalable. That means refraining from one of the biggest mistakes I see authors make: bulk emails. They usually read something like, "Dear Friends, I never normally do this but I have a book coming out and it would mean the world to me if you would buy it . . ." The authors are going for efficiency, and it stinks. It might work on your aunt or your BFF, but who else is going to feel moved by such a plain-vanilla, impersonal missive like that?

Before the launch of my last book in November 2013, I spent all of August writing email after email to people from whom I wanted help. "Dear Bill, it was so great seeing you last month at the conference in Reno. Did you connect with those people I set you up with? Anyway, I'm writing to you because I have a book coming out, and it would mean the world to me if . . ."

See how it's done? And I did it over and over again, personalizing every email so that the recipients knew that I was paying attention to them and that I truly valued our relationship. And I didn't just ask them to buy as a favor to me. I gave them real reasons why I thought my book might be of use to them, their friends, or their employees.

Fifth, create opportunities. In the fall of 2014 the podcast scene was starting to really happen. So I did a ton of interviews with all the emerging podcast people, achieving something I call equity arbitrage—where two people or entities get ROI based on the mutual exposure they gain by joining forces. I barely mentioned the book during the entire thirty minutes I was on the air. Instead

I focused on providing as much value as possible to their listeners. It was my one shot to let them know I was someone to trust and take seriously. Since then this has become a popular tactic, but now there are so many more podcasts and so much more competition for ears that it's not as valuable as it once was to be a guest, though it's still worthwhile to appear on them and promote. But as you read this book, there is probably some new platform that has come out just waiting for someone like you to use in a creative way that gives you leverage and visibility.

Finally, remember that whether selling books or Barcaloungers, on social media or in a brick-and-mortar store, you won't convert unless you appeal to your consumers' emotions. When you've got that, you show them your value proposition. And then you stand back while they pull out their money. Heart, Brain, Wallet. Every time.

# CHAPTER 9
# THE PLATFORMS

## IN THIS CHAPTER I'LL TALK ABOUT WHERE THEY ARE AND WHERE THEY'RE GOING.

Debating the current state of the Internet has become as much a passion for some people as sports, music, and celebrities. For years now the five to fifteen platforms that dominate our society, whether Blogger and MySpace a decade ago, or Instagram and Snapchat and Facebook today, have been fuel for conversations around what stock prices will do, where society is going, and where creative things are happening. These hubs have become integrated into our daily lives as much as television, radio, and magazines used to be, and there's no more interesting time to talk about them than while they still capture the consumer's imagination.

It's a challenge to answer questions about social platforms because in the time it takes you to utter one sentence, they've usually changed again. However, as I updated and elaborated upon these answers, I realized that the real value isn't just in the analyses, but in the overall pattern that emerges. This isn't the first time we've seen tech wreak enormous cultural and social change on our world, and it won't be the last. And we're all still here. Businesses are still being built, people are still innovating, and the world keeps turning. My hope is that reading this chapter will help more marketers and brand managers welcome change rather than fear it.

## The Big Picture

---

▶ What will the next big social network have to do to challenge Facebook, Twitter, or Instagram?

---

There are two keys to the success of a social network.

1. Win over the youth market. The network that makes Snapchat feel like it's for old people will be the next social superstar.
2. Be extraordinarily useful. Instagram was just a place to post pretty pictures until people realized it actually made them better photographers. The visual intimacy of the pictures made people feel close to other users, and eventually the social network developed to support that closeness.

In sum, if you're trying to develop the next big platform, create something the youth of the world didn't know it couldn't live without.

---

▶ Which currently popular social media platform will likely be extinct by 2020?

---

The two most vulnerable platforms today are Tumblr and Google+, mostly because big conglomerates own them. For all my concerns about Twitter, I have faith that Jack Dorsey will figure out a way to make it relevant and new-user-friendly again. But Tumblr is owned by Yahoo, and despite all those politics of being independent it's still part of a big holding company. Google has shown a tendency to cut bait if something isn't working, no matter how much they invested in it, and there's no doubt that Google+ isn't working. It's possible Google will cut Google+, retool it, and reintroduce it one day, but I think it's a fair bet that Google+ as we know it will not be around in a few years.

---

▶ Social media marketing is not as dominant in other countries as in the United States. For example, in Germany a meerkat is still nothing more than a cute animal. Is it really worth our time to put content on these platforms, then sit, wait, and hope they gain traction?

---

Meerkat was once just an animal in the United States as well. A face book was a college directory, a twitter was the sound of a happy bird, and a periscope was that thing sailors use to see out of submarines. Every platform has potential, but it will be infinitely more valuable to you if you get there first and make your name for yourself before the masses show up.

I have plenty of cash, and yet I sit on practically unpopulated platforms. It is beyond me how some entrepreneurs who have no cash, whose only assets are raw talent and time, could possibly question the value of getting in on a platform before it has proven worthwhile and started monetizing. You're going to cry because you don't have enough money to compete with the big guys, but then you'll cry about wasting your time on something that's free? Where's the sense in that?

The upside of being an early mover in a new platform is so much greater than the downside of waiting there for months only to find that it didn't pop. I'll sit on a platform and hold my breath for five to seven months when it's not particularly valuable so that I can be there when it is. And then I can ride that wave for twenty-four months before the platform adds an ad product that makes it more expensive. So, yeah, I'd say experimenting with unproven platforms is definitely worth your time, no matter what country you live in.

That advice goes double if you're a small business or start-up. The only assets you have against bigger, wealthier competitors are raw talent and time. So use the time from 3 to 7 A.M. if you must to establish yourself on new platforms and overindex there before money starts becoming a variable. Corporate America isn't as nimble as you. You'll have made plenty of inroads by the time your larger, more established competitor notices that the new platform has gone mainstream, and then in all probability it will take them a ridiculous amount of time to get approval to divert resources to it. Meanwhile, you'll keep making inroads, getting a stronger foothold, and building your connections and brand awareness. Extract the value of the platform before its ad product becomes mature so that by the time it becomes expensive you'll be ready to move on to the next new frontier.

## YouTube

▶ I make my living off YouTube and lately people have been asking what my next step is because they don't think YouTube can last forever. I think it will only continue to grow. Should I hedge my risk by expanding to other platforms or stick to YouTube?

The guy who asked this question, Matthew Santoro, has more than 2 million subscribers on YouTube.

I'd venture to say he knows what he's doing.

Always follow your gut and do what you know. If you're putting up content and blowing up on a platform, go with it. And if you're wrong and the platform starts to crater, it's not the end of the world. Early in my career I loaded my videos exclusively on Viddler. Once YouTube came out it didn't take long to realize going whole hog on Viddler was a mistake and I made the correction, jumping to YouTube. As long as you adjust in real time, you can't go wrong.

---

▶ Why do you rarely recommend YouTube in your digital
recommendations despite the 1 billion active users per month?

---

I'm not good about admitting to mistakes, mostly because I honestly don't believe I've made that many in my career, but this is one of them. I think YouTube's value is so obvious, second only perhaps to Facebook, I just forget to push it. In fact, one of the reasons I decided to do *The #AskGaryVee Show* was to increase my presence on YouTube.

## Twitter

---

▶ Is there value to following thousands of people on Twitter, or
should you only follow those who bring value to you?

---

Everyone likes to be noticed, especially by someone they respect or admire. I freaked out when former New York Jets player David Nelson followed me on Twitter, and I'm always amazed by how much it means to people when I follow them, even though I'm only on the celebrity Z list. I'd like to see more people worry less about the value they gain from their followers and more about the value their engagement provides others.

I initiate a lot of strategies toward increasing my reach—what I call the length game—but when I'm on Twitter, it's all about depth. I want to give people what they want, and if they want engagement or time or attention, I'm happy to provide it. That's why I film *The #AskGaryVee Show*, too; it gives me a chance to go deep and detailed. It's not always easy to go deep, because we're busy running companies and living life, but it's crucial to building that relationship that will make all the difference when your customer is ready to buy.

▶ I understand that marketers ruin everything, but is Twitter's latest algorithm change going to damage user experience and the essence of Twitter?

When Twitter announced it would be following Facebook's lead and switch to an algorithmic feed instead of a chronological one, a lot of people predicted the end of Twitter. Because that's what always happens when a platform makes a change—the die-hard users cry and threaten to take their toys and go home, and then whaddaya know, they stick around and adapt. So long as Twitter continues to offer value, it will keep its user base. The experience will only be irrevocably ruined for those people who are irrevocably put off by the 7–10 more tweets that appear in their stream.

Have you ever dated someone who's drop-dead gorgeous only to discover he or she is not that nice? Maybe you broke up with that person right away, but a lot of people wouldn't. They value the beauty so much they keep going out with that mean person even though he or she is mean to their friends and hurts their feelings.

It's only once the value of the beauty no longer outweighs the nasty disposition that they quit the relationship. Of course that process would probably speed up if another drop-dead gorgeous person, this one with an awesome personality, were to come along. The second that something loses value to you, you stop paying attention to it.

So will Twitter's switch to an algorithm that tries to make the deluge of information on the platform more relevant to users kill the platform? Only to those people who don't value everything else Twitter does for them.

▶ I don't understand why I barely see @garyvee in my Twitter feed, but you're all over my Facebook account.

Because Facebook has done a better job with its data and makes sure that what you see is relevant to your interests. Twitter is a busy, busy place, and it's exceedingly difficult to get noticed there anymore. Hence the changes to the algorithm. Believe me, if you're not seeing me in Twitter, it's not because I'm not tweeting away.

▶ Why is Twitter so much like a wall in a public bathroom?

I would argue that it's not. Anonymous apps like Yik Yak offer far better opportunities for people who want to make statements and take positions they might not want the whole world to know are theirs. I'm always far more scared of the people on Twitter who say scary shit and don't even mind showing their faces than the people who hide.

eople afraid of Snapchat, especially

Because most people want to do what they already know. Ninety-five percent of digital and social agency marketers have never even tried to use Snapchat and don't understand how it works. It's not like other apps; it moves left to right instead of up and down, it has the Discover tab. It's weird. And they've read in the headlines that it's the app that lets the fourteen-year-olds send naked photos to each other. They have not taken time to figure out if there's a way to adapt it to suit their purposes. And that, in a nutshell, is why most marketers suck.

Not because they've rejected Snapchat per se, but because the suspicion and reluctance with which they approach it is the same they have for every new app. It's why they're late to the party every freaking time and then spend an inordinate amount of money and effort scrambling to catch up once they get there.

Marketing today is for the forward thinking, the brave, and the young at heart. If you're scared to innovate, you're too old for this and you stink.

## Facebook

▶ What are your thoughts about Facebook's ban on like-gating?

I think Facebook is maybe one of the worst PR companies in the world. At the end of 2015 they made a move that will help ensure that when people like a brand, they really do like it and aren't just liking it to win a prize or get some more points on a video game. The only people who should have been upset about this are those with no imaginations and no confidence in their brand. Making sure that users are seeing things in their feeds that they actually want to see is good for everyone.

---

▶ Marketing to the next generation through Facebook is on par with putting ads in the Yellow Pages. Facebook is dead. What's next?

---

Facebook is so not dead. If anything, it's just starting to grow. I've made the mistake of counting out a platform or service prematurely. In 2003 I predicted that SEM and Google AdWords was dead, when in reality it was just starting.

I'd say that Google search is destined for Yellow Pages obsolescence. You used to have to go to Google to look up what you wanted. Now it's all just coming to you, not on the right side of your desktop but in your actual feed. If you know how to target and create content properly, your consumers will have a constant reminder, in the best way, of how relevant your brand is to their lives.

---

▶ I don't get it, Facebook. You decide to not show my book page to people. Do you think a lack of success will make me give you more money?

---

I wish people would stop complaining about the cost of doing business on Facebook. It is like any other medium in the world. TV channels aren't going to run your ads for free. The post office isn't going to ship out flyers and advance copies of your book for free.

This idea that because Facebook started out as a free social network it has to continue giving away organic reach is crazy. It's one of the most efficient ways to deliver content to people in the world. You don't think that's worth a little money?

To anyone who feels he or she has a legitimate gripe, by all means use the free alternative to Facebook to alert people to your brand or book or business. That would be email. I'd love to see you get results even close to what you could do with Facebook. You can rant and rail against the cost of Facebook, but in the end you're just talking to yourself, because Facebook doesn't care. Nor should it.

---

▶ Will Facebook video become a rival for YouTube as a monetized video platform?

---

It already has.

Some viewers noticed that I started uploading *#AskGaryVee* shows straight to Facebook instead of attaching a photo linking to my website or the YouTube video. I did that because posting natively is always the way to go. I like to say that I don't pay attention to data, but what I should say is that I don't pay attention to data unless it tells me something important. And Facebook has some of the best data out there, including some that tells me if I upload my videos natively, about 20–30K more people see them than if I link to YouTube or my website. On top of that, Facebook now shows view count so I can build brand with perception in the same way as I build it on YouTube. It allows me to embed videos on other sites. I'm eliminating friction and making it easier for more people to see my content, which is valuable. And providing value is always what I care about the most.

So I suggest that those of you out there doing YouTube shows should start doing Facebook shows, too. Now, of course, the caveat here is Facebook video requires a budget. It's worth it. The dollars go on a long way; with the precise targeting we have available through the platform, you are sure to reach an audience with an interest in your subject matter.

At the time this question was asked, in March 2015, I predicted that six months later my primary embed would be Facebook videos over YouTube videos.

I'm not saying you should give up on YouTube. It's still extremely relevant and important. But if you're creating content for YouTube, throw it up on Facebook as well. Not with a link to the video—you won't get the reach you want that way. Remember, native is the way to go.

I actually think this will be good for YouTube. Competition breeds innovation, and YouTube has been pretty stale for half a decade now. It might be motivated to push for some quality innovation soon, which will then probably compel Facebook to innovate some more as well. Everyone could win, especially us marketers.

---

▶ Three seconds count as a view for Facebook video—moderately misleading metric, or incredibly bullshit metric?

---

Marketers have got to stop valuing width over depth. Is three seconds of pre-roll view on Facebook more bullcrap than people buying views on YouTube as pre-rolls? Those on YouTube are actual ads whereas Facebook is putting them in feeds.

I don't care about width metrics. Any brand start-up using the number of views it receives to gauge its success doesn't realize that tech can game that game. I'm looking at the engagements, the comments, the click-throughs to the product. If I am paying attention to something like number of views, I'm taking the width at width value. If I want 800K people to see my face, and they do that, then I consider those three seconds I just got to be worthwhile. It depends what you're trying to accomplish.

> My little sister has Insta and Snapchat but has no interest in Facebook. What do you think the future holds for Facebook?

Facebook's Mark Zuckerberg is an assassin. There's a reason he bought Instagram and there's a reason he tried to buy Snapchat for $3 billion—he wanted the teens. I doubt Facebook is going to get them, though. Instagram is going to become more like Facebook, but if Facebook keeps crushing it, it should be able to hold on to the thirty-five-and-older crowd, which of course is an enormous business. Over time the population will diminish, but I believe Zucks is going to keep going after that youth market. Facebook missed Snapchat, but it bought Oculus, and I'm sure there will be more. Don't ever count Facebook out. It's going to be the infrastructure for over-the-top TV, or free Internet, or the best phone we've ever seen. Just you wait.

## eBay

> Do you think eBay will become irrelevant if they don't innovate?

My friends and I were predicting the end of eBay back in 2005, and it hasn't gone anywhere. I think until there is an alternative to eBay in the world, they don't have to worry. I loved the old eBay—I taught AJ to be an entrepreneur by going to garage sales and showing him how to sell his finds on eBay. Now eBay sells so much new product it's more like Amazon, and people are frus-

trated with the new fee structures, but there really isn't
else to go.

There is a billion-dollar opportunity in a new eBay, one that
exclusively deals in used product the way the old eBay used to.

## Blogs

> ▶ Blogging doesn't seem as popular as it was a number of years
> ago. Does it have a future when everyone is "renting" social media
> space?

No one talks about email, but that doesn't mean it isn't important.
Same with blogging. It just goes without saying that if you're in
business, you've got a blog. If you're putting out content on social
networks, you're blogging. Bloggers used to have to use SEO to
get people to come to their blogs, but now they can simply bring
their content straight to their readers. It's a huge improvement over
talking to yourself and hoping you can get someone to come along
and pay attention.

Now, does that mean that personal websites are irrelevant today? Not at all, especially when a lot of brands are reassessing the
idea of "renting" social media space after all. If you're putting your
content on a site that you cannot control, you lose ownership of that
content. This has proven catastrophic to some brands when Facebook's ever-changing algorithms wreak havoc on their carefully
planned Facebook campaigns. So many are redoubling their efforts
on their sites, and offering their social engagement as the gateway
drug to get people there.

People's attention is short and unfocused. They are more than
willing to consume; they're just not as willing as they used to be
to leave platforms in order to do it. It's perceived as too much

trouble—until they spot something that makes it not. And that's when you've got them. If you're going to retain control over your content and drive people from social networks to your website, your storytelling, which may have already been good, has to get even better. You've got to get smart. Really smart. And that's something to embrace, because raising the bar on one's work has never hurt anyone. Ever.

## Instagram

---

▶ Numbers of monthly users aside, do you think Instagram is actually a larger social network than Twitter?

---

The media made a big deal out of the fact that in 2015 Instagram reached 300 million monthly active users, surpassing the number on Twitter. They made it seem like a platform's number of users can predict its success and staying power. But while obviously the number of users is one indicator of how a platform is resonating with the world, it's not the only one. And it's not even the most important.

Instead of how many users are on a platform, we should all focus on how much attention its users are paying to it. Which platform is more valuable, the one that's always on in the background but rarely looked at, or the one that has users' full attention when they're there? That's the big difference between Twitter and Instagram right now.

Twitter has a serious noise problem. Six years ago, I had less of an audience on Twitter than I do now, but I could send a tweet and get more engagement because that audience was paying closer attention. The amount of information and users on the platform is so intense that it's hard to make yourself noticed, much less engage. On the flip side, *no social network in the world right now has more of*

*its users' attention than Instagram.* When people are there,
percent there, looking at each photo that passes by. In some ways
even got more depth than Facebook, because there aren't all the dis-
tractions that can come with the emotional ties there, like spotting
ex-boyfriends and avoiding family drama. Instagram isn't winning
because it has more followers; it's winning because people are there
to wholeheartedly consume content. It's not just in the background.

When people want real-time information about what's going on
in the world, they still run to Twitter for the conversation and live
updates. But until Twitter figures out how to control the fire hose
of content that hits people when they're there, Instagram is going
to be a better place to engage with consumers because you have a
better chance of being seen. That's why I've moved so much energy
toward Instagram myself. I still love Twitter, but survival of the
fittest doesn't just apply to the animal kingdom. If Twitter doesn't
evolve, and soon, it's going to die.

---

▶ How will Instagram evolve in the future?

---

It's evolving now; it's just somehow it manages to do it in a more
subtle way than Facebook does, and therefore elicits less angst from
its users. One thing is certain: If Instagram were ever to layer Facebook's targeting capabilities on its platform, it would become one
of the great ad products of our time.

It wouldn't surprise me if it transcended mobile photography
and started developing smart photo tech, like the best new smart
camera or maybe contact lenses that could take Instagram shots.
Why not? CEO Kevin Systrom is a thoughtful leader who cares not
only about his product but also about his audience. I bet he'll take
the platform into an interesting new space, and without ruining it,
too.

▶ Facebook and Twitter make it easy to manage separate pages and accounts, but not Instagram. Is there a way to successfully use one account for all three things without it being shit, jumbled and ineffective?

It's easy to forget that Instagram is really, really young, and young platforms need time to work out their kinks. Before business pages existed on Facebook I had to use fan pages, and it was a pain in the ass. But I sucked it up because that's what you do until the platform evolves or responds to its users' needs.

▶ People who write essays as their Instagram captions—what the hell are they thinking? We're there to look at pics, not read endless shit.

You are. But plenty of other people like the long form on Instagram. You do you and create your own experience. But don't be surprised if you start to see more and more of this kind of thing. There is a growing opportunity, and if it works, other people are going to start trying it themselves. Platforms evolve; that's just the way it is. In fact, as of this writing, I am finding myself more and more attracted to longer-form text on Instagram.

▶ Like, why is my dad following me on Instagram? Like, no, that's unacceptable.

I have bad news. You are going to see your dad following you on every social media platform that hits scale—for the rest of your life.

That's how this stuff works. The youth establishes the community centers, and then everyone else follows.

---

▶ People ruined the artistic intention of Instagram. Like now people try to sell refrigerators on it. The fuck?

---

What do I always say? Marketers ruin everything. People will try to sell on whatever platform has the public's attention, and clearly it's Instagram's time. If it becomes oversaturated like Twitter, they'll move on to the next one.

---

▶ Instagram posted that they're going to start advertising on the timeline in the United Kingdom. More than 6,300 comments protested that they're going to ruin it and threatened to leave the platform. Your thoughts?

---

Different strokes for different folks. A lot of video hosts wouldn't let someone precede a question on the air with a nine-second self-promotion, but I do because I love to reward people's hustle. Not everyone using Instagram cares whether ads show up or not. And of those who say they do, I'm willing to guess that they're just venting, and will ultimately be too lazy to follow through on their threat to leave. Do you know how many Americans said they would move to Canada when George W. Bush was reelected, or Obama? The gap between what we say and what we do is pretty big. I'm willing to bet that if you went back to that Instagram announcement and clicked on the people who said they were quitting the platform, you'd find that most are still there. The number of things we say versus the things we do is pretty big. Go back to that post and look at how many people have posted pictures since swearing they were saying bye-bye to Instagram. My guess is quite a few. Instagram will find its rhythm the way Facebook did, and it will be a nonevent.

▶ I am wondering what you think of Direct Message on Instagram. Is it an untapped resource?

Don't go where you're not wanted. DM is like texting—it's private, and a place where no one wants to be marketed to. I hear anecdotally that most of the conversations happening by DM are flirtatious and maybe even inappropriate. Few people are following anyone they don't want to follow, either, so an unexpected DM from you would feel more like a spam intrusion than it might on a different platform. Stay away.

## Podcasting

▶ What's your take on podcasting? You're playing in the space, but not all in. Not worth it yet?

The only reason I'm not all in right now is I'm too busy, but I think it's a tremendous opportunity. People can consume your content while driving the car, jogging, or riding the train. They don't have to stop what they're doing and they don't even risk getting hit by traffic while they cross the street because their eyes aren't focused on screens. And podcasts are probably easier for more marketers to do well. Besides, I'm particularly strong on video, so it makes sense for me to put my energy there (focus on your strengths, remember?). Since video can make a lot of people self-conscious, podcasts are an excellent alternative.

## Pinterest

---

▶ As a man I find it extremely hard to accept that other men use Pinterest. How do I get over this bias?

---

Quit being a jerk. If you're targeting 15–19-year-old guys to sell them sports equipment, then maybe you don't need to be there, but if you're a man who is trying to market or sell or storytell or create awareness to women, you do. Your BS bias is not helping you.

---

▶ There is buzz around Pinterest advertising and they are slowly letting in business accounts. Are you optimistic?

---

When this question was first posed, Pinterest had just launched an ad service called Promoted Pins, which not only serves pins featuring your product to people their demographic data tells them might be interested in buying it, but also allows you to target them based on items they have searched. It's early Google AdWords all over again, which is a big, big deal.

I was the first person to sell against the word *wine* back when Google AdWords first launched. I bought it for five cents, and it was nine months before anyone bid me up. Google became huge, and I reaped the benefits. I saw similar results with Pinterest almost immediately.

With Pinterest blocking affiliate links and introducing a "Buy" button on pins, it's positioning itself as a major e-commerce contender. Back when I answered this question, I predicted that eighteen months from that day I would come back with an update. But I might as well tell you now: For better or worse, nothing has really changed. At the time of this publication, Pinterest has moved fairly slowly, so there are no new major updates to discuss. I still feel bullish, though, and still confident that when people understand that it's a search engine for visuals they'll figure out how to use it. If, however, Pinterest continue to be as slow as they have been for another six months, I'm going to start to get concerned.

## Kickstarter

▶ What are your thoughts on using Kickstarter to start a business?

Oculus Rift did it, raising $2 million to put out its first prototype, and later sold to Facebook for $2 billion. Lots of other people have tried to do it and failed. The difference? The founders of Oculus Rift built a great business. So yes, it can be done—if you've got skills. None of this stuff works unless you have the talent to execute.

## Ello

▶ What do you think of Ello?

Hundreds of people have asked about this ad-free social network that promises not to sell personal data. It sounds so great, but what's the business model? You can't make a profit on free.

A lot of people say they resent social networks like Facebook selling their data. But you know what they hate more? Paying for them. From what I can see, people don't mind ads when they don't look or feel like ads and bring us some sort of value. I think that's where Ello is going to have to go.

## Listicles

---

▶ What's your opinion on listicle sites?

---

Many of my friends and contemporaries who loved growing up reading the *New York Times* and the *Wall Street Journal* bemoan listicles, but I think they're great. The past is the past, and now people want their news fast, colorful, and pithy. BuzzFeed, Upworthy, and Gawker have built tremendous businesses around listicles, using them to explore everything from racism to the challenges of motherhood to the Palestinian-Israeli conflict. The problem, as I see it, is they're being overrun. Too many lists like "12 Things the Cat Did While It Ate Its Food" are crowding out the valuable content that people used to count on.

It's the same argument we had over reality TV or daytime game shows. There's a huge misunderstanding of how these things work.

What do I think of listicles as a business? In October 2012, twenty-four months before this question was asked, I would have said it was a phenomenal opportunity. At the time I discussed this topic on the show, I thought it was superstrong. As I write this book, almost a year later, I think it's a pretty good idea. In two years, I'd be careful. Listicles will follow the same path as all other media, in that the best opportunities arise when a platform is new, and it loses value as more and more people pile on.

## Email

---

▶ Do you think email will be more or less relevant in the next five years?

---

I think it's so important I've put it at the top of my marketing strategy. Email open rates may no longer be 80 percent like they were back when I was selling wine in 1997, but that doesn't mean email is dead. See, people used to sign up for emails without thinking twice, the same way we used to click thousands of likes on Facebook. As time went on, we started being more selective. That means that if someone takes the time to sign up for your emails, you'd better deliver quality content. If you succeed and prove to people that they will like opening your emails, your email open rates will be high. You just have to deliver on your promise to provide amazing, exclusive, relevant content.

The other advantage of emails? You own them. You're in total control of the creative and the distribution, and you don't have to worry that your platform is going to make a change that alters whether the consumer who opted in receives it.

I think as long as people have email accounts email will be relevant. It won't be as valuable as it once was, but it will still be a player.

## Reddit

---

▶ What are your thoughts on Reddit? Is it even social? Is it useful?

---

Reddit's big advantage is that it has a solid community, which means the brands and creative shops that can make their content natively

"Reddity" should see excellent returns. But as with all platforms, if you barge in there without bothering to learn the language and fail to understand why people come to Reddit, you'll get nowhere.

Now, of course, once brands start having an impact on Reddit, the platform's die-hard users will accuse it of selling out. They will threaten to leave. And then I think they'll get over it.

## Google +

---
▶ Why do you continue to use Google+?
---

Because it's there. It's definitely a failure, but there is still a niche of early adopters who use it. I have an audience there, so I give them content. Why wouldn't I? How much effort does it take to post a video and check in with a few people who like my stuff? I respect that community and want to serve it.

Can we please try to remember not to think about social networks as all or nothing? Invest in the hugely successful ones, of course, but don't turn your nose up at the others. The members of those communities are consumers, too. Would you turn away their money if they wanted to give it to you?

## Yik Yak

---
▶ What are your thoughts on the marketing opportunities in Yik Yak?
---

If you're marketing to the 18–22-year-old college demo, you need to be there. The challenge is: How do you market yourself or your brand when it's a place that values anonymity? You could use humor, like "I hear the chef at Burger World is hot . . . ha ha, it's me." The trick is to be authentic and not spammy. It's a tough one.

## Meerkat

---

▶ Which industries do you think will leverage Meerkat the best? Who is their target user?

---

Plenty will, but I think it will prove particularly useful to retail, entertainment, and sports. Can you imagine the QVC 2.0 opportunities? I could schedule a show from 6 to 9 P.M. where I sell and talk wine. Sponsors could jump on live sports events. Or you could charge money for special shows. I'd happily pay $2.99 to watch a live street-fighting match.

Twitter's acquisition of Periscope hurt Meerkat for sure, because it allowed for a seamless transition between the apps that Meerkat didn't have. Twitter users can see embedded images and even the ability to watch live streams in feed; Meerkat pushes a tweet out on your behalf that is nothing but text and a short link. Obviously Periscope has the advantage (which sucks for me because I invested in Meerkat).

## Yo

---

▶ What do you think of Yo's new updates? Can businesses use them to communicate to customers?

---

At the end of the day, communicating with your audience is the number-one thing you should be doing at all times. If you think the Yo app allows you to do that, be there.

## Tech

---

▶ How will the world change in 2018 once the Apple Watch has probably become a vital part of everybody's lives?

---

If there's one thing I know for sure, it's that the phone will be trumped. And it doesn't end with the Apple Watch. Smart tech is coming not only to our wrist, but to our collar, our sneakers, our hats, maybe into our actual bodies. And don't be surprised if we return to our communication roots. Our main form of communicating across distances used to be letter writing, then it was the phone, and now it's through our thumbs, but who knows, we might start talking again. I'm invested in a company called Cord Project that's bringing voice messaging back into play. It could happen.

---

▶ Disney's MagicBand: How do you see this space evolving? What do you think about the necessity for these online/offline bridge technologies?

---

Smart, wearable technologies are going to eat up the world. Everything will be smart. All of it. Your shirt. Your pants. Your underwear. Your socks. As your coffee gets cold in the cup, it will tell you, "Drink fast! It's getting cold!" Don't believe me? For an actual present-day example, look no further than Amazon's new Dash Button. It's not on the level that we just discussed, but you have to agree it's pretty damn close.

All this is coming in the next ten to thirty years. Wearable tech allows things that are physical to go so much further in the digital world. We are always looking for ways to represent our physical experiences in a digital space: posting photos to Instagram. Tweeting about a concert. Facebook statuses. The next natural step is for the digital to enhance the physical experience. That's where Disney's MagicBand succeeds.

The MagicBand is a wristband that allows you to do everything from open your hotel room to purchase a hot dog to enter the parks. It also gives Disney an extraordinary layer of data and ammo. It lets visitors recall steps during the day so they can create their own personal timeline. It pushes out content and unlocks new virtual features. In addition, it finally cracks open a path to efficiency, one of the biggest goals for every retailer.

One of the biggest frustrations for any visitor to Disney is the long lines and how hard it can be to navigate from one end of the park to the other. The MagicBand fixes that. Disney can see where people are getting stuck and where there's open space, and use technology to encourage people to head to the underused area, for example by relaying through the band that there's a code they can unlock over at Splash Mountain that will give them a coupon for a free ice cream. The technology actually speeds up the flow throughout the park. Disney can directly affect purchasing behavior by giving people reasons for spending more time in a space, thus perhaps creating more occasions to shop, or exposing them to two or three additional hot dog stands until they finally realize they're really hungry, and improving their mood because the lines aren't ridiculously long.

Wearable smart tech feels the same way social networks and the Internet felt to me in 2005–2007. It's going to infiltrate everything we do. I'm telling you, the smart beard is coming soon.

## Traditional Media

---

▶ What are your thoughts on Facebook advertising on
  television?

---

I've always said that social and traditional media should play Ping-Pong, working together to extend stories and pique people's curiosity with fresh content. And I've also said that my beef with traditional media isn't that it doesn't serve a purpose, but that it's overpriced for the limited audience it reaches.

Except for when you're actually trying to reach that limited audience.

A small company probably shouldn't spend a lot of money on TV because it can get far more reach by building stories that spread through word of mouth on social media. But today Facebook has 1.8 billion users—it already has everyone's attention. The only people it can't reach are the people who balk at using Facebook, namely the 13–15-year-olds, and the senior citizens. Like, the 70–90-year-olds. The kids don't watch much TV, but the seniors are there. The TV ads are still overpriced, but you can absorb that cost when you have a market cap of $225 billion.

Facebook isn't the only one going old-school. Airbnb launched a print magazine. Warby Parker, the online prescription eyewear vendor, and Birch Box, a monthly cosmetics subscription service, both opened brick-and-mortar stores. Why? Because there was an audience there and they wanted to make sure to reach it.

Don't ever lock yourself into one strategy or platform. Use a healthy mix that optimizes your reach. And though everyone has to market in the year we live in, it is possible that your year still includes traditional print and TV.

▶ I just bought an indoor billboard company. How do you feel about
advertising in the bathroom?

An ad placed smack above a urinal or on the back of a bathroom
door is a great investment—unless you're doing it in a year when
people read their phones when they pee and no longer look at the
wall above the urinal or the back of the bathroom door. You've got
to think about the attention graph. Where is people's attention going? That's where your marketing should go. It's not that marketers
shouldn't put their ads in the bathroom; it's just that the value of
urinal and bathroom signs isn't nearly as high as it was even three
years ago.

No matter what you're selling, you've got to pay attention to
the attention graph, not just how it looks now, but how it will look
in the foreseeable future. Phone culture and wearable tech opens
up tons of marketing opportunities, but it makes us vulnerable,
too.

▶ When will social marketing spending be bigger than television
commercials?

Maybe in about two decades. These things take time. Let's remember that the Web has been around since the mid-nineties offering banner ads and email and Google AdWords, and none of that
made a dent in TV. I think television advertising today is in the
same position as newspaper advertising a few years after Craigslist
took off. The DVR and Netflix have chipped away at it, and social
is going to bring it to its knees. Eventually ads won't look like ads
anymore; they will all be natively interwoven into the platforms,
and we'll consume them without even knowing it.

▶ Do you have suggestions for me and other photographers about other ways to drive local print sales?

To me, physical goods don't just disappear in a digital world. Obviously we're living through a transition in all industries, but the fact of the matter remains that at the time I was writing this book the media was reporting that about a trillion photographs would be taken by the end of 2015. At the end of the day, every business needs to respect the supply-and-demand curve of what's happening in the marketplace, and people are still going to go into physical stores, and hang physical pictures in their houses. Now, I'll be totally honest, I'm kind of surprised we're not further along with digital picture frames, but tomorrow Apple may decide that their next natural move is the iFrame, and then we'll all have thirteen of them in our homes, and away we go. As someone who respects the market, if that happens, well then . . . tough luck.

I think what you need to do is focus on capturing the great pictures. What doesn't go away is the iconic shot. You need to focus on the product that can be delivered both physically and digitally.

And finally . . .

▶ If you created a social media platform, what would be the key feature and why?

I love restrictions. I think they force us to be efficient and creative. So my social network would only allow you to post one piece of content—blog post, video, audio, whatever you wish—every twenty-four hours. Imagine how that would keep the volume down and raise the quality bar. You'd have to think hard about what was truly important to your consumer, and at the same time your consumer would know what was truly important to you. I think it could be a billion-dollar idea. I'm not in a position to do it. Who else wants to try?

# CHAPTER 10
# FACEBOOK ADS

## IN THIS CHAPTER I´LL TALK ABOUT TAKING ADVANTAGE OF OTHER PEOPLE´S EMOTIONS, HOW TO MARKET PRODUCTS PEOPLE ARE EMBARRASSED TO ADMIT THEY USE, AND HOW PRACTICE MAKES PERFECT.

As of the writing of this book in late summer 2015, Facebook ads, also known as Unpublished Page posts, are the single best advertising digital product for entrepreneurs and Fortune 500 companies that I've seen since buying the keyword *wine* through Google Ad-Words in 2004.

I didn't realize it at first. Facebook has been an evolving ad product for the last few years, starting off slow, with ads on the right side of the desktop like any other banner advertising. When I started to see ads in the newsfeed it made a lot of sense to me; it's huge and in-your-face when you look at the screen on your phone. Still, I didn't have a eureka moment until a few months later, into 2014. It was only when I looked at the data and the results of the early Facebook ad campaigns that I started getting bullish and recognized that this was going to be a game changer.

So did a few others, but not everyone. In fact, a lot of people were hysterical in 2014–15 that Facebook would make changes that would compromise its organic outreach on fan pages in favor of ad pages. Journalists, pundits, and execs who had never run a Facebook ad were publishing articles about how all the young people were migrating to Snapchat and Instagram and threatening Facebook's domination. People were so angry and emotional they resisted exploring Facebook's capabilities and trying out the new ad product. But I and other real practitioners, the kind of people who spend lots of time in the dirt, recognized that this emotional narrative was creating an outstanding arbitrage opportunity, and we jumped in to take advantage of it.

The more people bashed Facebook and swore its effectiveness was on the decline, the fewer people were trying out the new ad platform. And since Facebook is a supply-and-demand marketplace, the price only goes up as advertisers bid for audiences, just like Google AdWords. There was therefore an incredible golden era in 2014–15 where the intrepid marketers who weren't wasting their breath complaining and were willing to experiment could get tremendous reach to the exact people they wanted with a bunch of different creatives, and see tangible results. That, my friends, reflects the difference between how practitioners and headline readers operate.

We've never had an ad product with incredible accuracy, one that could target to age, sex, occupation, and on top of that, behaviors and interests. By partnering up with data mining companies, Facebook can now tell us not only the demographics of its users, but their buying histories, both online and off. You can literally target one ad to nineteen-year-old men with facial hair who live in Phoenix and drink Red Bull, and send another one to twenty-three-year-old women in Detroit who wear contact lenses and play golf.

I'm a forty-year-old male who lives in Manhattan and loves the Jets and root beer. Imagine what a phenomenally cost-effective transaction you could instigate if you hit my emotional center by putting in my line of vision a root beer with green football thematics. The only challenge is figuring out the psychology of your audience and determining what story will most likely compel them to make a purchase. If you learn to interpret the available correctly and deploy it with creative calls to action against the right demo at the right time on the right platform, you're golden. Theoretically, Facebook ads could allow you to create a unique, native, relevant ad to every user on Facebook. I'm convinced this period will be heralded as one of the great eras of advertising alongside early TV advertising, early direct mail advertising, and early Google AdWords.

By the time you read this more people will be flooding this product. It's possible that Facebook ads will no longer be as effective as they once were now that more people have caught on to their extraordinary capabilities. Slowly the supply and demand will force the ads to a more appropriate price. I'll still be bullish about it and I believe it will be a monster platform in 2016–17, even becoming the bedrock of people's advertising plans. And as always, even in the most saturated market, there is ROI in putting your content on anything that consumers pay attention to, so long as you know how to execute, preferably better than anyone else.

---

▶ What's the best way to use Facebook ads and the right price to
  pay?

---

The answer is the same whether we're talking about the best way to capitalize on Facebook ads or Instagram, Pinterest's ad platform or native ads on Outbrain, Taboola, and Hexagram: Get in there and figure it out. The only way to get good at anything is to do it. There are hundreds of papers, articles, and video tutorials that will teach you how to create Facebook ads, but what will determine whether yours work or not will be how much time you spend listening to your consumers and gauging what content will best speak to them. The only way to figure that out is to experiment and see what happens.

As for what ads should cost you, that's always going to be a different answer from day to day depending on the supply-and-demand curve of the open bidding marketplace.

---

▶ What's the best way to use Facebook ads to grow audiences on other platforms?

---

You shouldn't. It's the wrong strategy when you can buy an audience on YouTube with pre-rolls at 5–7 cents per view, and Pinterest and Instagram now have their own ad platforms. You will find that dollar for dollar, you will win by building audiences within the ad product of the platform. Native content is always the best way to reach consumers, so leave your Facebook ads on Facebook.

---

▶ Which marketing vehicles are working best to grow the start-ups you've invested in?

---

At the time I answered this question, every start-up I was investing in was using Facebook ads and if they could have spent every dollar they had on them they would have. It was as effective as Google AdWords was back in the day for Amazon and eBay. At that time, while many dithered and debated the ROI of Google AdWords, these two Internet companies went all in, which allowed them to gain tons more market share at an undervalued price.

▶ As a rookie, how much should I allocate to Facebook ads for a Teespring campaign?

With a platform this powerful you should be spending as much money as possible on it. You could have so much fun with a campaign for such an easily customizable product. Imagine if you made a T-shirt that said, for example, "Denver Truck Drivers Rule." You could then create a Facebook ad targeted toward truck drivers who live in Denver. It would crush.

▶ How should marketers engage with an audience that is generally reluctant to talk publicly about the needs we can fill, for example hair replacement products?

First of all, you might be surprised what people are willing to talk about in public. Ashley Madison aside, there isn't much left that's truly taboo or embarrassing. Rogaine has 36,000 likes on its official Facebook page. Depends has 26,000. So you can certainly start there, and you can make an educated guess that a sizable portion of men and women between the ages of 35 and 50 might have hair loss on their mind. In addition, however, because of Facebook's data mining capabilities, you can gauge who your audience might be based on their purchasing behavior.

Second, don't forget you can go after people indirectly, too. Look for specialists and doctors with fan pages and tap their audience. Analyze the similarities among all of those people and create a general profile for the individuals who would probably be interested in hearing about your product or service, and target them.

Finally, search ads would be a powerful tool for anyone with this dilemma. Buy the right keywords on Google so that when someone does take it upon themselves to start looking for information, yours shows up immediately.

---

▶ Is it worth paying for a course to learn all about Facebook ads, or is it all right to rely on the free info on YouTube? Are Facebook ads really that complicated?

---

Facebook ads are not hard in the same way that using a screwdriver or shooting a basketball is not hard. *Being great at the execution is what's hard.* Use your time to educate yourself on the options available to you with the tool, and then start experimenting with it. The more you practice and analyze your results as you go, the better you'll get. Being a practitioner is the only way to achieve meaningful success. We live in a world of headline readers and shallow pundits. I want you to be different. Go deep.

# CHAPTER 11
# INFLUENCER MARKETING

---

## IN THIS CHAPTER I TALK ABOUT WHERE THE BIG BUCKS ARE GOING NEXT, THE TWO BIGGEST INFLUENCER OPPORTUNITIES, AND HOW UP-AND-COMING INFLUENCERS CAN GET ADVERTISER ATTENTION.

---

We all know that the thank-you economy is based on the power of word of mouth. With one click—or tweet or share or favorite or any number of other social digital acts—consumers' messages can be spread and their voice amplified well beyond the boundaries of their neighborhoods or even the industries where they work. And that's just the ordinary Joes who aren't actually trying to make names for themselves. There are others, of course, whose WOM is even more valuable. These are the people who put in the hustle. Celebrities, for sure, and experts in their fields, but also those people who aren't celebrities in the traditional sense and yet who are so entertaining, different, or funny, *and* so good at creating native content, whether six-second Vine videos or pithy tweets or insightful blog posts, they develop a disproportionate effect on popular culture and opinion. Marketing today is about going where the eyeballs go, and the eyeballs are on all of these influencers. Will they see your brand there? You're missing out if they're not.

I've known for a long time that one person's passion and personality could carry a brand, especially via video. Companies were reaching out to me as early as 2006 asking if I would integrate their products into *Wine Library TV*. I didn't take their offers because I wasn't yet sure what the negative side effects might be, and though 5K was a nice sum I was making enough that it didn't seem worth the risk. Now the practice has become so commonplace and acceptable I'm considering getting a sponsor for *#AskGaryVee*. Can you imagine it? "*The #AskGaryVee Show*, brought to you by the New York Jets."

Back in 2009, when I first wrote about influencer marketing in *Crush It*, people were still debating whether YouTube was really a major platform. Today YouTube is *the* video platform of our society, with Facebook video hot on its heels. Influencer marketing is an exploding category, yet for all the thousands of dollars being paid to people to post things on social, it is still grossly underpriced below its market value. I always say that I don't like to make predictions, but I'm comfortable predicting that whatever the dollar amount influencers are being paid to market services and products in 2016, that money will be dwarfed by 2019. Corporations are going to give massive amounts of money to individuals to help bring awareness on platforms like Snapchat and Instagram and plenty more that don't exist yet.

When I first advocated for this kind of marketing, people were still skeptical of the idea that everyone and anyone could develop a personal brand. It was weird. Now it's the norm. Every fourteen-year-old knows that if she can get enough followers on Instagram companies will send her free stuff and pay her to put pictures of their product on her feed, and not one fourteen-year-old watching her is going to think badly of her for doing it. You'll see—

influencer marketing is going to be one of the advertising be...
of the next decade.

I believe in this form of marketing so much that in May 2013 I started a talent agency with Jérôme Jarre called GrapeStory to represent the star storytellers of Vine and Snapchat. Since then I've watched the careers of Logan Paul, Marcus Johns, KingBach, Lele Pons, Nash Grier, and Shonduras explode, turning them from unknowns into bigger stars to the average fifteen-year-old than Rihanna. If you're twenty-five years or older, these names may not mean anything to you, but for anyone ages 14–24, these have been household names for well over eighteen months.

---

▶ Where do you see the biggest untapped opportunities in the social media influence space? Where is the next big thing coming from?

---

Influencers have more power than ever because now they're in a position not only to create content, *but also to create meaningful distribution*. The two biggest opportunities are product and retail. I could have sold stemware and glassware thanks to my influence in the wine industry. Think infomercials. Don't laugh. Have you any idea how much money QVC makes in five minutes when they've got the right person selling the right product? It's a $3 billion company. Make yourself the QVC 2.0, and you'll have something tremendous.

---

▶ How do you define influencer?

---

I define an influencer as anybody with a public social profile. That's it. If you have forty-two people following you, then you are influencing them with your content. You may not be the influencer that BMW needs to impact its sales goals that day, but that doesn't change the fact that you *are* influencing *someone*. I have long been a fan of chasing the long-tail end of the graph by using tons of smaller influencers. The bottom line is, whether you're in competitive sports or in wine, you can head over to platforms like Instagram or Pinterest and round up *everybody* with more than 100 followers and find a way to use them. In fact, let's take a left turn and talk about something else: this book.

I am going to spend a disproportionate amount of my January vacation (or at least the downtime when Liz's parents have the kids) reaching out to as many people as possible and getting them to agree, when the weather warms up, to post a picture of their hot dog legs with my book on them accompanied by a hashtag like #SpringBreakBookOfTheYear (or . . . something). Seriously. I will spend my (incredibly valuable) time chasing down 100–1,000,000 micro-influencers to post a picture of my book.

The long tail matters. Everybody is an influencer.

---

▶ Now that you're running an influencer space with GrapeStory, what are the biggest challenges you're facing in scaling the business model, and which brands are doing a good job using influencers in social channels?

---

A lot of companies are doing it well. Our client GE was the first to jump on it with a six-second science experiment on Vine that led to a much bigger campaign. Virgin Mobile, Hewlett-Packard, and Samsung are also companies that have seen success using influencer marketing. They're just the tip of the iceberg. By the time you read this book 90 percent of large businesses will be considering spending on influencers, and by the time 2020 gets here many small businesses will be reaching out to local celebrities. And when I say local, I mean neighborhood moms with 329 Instagram followers. It works because people like to buy from people they trust. You're going to see a whole lot more of it everywhere, from Pinterest to YouTube.

As for GrapeStory, the real problem we have with scaling is that we do too good a job. We help people with talent get big, and then they get so big they decide to move on to more established agencies like Creative Artists Agency and William Morris. But then, CAA and William Morris face the same challenge as well. That's what happens when your business model isn't based on building an asset, like a piece of tech, but on your own skills. Like a lawyer, you're only as good as your last billing cycle.

But I bet on my strengths, which are 1) interacting with people, and 2) noticing trends and taking advantage of them. This business is built on both. And I'm telling you, I've seen all of this before, back in 2007 when Twitter started its rise. My strategy is to ride the wave first, and do it better than anybody else ever will.

▶ What's the difference between influencer marketing and product placement?

Because of the visual nature of modern advertising, product placement is at the core of the influencer executions. When people think about influencer marketing, they don't realize just how many different ways product placement can be handled, especially when you consider how the primary platform for this kind of execution, Instagram, is dramatically maturing. I see a brand like Protein World spending a ton of money on Instagram influencers, but it's always the same old thing. Some good-looking kid is holding up the product. I think we're past that. They could be doing it much more intelligently, and seamlessly.

For example, forced product placement like a fifteen-second MTV *Cribs*-style tour of an influencer's apartment where the product just happens to be visible in the kitchen would be more honest and natural. Or instead of hiring some random attractive person in a bathing suit to hold up a can, you could create a brand ambassador where people actually buy into his or her brand, so it means something when that person shows up at your branded events, or your box at the Kentucky Derby. The best influencers are so creative, they can make the product feel totally seamless, like it's a natural part of the event. It's why GoPro has done so well. Their product is, by its very nature, a seamless part of the scenarios with which they want it to be associated.

There's also the reverse move. Some brands can go in the other way and actually openly laugh at the marketing play. Having an influencer shove the product into the camera while they peek out from behind it lets you in on the joke and paradoxically makes the whole thing more natural and understandable.

---

▶ What is the role of influencers in my overall media strategy, and how do I evaluate them relative to other marketing channels?

---

The only thing that makes influencer marketing different from any other marketing channel is that you're paying for both content and distribution on the same line item. That's it. Otherwise, you quantify it the same way you quantify any other medium. When you buy banner ads, you quantify it against impressions or clicks. Why wouldn't you do it the same way with an influencer spend? Speaking of impressions, a lot of digitally registered "impressions" that you pay for with display advertising don't even correlate with an ad actually being seen. With an influencer, you know that consumption is going to be substantially higher because his or her audience is truly engaged, not quickly scrolling through in order to get to the real content. That's the attention that I care so much about.

So for me, it's easy to measure one platform against another because I'm almost always pointing to a page or a transaction that can be tracked. If you're not fortunate enough to be in that position, and instead are going for broad awareness, you still need to be able to track by impressions. In my opinion (and if you're reading this book, hopefully you care about my opinion a little bit), an impression generated by an influencer is far more valuable than an impression generated by a generic "digital media spend" that puts some image in the right-hand rail of a website.

---

▶ How do I evaluate the cost of an influencer on a case-by-case basis?

---

To answer this question, let me begin by telling you a story. Late 1997 was a new frontier. I was out of the gate with WineLibrary .com before most people knew what the Internet was (much less that they could buy wine there), and I had an email service that was doing shockingly well. Then along comes Luxury.com (yes, Luxury.com, I'm calling you out again) saying, "Hey, Wine Library, would you like to buy an ad on our ONE MILLION PERSON email list?"

At this point, my head exploded. I couldn't even fathom a million people actually being on a mailing list. Mine was only in the tens of thousands at that point. So I spent what was at the time an ungodly amount of money, something like $40,000, a huge chunk of my marketing money for the year, and went for it. I thought there was a huge opportunity to siphon off their users and build huge LTV (lifetime value). To me, the math made sense.

The morning of the email, it was all hands on deck. We called in every warehouse, sales, and part-time employee we had in preparation for what I thought would be our biggest sales day ever. We were getting two, three, four orders a day at that point, so I thought that maybe it could be HUNDREDS!

Nine o'clock rolls around, the email goes out, and I'm refreshing the order screen like mad. It's 9:03 A.M. . . . 9:04 A.M. . . . nothing. For the next fifteen minutes I'm completely scared until "Ah! I know what it is! They must have had it scheduled for nine A.M. Pacific Time." So I email them asking if that's the case, and whether I should be waiting until noon to see results.

I get an email back two hours later saying, "No. It went out at 9 A.M. EST." At that point, one order had come in using the code LUXURY at checkout.

I was shocked, I was scared, I was upset. And then I realized, it doesn't matter how many people are on your list. What matters is how many of them OPEN it. What matters is how many of them CLICK the link. What matters is how many of them BUY your stuff. One could argue that this moment was the seed behind what everything my life, my companies, and this book is about. This was when I realized it wasn't about width, it was all about depth. It's about how many people care, not how many people you have. And let's call it what it is: When I say "care," what I really mean is "who will convert for me in a transaction."

So how do you judge an influencer? By a ton of things. Who is following them? If you're going after some fifteen-year-old kid with a fan base of screaming girls, but you sell Pampers to middle-aged moms, you're going to miss the mark. So you need to know who they're reaching. Once you know that, you need to look past that top-line number of followers and look at the actual engagement happening on each individual post. First off, on a quantitative level, you're looking for what that engagement is as a percentage of their overall followers. Then you need to look at each of those interactions from a qualitative standpoint to see if those interactions are superficial or if they're actually interested and engaged. I may not have the biggest following on Instagram, but I know that my posts could do a hell of a lot more for Office Max or Staples than another user with forty times my following because my people aren't just following me because I'm hot (although to be fair, since I've started working out, I've gotten significantly more attractive); they're in it for a much deeper reason.

---

▶ My brand doesn't even have a Vine account. Should Vine be a platform I consider if it's not somewhere we're already active for brand development?

---

Your brand should be on any platform that has meaningful scale within your target audience. It would be crazy to not be present on a platform on which your customers are also present. (This also applies to platforms that your audience might be on in twenty-four months, too. Please recognize what's happened to Facebook, Instagram, and Snapchat over the last decade as their user base has matured into a much older one and as parents have been forced to go there in order to communicate with their children. Let's make sure to wrap our heads around that.)

Here's another way to look at it. This is like asking if your brand should run TV commercials even though you don't have your own TV show. Of course. You're looking for awareness and contextual relevance. It's not just about siphoning that influencer's followers off onto your own fan base within the platform. If you're selling to that audience, and a Vine celebrity can get you that reach and that association, you're winning.

That said, of course it would be a more ideal execution for you to already have a Vine page that can be tagged and allow you to get those extra 4,000 followers. Then you can remarket to them over and over, and ultimately drive down the cost of acquiring them by increasing their lifetime value. Work on that, because you should be there.

---

▶ When you contract with an influencer, do you instruct them
to continue to make the kind of content your brand is already
making, or should you let them speak with their own voice and on
their own terms?

---

This is the biggest debate that I see going on between brands, entrepreneurs, and influencers. I am a humongous believer in letting the DJ do her own thing. If you write a song, and one of the biggest DJs in the world wants to sample it in her set, get the hell out of the way and let her do it. That DJ is famous for a reason. She knows what she's doing. No brand is going to know an influencer's audience the way the influencer does. And to be honest, influencers have to bring that context to their audience for the sake of their own brand, not only so that they can continue to monetize, but for the sake of making *your* content. It is in your best interest for them to put your product in their own context. Now, you may not like that. There's typically a huge disconnect between the talent and the decision maker on the brand side. At the end of the day, it's your business, and you always have the option to say no. In fact, I think you should absolutely have approval. Obviously I'd never recommend anybody pay money for a product they don't get to see in advance. But that approval really only exists for the fringe 1 percent of craziness, not for you to add your creative two cents.

There is a reason you're paying an influencer to reach their audience. They know what they're doing. Even if all you want are their followers, you still need your product to be presented in the right tone. I often like to hedge on answers, but in this case I'm very comfortable being definitive. Let the talent do his or her thing.

---

▶ Can an influencer on Vine, Snapchat, or Instagram drive app downloads given the platform limitations against linking out? How can we prove that their content directly affects the KPI?

---

The first half of this is a silly question. The answer is "Of course!"

For one thing, Instagram now *does* have ads that link out. You could use an influencer's content to get the recognition, and then market against his or her fans with an ad that contains a click out. You're paying twice, and taking a bigger risk, but that is an execution I believe would work.

Otherwise, simply run a controlled test. Establish a baseline of daily app downloads given your current ad spends and measure against it. If you're getting between 300 and 500 downloads a day, and then you get 1,000 on a day when you run an influencer post, well, then you know something is working.

Way too many people are looking for the reason that something isn't working instead of the reason that it is. It's basic. Snapchat is just awareness, I get it, but at a certain point, you're going to hit a point of consistency in downloads that you'll be able to measure against. That's when you want to get into something like influencer marketing, because then you'll be able to measure in a controlled state.

PHILLIP GIMMI
@PHILLIPGIMMI
www.PhillipGimmi.com

▶ What is the tactical and strategic pathway to become an influencer? I am all in when it comes to all forms of marketing. How do I connect with influencers, leverage their brand equity, or grow my own?

Asking "how do I become an influencer?" is really no different from asking "how do I become a star?"

The really funny first answer is that you have to have talent.

The next funny answer is that you have to put in a ton of work.

These are both very clichéd, basic answers, but they happen to be massive truths. I will say that the one new truth is speed of adoption within a new environment. If you pay close attention to the people who popped on Vine, or the people who popped in the early days of Snapchat or Instagram, they all happened to be the Christopher Columbus of their platforms. They were early. So as those platforms took off, they developed disproportionate amounts of followers as new users joined and found them.

These days it's going to be way harder to be the next The Fat Jew or Fuck Jerry (even though many have tried) because they succeeded in the landgrabs of the early days of their platform. So if you want to be a video influencer, you can go and attack YouTube, Instagram, or Snapchat, even though they're established markets, or you can use those platforms to hone your talents. Become an expert, and then when the next big thing in video comes out, use your new skills to jump on it and become a first mover.

So the biggest move here is to be a first mover on a platform I don't even know about yet . . .

And then have tons of talent . . .

And then do a lot of hard work.

# CHAPTER 12
# STOP WITH THE EXCUSES!

---

IN THIS CHAPTER I´LL TALK ABOUT *GONE WITH THE WIND*, HOW TO MAKE DEPRESSING CONTENT PALATABLE, AND RAISING THE DEAD (INDUSTRIES).

---

Throughout the relatively short history of *The #AskGaryVee Show* I've fielded numerous questions from people convinced that their especially dull or outdated industry or uninspiring job poses a special marketing challenge. It's stunning how many remarkable reasons and circumstances people can come up with to explain why they haven't met with success. Of course, the problem doesn't usually lie with the type of industry or job. The problem lies with the individual who can't see opportunities when they're right in front of his or her face. There might not be any easier place to make your mark than in an environment where few people, if any, are putting much effort into making their mark, or where everything has stayed the same since the dawn of time.

What I find heartening is what often happens after I answer these kinds of questions. A high percentage of people will email me afterward to say, "Hey, you were right," and tell me that my answer sparked the beginning of a mind shift that led to rapid gains. I have no interest in being a motivational speaker, but it's scary and exciting to see how little it sometimes takes to change someone's perspective. Maybe we all look for excuses to explain why we don't achieve what we want to, and we should be more self-aware and recognize how much control we actually have over our own fate, even taking into account the barriers like racism, sexism, and nationalism that many of us have to face. It's amazing how as soon as you make the shift from "I can't" to "Why can't I?" you go from defense to offense, and as everyone knows, the best place to score is always on offense.

---

▶ How do I create interesting content for a boring product or a stale industry?

---

A white lawyer defends a black man in a small southern town. A spoiled rich girl gets married three times and survives the Civil War. Boy meets girl. Recognize any of these? Shaved down to their core, *To Kill a Mockingbird*, *Gone with the Wind*, and *Romeo and Juliet* sound pretty damn boring. Their lasting power lies in the fresh, imaginative, daring, surprising storytelling of their creators. There is no boring if you tell your story right.

If you're asking this question, your problem isn't your content; it's your mind-set. You have to shift your thinking immediately. You cannot change your output unless you change your input.

Start by thinking of every possible way your business, brand, or product touches people, from what they eat, to their hobbies, to their conversation topics. Don't box yourself in. Use your imagination and map out all the options if that's helpful. For example, a hardware store. You are sadly mistaken if all you see are tools, adhesives, and paint. Other people see their dream home, their kids' fort, a finished honey-do list, a new vegetable garden, or a bird feeder. They see their problems solved, their rainy days filled, or their closet space doubled. They see Habitat for Humanity or Eagle Scouts or Pencils of Promise. They might see sweat and exercise, or inspiration, change, craft, and fun.

Next, think outside your industry altogether. When I was still selling wine, people would always tell me about other retailers that were doing interesting things and suggest I go for a visit. You know what my answer was? "I don't give a crap." The truth is despite all my years in wine, I spent an amazingly little amount of time within the industry itself. The same can be said for the agency industry, even though I'm working in it now. I've been to maybe six other agencies in my life. I don't follow industry news. I try not to listen to what else is going on.

And that is why I have been able to innovate over and over again. I don't want to copy what everyone else is doing—I want to stand out. So I stick to what I'm really good at, and I search for inspiration where everyone else isn't looking. My experience in toy collecting and baseball cards gave me the perspective to attack the wine-collecting world in a new and fresh way. I looked to Silicon Valley and Hollywood to create *Wine Library TV*. I used my business skills to create an agency that focused on business results more than creative, I used what I had learned from SEO, email marketing, and content marketing in the late 1990s and early 2000s to figure out how to create strategies for the new social media platforms. If you're launching a fitness app, pay attention to what's happening in the food industry, the rock climbing industry, even hip-hop or sports. Think completely left field. The best way to stagnate is to pay attention to everyone else because they're doing the same crap over and over. And guess what? The same old crap sucks.

Taking an open, optimistic attitude will keep your content fresh and exciting, and allow you to change the world's perception of your "boring" product.

---

▶ How can a nonprofit that works to solve a serious problem, like human trafficking, make depressing content dynamic?

---

No one ever said content had to be fun or light. You have to respect your topic and contextualize it for your platform. Though you probably can't make your content light, you can certainly work on keeping it simple and easy to absorb. Create narratives through infographics, slide shares, videos, pictures, and quote cards that get your story across without requiring people to dig too deep. Make sure you pay attention to the colors you use and the music you choose.

---

▶ My goal is to wake the dead, aka the funeral business. What are your thoughts on bringing relevance to a gray-haired industry?

---

I'm fascinated by this business. This wasn't the first time someone in the funeral industry asked me for some ideas. I once recommended to a funeral director that he should become the number-one flower content site on the Internet, thus creating a positive connection to his work. That's what I'm talking about when I say that companies need to become media companies and start writing content for and getting involved in areas that are related to them. Don't comment on your competitor! Instead, comment on something completely out of the ordinary yet surprisingly relevant.

Whenever someone breaks new ground in any industry, especially one with as much history as funeral direction, they will likely be accused of disrespect. And maybe they're right. Maybe innovation is inherently disrespectful of what has come before. Anyone in a highly sensitive business, such as funeral directors, hospice workers, and the like, would have to tread especially carefully, of course.

Their job is to guide people through a difficult time when they're at their most vulnerable. But even as we entrepreneurs and innovators disrespectfully bring progress to our industries, we can avoid offending consumers by being understanding, compassionate, and empathetic. And that's not just people whose business is to help the grieving. It's true for all of us.

Innovation is what wakes up sleepy, gray-haired industries. When I started in the wine business, wine was serious and sophisticated, and its experts were sixty-year-old gentlemen, not twenty-five-year-old Jets fans from Jersey. So I came in and I innovated. I started a dot-com in 1996. I started a YouTube show less than a year after YouTube launched. I started posting content on Snapchat and Pinterest before almost any other entrepreneur knew what to do with them. When you get in early, you have the freedom to play and improvise and figure out what works best.

# CHAPTER 13
# GRATITUDE

---

## IN THIS CHAPTER I TALK ABOUT WHAT I DO WHEN THINGS GET TOUGH, HOW TO ROMANCE YOUR AUDIENCE, AND HOW TO BUILD LIFETIME VALUE.

---

I'm often asked what fuels me, and 80 percent of the time my answer is gratitude. I'm glad I was born in a communist country and got to move to this country, where capitalism is revered and appreciated. I'm thankful that I haven't had a lot of pain in my life, though it's because I lost three of my four grandparents before I ever knew them. I'm grateful for the best mom in the world, for the best wife in the world, for a dad who taught me not to be full of shit, and for all the people I love.

I won't say I know how to teach you to have more gratitude, but I can say that if it is something that can be developed you should go figure out how. Gratitude is my weapon in my day-to-day life. Period. Being an entrepreneur or a CEO is a stunningly lonely job. That's not talked about much (though it did get discussed more frequently for a while after a spate of suicides within the tech community). As the head of a company, you are the last person in the line of defense. You are entirely responsible for *everything*. It's a huge eye-opener when you realize that you are responsible not only for yourself and your family and loved ones, but for other people's, too. The enormity of that obligation hit me hard when I was a kid building up Wine Library to 150 employees, and weighs on me even more now that VaynerMedia has nearly 600 employees. Keeping that commitment front-of-mind while battling all the competitors trying to beat you and put you out of business, all while navigating dynamics you can't control, from Wall Street to geopolitics, can weigh heavily even when you're not faced with a business catastrophe like losing an important deal or going out of business.

Gratitude is what has gotten me through my toughest moments in business (yes, there have been some, though I don't talk about them much). Whenever I have lost a deal to a competitor, or an incredible employee, or millions of dollars in revenue because a state changed its shipping laws and won't let me sell there (damn you, Texas!), I default to gratitude. Because I recognize that even if I had invested in Uber, and Woody Johnson decided it was time and I did buy the Jets tomorrow, none of it would matter to me at all if the next day I got a call that someone I love was sick or had died. Keeping that perspective allows me to handle anything and everything. Whenever I've been in my loneliest place with my biggest headache, thank God I've been able to step away from it and remind myself of all the great things I've been given. It's impossible to complain and get too down when I do that.

Gratitude is what allows me to live my life the way I do, but it's also a core element to the way I do business. I never, ever take it for granted when people take minutes out of their ridiculously busy worlds to watch my show or read my blogs or books. I spend much of my time online trying to thank my fans, followers, and customers as often as possible. I don't understand why more brands and businesses don't make that their mission, as well. It's not as if consumers are limited to their neighborhoods or even their cities to find what they need or want anymore—the world is at their fingertips. It seems to me that when the competition is that widespread, you should be falling all over yourself thanking every damn customer who decides to spend some of his or her hard-won money with you.

---

▶ Any thoughts on how to use social to promote nonprofits that are selling an experience and culture rather than a product?

---

The companies that have struggled the most to use social media correctly are generally charities and NGOs.

My big issue is with their manners. Many businesses with sizable audiences, including mine, get hit up every day by charities that ask us for donations or for us to share their content via a retweet or post. And you know what? Rarely do they even say hello first.

Can you romance a girl a little?

The rudeness and entitlement illustrate for me the fundamental problem charities have when they're looking for help raising money: They've forgotten that we're living in a thank-you economy (yes, that's a book plug). Most of the nonprofits that ask me to help them assume that I'll be compelled to give my money or use my clout on their behalf just because they're working for a good cause. But when my time is limited, I'm going to focus my attention on the organizations that have bothered to build a relationship with me, not the ones who approached with their hands out. And I think the same is true for the rest of the population. Many charity organizations think that merely putting up heartrending photographs will be enough to move people to support them, but they're overlooking the fact that it's never the photograph that compels people to help—it's the greater story it tells.

For NGOs and charities to succeed in social media, they have to do what all the for-profit businesses out there are doing—hustling, listening, creating dialogue, solving problems, building relationships, and storytelling. (For a good example of how nonprofits can execute this strategy, check out Charity: Water. It's not only an excellent organization; it's also got a killer social media strategy.) And then, like all businesses, they have to express gratitude and appreciation whenever anyone so much as looks in their direction. Social media is a wonderful place to express gratitude, even for organizations whose members prefer to remain anonymous. It's so easy for a nonprofit to create a video or other public announcement of their thanks for the people that support their efforts.

Nonprofits that focus on expressing appreciation instead of expectation will be the ones that crack the code to success in social media.

---

▶ Do you still believe marketing is headed toward one-on-one marketing?

---

More than ever. You know why? Because despite all the evidence (I put a lot of it into my book *The Thank You Economy*) about how good business gets done today when you listen to your consumer, most brands are still talking away. They're like the guy at the party who won't let you get a word in edgewise because he's not really interested in what you have to say. When you're in that situation, how long do you last before coming up with an excuse to walk away? The scene on social media is no different, except the consumer doesn't need any excuse. When they've had enough, buh-bye. They unfollow, they move on, and they don't come back.

One-to-one marketing takes time but the ROI is tremendous because so few businesses are actually doing it. I finally figured out that's why my results are so often the exception instead of the rule. When you're listening and other people aren't, you look like a star. I'm still amazed at how much it means to people when I send them a Twitter video response or reply to them on Instagram to thank them for their follow. Almost every single Twitter video I've sent has been liked and retweeted. Why are people so excited? Because nobody else does it! But you can and you should. People love when you take an extra second out of your day to acknowledge them. It's the equivalent of a nicely written thank-you note, except it takes less time to do and it doesn't take two days to get to its destination.

Expressing gratitude helps you build lifetime value—"LTV." When you're small and still climbing the mountain, sometimes it's practically all you've got to give. So spend your time being generous and grateful for whatever time and attention your customer gives you. You'll see that it comes back to you eventually via word-of-mouth recommendations, sales, and legacy.

# CHAPTER 14
# LEADERSHIP

---

## IN THIS CHAPTER I´LL TALK ABOUT THE BIGGEST LESSONS I´VE LEARNED, BUILDING CULTURE, AND WHY REPEATING YOUR MISTAKES IS SOMETIMES A GOOD THING.

---

I suspect the topic I will most want to talk about when I get to the end of my career will be leadership. It's a skill that came naturally to me at a young age. Yet as proud as I am of my leadership skills and effectiveness, I still work on it every day, and it's an aspect of myself where I feel I am continuously growing. This chapter allows me to thank my employees, whose smarts, talent, and hard work always push me to raise the bar and hone my abilities. They have afforded me the chance to take my leadership skills to a much higher level than I ever realized was possible.

My philosophy on leadership is very simple: Everything in business stems from the top, whether you're the boss of two people in a three-person team or the head of a Fortune 500 company. And everything that happens in a company is 100 percent the CEO's fault. After all, the CEO is the person who puts people into a position to make good or bad decisions. It's no accident that when some companies change their CEO they go from winners to losers or vice versa. It may be the most important variable for success in running a business.

Being a leader today is a greater challenge than ever because of social media. It has completely changed the nature of the job. You used to be able to—no, leaders were *expected* to talk from the top of a mountain. You'd make your proclamation and not worry much about hearing anything back, certainly not in real time. But now that our communication channels have given everyone a voice, whatever you say from on high may invite a reaction. You might get it in-house, or you might get it from the masses. That's proving to be a challenging adjustment for some leaders, especially those further along in their career.

The only effective way to truly lead is to practice and model the behavior you want to see in others. That's why I once drove across state lines in a blizzard during the height of the Christmas rush to deliver a single case of white zinfandel to a customer whose order had been delayed. I know my team is watching me. I can't tell them to go the extra mile if I'm not willing to do it myself. If the DNA of any business stems from the top, the top has to ensure that its values, beliefs, and attitudes trickle down to shape the culture and encourage a productive, innovative, creative, and even happy environment.

One hallmark of a good leader is to ask questions. It's the best way to show your team you recognize they're more than just cogs on a wheel. "Hey, how are things going?" "How's the new baby?" "What are you excited about lately?" "Do you have any ideas you'd like to discuss?" It's also the best way to solve problems. Don't ever start offering solutions before asking tons of questions: "Why are we two weeks behind?" "What do you think is the issue?" "What do you need?" And then for God's sake, listen. Be compassionate. Be fair. Hire people who embody those characteristics, too. Celebrate successes, and when you have to reprimand, hark back to all the times you screwed up and remember that those mistakes have everything to do with who you are today. Great leaders aren't born; they're made.

I think this chapter offers a lot of value. After reading it, look in the mirror and think about what you do well and how you could do even better. Leadership needs to be a big pillar in your development if you have ambitions of building a business. The answers you see here may be the secret sauce to any success I've enjoyed in my career.

---

▶ What are the most important lessons your father taught you about building a business?

---

My dad is responsible for the single most important advice I've ever received:

Your word is bond.

I wasn't old enough to drink when I started working the floor at my dad's liquor store in Springfield, New Jersey, but that didn't stop me from being a great wine salesman. Not only had I memorized everything I had read in *Wine Spectator*, but I was naturally charismatic. Now, before I started at the store, I was also a bit of a bullshit artist. I would say absolutely anything to sell a baseball card. Maybe that's no surprise; a very, very fine line separates salesmanship and bullshit. My dad, however, made sure everyone working in his store knew the consequences would be severe for anyone who tried to cross it.

He taught me that when you make a commitment, you stick to it. If I bought fifty cases of wine, I was in for those cases no matter what. If the market changed or the wine received a poor rating, I was to stick with that purchase. You take it, you eat it, you drink it.

Those lessons made me into the man I am today. They showed me that I could use my charisma for good, and that I didn't need to cut corners or treat people poorly to succeed. For this reason, I've been able to hold on to business relationships for decades. Being honorable always pays off in the long run, even if it occasionally makes you a little less money in the short term. The marathon truly has greater value than the sprint.

---

▶ How do you change a firmly established culture into one that genuinely cares about the customer?

---

Everything that happens at VaynerMedia is my fault. Because I empower everybody I work with to create the culture at my company, the responsibility to build that culture is entirely on me. If I fail, we fail, so I work my butt off to make sure I don't.

Unfortunately, not everyone sees it that way. Some leaders at the head of a floundering ship might try to make excuses. They'll say there's some facet of the business that makes the current culture necessary. That's bull. Who is in charge of that facet of the business? The leadership. No matter how you slice it, a company's culture is completely dependent on the people in charge of it.

So there is only one way to change the culture when it's broken—kill the leadership.

Have you ever seen a recently pruned rosebush? It looks stunted, bare, and shrubby, like you've killed the plant. Until you come back six weeks later. See, rosebushes thrive best when old growth and dead branches are cut way back. It looks awful at first, but you'd be amazed at how rapidly those new branches and buds start to grow. Within just a few weeks of pruning a rosebush can be exploding with flowers.

Now, you can't just hack at the thing; you have to do it right.

There's a certain angle at which you cut to make sure the flowers grow in the right direction, and all sorts of other precautions someone who cares about roses a lot more than I do would know. My point is, sometimes you have to get rid of the old, tired stuff at the top to give something better a chance to bloom. And the same can be said for old, tired ideas or old, tired ways of doing business.

Obviously I'm not proposing murder, so how could you go about "killing" a company's leadership to give a new culture room to grow? You might try to express your concerns directly to the people in charge and pray they're open-minded enough to listen. You could try talking to influential people within the company who aren't part of the leadership team and hoping they'll take up the cause. You could do as much as you can within your small sphere, then work hard so that you rise up within the company and your sphere becomes bigger and your influence more broadly felt.

What if you're working for a family business or a new CEO, and there's no hope for change? Get the hell out. Sorry, there really is no other solution.

---

▶ Who are your idols or the people who inspire you? Did you ever have a mentor?

---

I've never worshipped any so-called business idols, but two people that I always admired were Walt Disney and Vince McMahon, the wrestler and CEO of WWE (World Wrestling Entertainment), because they're great storytellers who turned their storytelling into businesses. But Disney died before I was born and I've never met McMahon, so you can't really consider them mentors. There are really only two people in my life I truly idolize and could consider mentors: Tamara Vaynerchuk, who taught me people skills and much about what matters in life, and Sasha Vaynerchuk, who gave me a work ethic and taught me honor and perseverance.

---

▶ As a business leader, what's the one thing that keeps you up at night?

---

The one thing I most worry about every day is my health and the health of my family. So long as everyone I love is healthy, I will not be afraid of anything—not the landscape, not possible market shifts, not competition, and certainly not internal issues. See, some people may reject the idea that a company is a direct reflection of its leaders, but this is why I embrace it. I don't have to worry, because everything that has to do with my business—how we navigate that landscape, how we react to fluctuating markets, how we spar with competitors, and how I handle those internal issues—is entirely within my control.

I hope you hear that. A leader is supposed to be in control. If you're staying up at night sweating, do something about it.

---

▶ Do you ever complain?

---

This question came in just as my son, Xander, was going through a whiny stage. He was only a toddler so there was nothing unusual about that, but when he's older and I'm looking at him fondly wishing I could turn back time, it won't be to that particular phase, because if there's one thing I'm fundamentally against, it's complaining.

What's the value in it? I was lucky to learn this lesson very early on from my mother, who I swear has never complained a day in her life, and she's an immigrant who lost her mother at the age of five and fled from a communist country, so you know her life has not always been sunshine and rainbows. Not that anyone's ever is. But that's my point. Problems happen. Life isn't fair or perfect. Complaining fixes nothing. Only taking action does.

Besides, I'm the boss. If anyone has the power to fix a problem it's me, because I'm the one with all the control. So here's what I do: assess the problem, find the solution, and get on the offense. And I do my best to empower my employees to follow the same process.

I think some of them find it intimidating at first. Do I really mean it when I tell them they don't need to come to me for permission to try this idea or solve that problem, but should just use their best judgment? The first time they stop worrying that they're too junior or going to step on someone else's toes, and just get in there and solve their problem, is a game changer. They're never the same.

When this happens, you, as a leader, can scale that success. Get people to break through and help you solve problems and build things and spread your religion, and things start to click really fast.

Positivity is a state of mind. Honey works way better than vinegar. It will be a few more years before Xander fully understands why these things are true, but I know that as I pass on what my mother taught me I'm giving him one of the keys to a bright, prosperous future.

---

▶ In what situations are you most comfortable?

---

I thrive in the midst of chaos. I'm great to have around when things go wrong because I tend to stay cool and calm. Which is funny because I hate calm. Even New York is too slow for me at times. As soon as I walk into VaynerMedia I'll ask someone to turn on some music, because I get pumped when there's a buzz and a beat in the air. The ridiculous volume of things that get thrown at me every day and all the demands put on my attention would overwhelm some people, but I love it. It's my drug. I need the action.

> ▶ If you could teach everyone in the world one thing you've learned, what would it be?

My dad taught me that word is bond, but as crucial as that lesson is, I think it's a lesson that was uniquely important to me because of my personality.

Here's the one universal rule I would try to teach everyone: Depth matters more than width.

That is, the smallest meaningful, intentional act will mean much more than a huge one that lacks intent or substance.

Believe it or not, I'm paying attention to many of you who are reading this book. I'm no longer able to engage the way I used to with every single person who says hello, but I'm definitely trying every single day. When I'm not in a meeting or writing or taking care of business, I'm hustling for depth with my community. I'm favoriting posts, leaving notes, replying, and saying hello, especially on Instagram (@garyvee). I try to catch your little moments and let you know that I noticed, even if it took me awhile to get around to telling you. It's amazing how much a tweet can still mean to people.

Sadly, a lot of the social media world is still going wide—gunning for more likes, shares, and right hooks, doing whatever they can to make their fan or follower numbers grow instead of paying attention to the quality of their engagement. We want the attention, but then we don't want to give it back. And no, offering a like in exchange for a like, or a share for a share, doesn't count. It's a crap move that takes no thought and has no substance.

This is my call to action: Go deep. Reach out, provide value, and be there.

---

▶ **How do you stay constantly motivated?**

---

One, I love what I do. I love the HR nightmares of a 500-plus organization, the headaches, the grind, the calls with an upset customer, all of it. It's easy to stay motivated when you know your day is filled with things that are getting you closer to your goals.

Two, I'm grateful every single day. I feel so lucky to have been born in the mid-1970s, during such a special moment in Soviet history, instead of the mid-nineteenth century or the 1940s, and to have been given the opportunity to come to this country. I'm grateful for my parents, my wife, and my kids. I made this bed; how can I complain? Gratitude is amazing fuel.

---

▶ **How do you keep others motivated?**

---

This question came from the epic Tommy Lasorda in episode 109, an all-time great baseball manager and motivator himself. I thought it was an interesting question since he's clearly figured out methods that work for him and his teams.

Motivating employees should be one of a leader's top priorities. You already know I believe in leading by example, not just when you're running meetings, but in your daily interactions, in the emails you send, even your posture. I hope that the way I carry myself and live my life motivates people to work hard and do their best by others.

But it's not enough just to do your thing and hope everyone else absorbs the energy you put out. You also have to pay attention. Everyone has different needs objectives, and the incentives that work for one type of person might not work for another. Some people live for their kids, some people are totally career driven, some people need to be constantly challenged or they get bored. I meet with every single new hire at my company within the first few months after they start, and throughout their time at VaynerMedia I try to get to know them as best I can. I ask them questions about what they want to do with their lives, and then listen hard and figure out what makes them tick, and put them in a position where they find that if they work hard and fast, they can succeed. I also recognize that people change, so I have to make sure my team knows that if I don't figure it out on my own, they can come to me any time to discuss how their needs have changed and what we can do to help them feel more productive and accomplished. Employees who believe that you support their desire to achieve their own goals will be more than happy to use their efforts and talents to help you get closer to yours as well.

---

▶ What advice would you give someone transitioning to a leadership role?

---

Surprisingly, moving into a managerial or leadership role can be more of a challenge than actually executing the job once you get there. Not because you're suddenly delegating orders whereas once you were just executing them, but because when everyone starts looking for answers, they're going to start by looking at you.

My advice in this case would be to learn to rely on empathy and emotion as much as your executive skills so you can empower your team to become leaders themselves and take ownership of their work. That's a much harder thing to do than just ordering people around, but the end result is far more rewarding and productive.

In addition, accept that now everything is on you. That means sometimes you're going to have to take the hit if your team isn't performing the way you hoped it would. But no one likes a boss that passes the buck to an employee when things go wrong. You need to be the best human being you can be to earn their trust and respect. Back your team up and don't pass blame, and you will earn their loyalty *and* their best efforts. And really, isn't that the best thing a leader could ask for?

---

▶ How do you instill soul and swagger into a physical product you create?

---

Do you have soul and swagger? Do you hire people who have it? If so, your product will, too. How many times has a brand or product suffered after the departure of the company CEO? That doesn't mean the next leader might not be great and continue the swagger, but it all depends on his or her DNA.

---

▶ Are there any common mistakes you repeat? Any tips on overcoming them?

---

I repeat all my mistakes over and over and over again.

You know why? Because while I regret—really, really regret—any trouble my mistakes at the office cause my team, for the most part I enjoy making them. For example, my team is constantly on me about biting off more than I can chew. Too often, I become the bottleneck, and that slows everyone down and causes them stress. I do try to do better, but somehow month after month it still happens because I love saying yes to things more than I hate being the bottleneck.

And, if I'm being perfectly honest, I'm not going to put in the work it would take to overcome these mistakes. I don't want to focus on my weaknesses; I want to bet on my strengths. I feel that way about everyone in my life, too. I have such confidence in my team I struggle to think of something we are not great at. There must be something, but it's not where I put my time and energy, so it doesn't really register.

Some people might think this is willful blindness, but I say betting on your strengths might be the most underrated strategy in modern business. At home, you have to pay attention when mistakes or weaknesses threaten your personal or family life, but in business, if you're an entrepreneur and the boss? Nah.

▶ Are you worried you might have created a Steve Jobs-esque "reality distortion field" around VaynerMedia?

What a flattering question. For those of you who don't know, *reality distortion field* is a term used to describe the magnetic hold the late Steve Jobs seemed to have on his designers. By sheer force of personality and charisma, he seemed able to dissolve any doubts or questions about his strategies or plans. I'm not worried about that because I know my intent is pure. Sure, I'm probably creating distortion. I think since our job is to get a large group of people to coalesce around common goals, most leaders have to, and it's all for good.

▶ Do you prefer to be around people who are the same or different than you?

A few years ago I noticed that some of my friends were surrounding themselves with yes men and women, and I took a step back to make sure I wasn't doing the same. Sometimes I know I can be so forceful in my opinions that I suck all the oxygen out of the room. Guilty. But I do value what other people have to say. A solid debate is as sexy as—and sometimes more so than—a mutual admiration society. For someone who talks as much as I do, which is constantly, I listen quite a bit. In fact, I'm watching and listening all the time, so when I do talk, I'm usually sharing the intel I've gathered. I don't talk just to hear my beautiful voice.

In the end, I don't meet a lot of people like me, and that's probably good for the world. In fact, I would say as I get older I am more and more interested in finding people who are different from me and can round out my skills.

---

▶ If you were to tragically die today, how well would VaynerMedia do long term without its CEO? Have you been satisfied with Wine Library's performance since leaving to focus on VM?

---

If the DNA of a company stems from the top, then it makes sense that it will stagger if something happens to a key player. My brother and cofounder, AJ, is ridiculously capable, but I'd assume if something were to happen to me he'd be pretty torn up. He'd better be, anyway. And knowing him, it's possible he would wonder whether there was any point in continuing. So it wouldn't surprise me if it were other people in the team who insisted on keeping the business going. We've built an interesting culture, and I think in the end it would survive and eventually thrive again, especially once AJ was ready to take the helm if he chose to.

As for Wine Library, I really thought it would suffer more without me than it does. It's all run by family and close friends, and they've done a great job. Do I think it could be doing better? Of course, because I think I'm great! They can't experience hypergrowth when I'm not there. That's what I'm best at. I can grow businesses fast as shit. But they have other great talent around.

---

▶ Would you be able to lead any type of company? Do you think leaders can switch industries easily?

---

I 100,000 percent believe I could run most $500 million or smaller companies (any bigger and I'd have to spend some time there to be sure). Now, I don't know crap about 93 percent of companies out there, but with my spongelike skills I could quickly learn what I need to know about any B2B or B2C by studying the data, the numbers, the culture, the marketplace, and the consumer, and then reverse-engineer it.

And you know what? I don't think I'm that special, either. I think anyone who is good at both sales and HR could do it, because there are two mandates to running a business—build teams and sell stuff. The level at which you will be able to perform will be capped by your level of talent, but anyone who's good at both is in a position to succeed at the helm of a company. Any company.

---

▶ Would you be willing to sacrifice your ethics for a business win?

---

No, and not just because I'm obsessed with the idea of leaving a good legacy, but because, practically, it's the right thing. For one thing, I've found that I make more money if I don't immediately grab what's right in front of me. For another, I've made it clear I think leaders should be role models and walk the walk. I have an assistant with access to my emails; he'd know immediately if I did something shady or unethical, and then he would have to question everything I've ever said to him, and he'd stop trusting me. That would slow us down, and ultimately he would talk, which would change the narrative of who I was and what I was trying to accomplish.

A healthy company culture built on trust and openness makes business go faster. There's debate, but no one is wasting a minute questioning anyone's motives. Over the course of my career I will probably end up leaving a lot of money on the table because I'll be judging my success by how many people I think will come to my funeral, not how much money I ultimately make. And I wouldn't sacrifice that at any price.

---

▶ I want to encourage people to do what I did and leave a very secure job to pursue their dream. But will my employee retention rate drop? Has yours dropped since you started building up your personal brand?

---

The only way to build retention is to make it clear to your employees that you want them to be happy and live their dreams. That kind of support builds insane loyalty. My employees know without a doubt that I want to win, but not at their expense. I want to buy the New York Jets *with* them. I am well aware that some of them have dreams that might take them away from this company, and me, and if that happens, they will have my blessing and my support. In the meantime, however, I will try to bring them so much value over the long haul that they will have to think twice, maybe even three times, before deciding to leave. I think it's sad when leaders and managers feel threatened or betrayed when they find out a valued employee is ready to move on. Our job as leaders is to empower our teams and root for them. Most of the time, if we do that right, we have a chance of building a relationship that can benefit us both whether we're working in the same company or not.

▶ How important is failure?

This question came to me when business icons Jack and Suzy Welch were hosting the show with me. Every one of us had our own story. As a young man Jack blew up a factory. Suzy was fired from the *Harvard Business Review.* When I was a kid I paid $400 for a table at a baseball card convention and not a soul showed up. It was my first business mistake and a huge failure; back then $400 seemed like a billion. Every one of us learned an important lesson from our awful experiences. We learned that failure doesn't kill you, and that the earlier you do it, the easier it is to recover. We gained empathy for others who have gone through the experience. As Jack said, it's not the failure that's so important as how well you ride after you get knocked on your butt.

You have to quantify your failure, of course. If you fail and you can't get up again, that's not a good thing. But if you're made of the right stuff, failure will just compel you to get back up and try harder. Any failure from which you can recover is a learning opportunity that will only make you stronger.

Don't fail too often, but don't be afraid of it, either. I tell my team I need wartime generals—leaders who can deal with things when they're not going well—not peacetime generals. I always know what's going well. What I need to know is where are we failing.

Yes, failure is really important. Failure makes you better. I like failure.

▶ How do you celebrate victories?

I am terrible at it, and that's not something I'm proud of, because when you don't celebrate your wins, you hold your company back.

Celebrating victories, in my opinion, is an integral part of building company culture.

At VaynerMedia we have big wins every day. We land big new accounts. We grow like crazy. We win awards. And yet I celebrate very quietly. You'll never hear us cheer, you'll never see a press release, you'll never see me pound my chest. Which doesn't mean I don't ever brag about our successes—three minutes of *The #AskGaryVee Show* (heck, three minutes into this book!) and you know I'm proud of what this agency has accomplished. But when I do mention our victories and accolades, it's usually long after they've happened.

It's all because I love the climb so much. Many entrepreneurs are like that. We're so focused on the journey, by the time we've gotten to the top we're already thinking about the next hill. You just get to the next battle so you can win it. But this can be dangerous and unfair to the people who helped you with that climb. Some people like to pause and enjoy the air up there. If you move right along without acknowledging their efforts and celebrating the moment, they can feel used and unappreciated, especially if you're the only one to reap the bulk of the rewards.

I know this is a weakness and it's one I think is worth working on. It's up to me to shape our culture, and I want my company to be a place where we celebrate our wins as a team. It's important to stop and smell the roses, but sometimes you need to hand them out, too.

---

▶ With such a busy schedule and so many obligations, how do you find the time to focus, be nice to people, and stay in the moment?

---

The *New York Times* published an article that said incivility in the workplace had risen over the last few decades, and when people were asked why they might behave rudely, they replied it was because they felt overloaded and just didn't have time to be nice. I call bullshit.

Being nice is a choice, and how you choose to speak to people even when you're pressed for time will reveal who you really are. It has nothing to do with technology or the generation gap. The jerks, especially the ones with power, who are making people miserable at work today would have been making people miserable at work thirty years ago. *Money and fame doesn't change people, it just exposes them.* When you're being watched all the time, it's harder to hide your true nature. Also, you know the consequences won't be the same if you decide not to play by everyone else's rules. Sometimes this can be for good, but sometimes it's a way for people to stop using their manners and indulge in their sense of self-importance.

I don't know that I have any other gear but the nice one. I may have a big ego, but I'm very aware of where I've been, and I try hard to stay humble and kind. I really do care about people, and they seem to sense that. I'll take a selfie with someone and then see him or her tweet, "Wow, GaryVee is a really nice guy." I wish they didn't seem so surprised.

For some reason the more exposure you get, the more credit you get for being a nice person, and that's just silly. We should expect more from people in the spotlight or who have built a platform. I not only try to lead by example, I also make it clear to all my senior staff that even as I expect them to execute and produce, I expect them to combat negativity and treat people with kindness and respect.

▶ When it's all said and done, how would you like to be remembered?

As the greatest human being who ever walked the earth.
    Too much?

As a very competitive entrepreneur who wanted to build the biggest building in town by actually building the biggest building in town, not by trying to tear down everyone else's buildings.

Or . . .

How about as someone who made an effort to help people do things that make them happy?

I actually do my best to make my daily interactions with people such that they'd want to come to my funeral. The only way to do that is to be memorable. Not in a showy way, but in being unimpeachable in keeping my word, backing up the sizzle, and dealing with others. In other words, all the behind-the-scenes stuff that doesn't necessarily get written about in the business trades. If all of us did business with that goal in mind, the world would be a pretty great place, don't you think?

Hopefully it will be a long, long time before my funeral, but I'm hoping for a shockingly big crowd.

# CHAPTER 15
# MANAGEMENT

---

## IN THIS CHAPTER I TALK ABOUT CREATING CULTURE, CUTTING MEETINGS, AND HOLDING TEAMS ACCOUNTABLE.

---

I love being a manager and I love talking about management. It's similar to the topic of leadership, but in my mind management is almost synonymous with mentorship. One of the great pleasures of running Wine Library and VaynerMedia has been the opportunity it has given me to show people how to be better managers. We all probably have our own opinions of what makes a good manager, but in this one man's point of view it's the ability to reverse-engineer every person that works for you and put him or her in a position to succeed at the task for which they've been hired. That's what I try to do for the people who report to me, and that's what I expect the people who report to me to do for the people who report to them.

In less than four years, VaynerMedia grew from thirty to more than five hundred employees. And in all that time, we had only one person in the HR department—me. That's how much my employees matter to me. Every company lies about how much they care about their customers, and how much they care about their employees. It's such an easy thing to say, but it's really hard to put in the work that proves it.

From the very beginning, when AJ and I were just starting VaynerMedia, we made a few key decisions and set standards that we swore would be upheld no matter what. We did this because we had seen too many companies become breeding grounds for unhappiness, places where uninspired, unappreciated minds went to wither. For that reason, my employees' happiness is paramount, to the degree that I tell my clients up front that I care about my employees first, their customers second, and them last. Interestingly, I've never lost business because of it, maybe because my track record speaks for itself. Clearly, putting my employees above everything else hasn't hurt my business. It could only help yours.

The quality of management in any venture is, like its cousin leadership, one of the core determinants of whether a business will succeed or fail. You want the people working with you to want to be there, to feel challenged, appreciated, and valued. People always respect and like the manager who's thinking ahead and guiding them to places they'd never thought of, but they love and admire when that manager stays with them until 2 A.M. working that deck or stocking the shelves. Is this you? A disproportionate number of the readers of this book are managers or will be someday. In fact, the day you launched an entrepreneurial venture you became a manager.

One of the reasons I was excited to write this book was that I knew it would allow me to freely explore some of the topics about which I'm passionate and that have made The #AskGaryVee Show so much fun for me. Management is at the top of that list.

▶ Where is the best place to hire employees?

I'm at a sweet stage in my career where I've become a known personality and my company has made its reputation, so people are coming to us. But don't let anyone tell you it's tough to find good people. It's actually really easy. It's only hard for people unwilling to do the work.

You can break this down in a few easy steps.

1. Go to Twitter Search and start looking for the people who are talking about what you do for a living. Search the terms that would line up with the responsibilities inherent in the kind of job you're trying to fill. If you need a Web designer, find people who mention website design, or graphic design, "landing page optimization," or any other term that might indicate they're talking about or interested in the kind of work you need done.

2. Find the most promising candidates, click on their profiles, click on their home page, click on their portfolio, and see which ones look like they have talent.

3. Email them and find out if they're interested in looking for a new position. Most will probably say no, but maybe one will say yes, and the other three would probably give you referrals.

4. Interview five people and hire one.

There. It might take you as little as eight hours. Eight hours of hard work, to be sure, but far less than the days and weeks it might take you if you go the traditional hiring route and wait for the right résumé or LinkedIn inquiry to land in your inbox. And yes, someone did try this approach and met with success, so I know it can work.

▶ What role does internal culture play in a company's success?

A starring one. Building a strong internal culture is one of the best ways to ensure success for your company. Sales matter, profits matter, customer relationships matter, but every one of those pieces of your business—in fact, every piece of your business—is affected by the culture. Culture is a product of people, and when people aren't happy and instead are constantly thinking of a way to get out, their work will reflect it. Wouldn't it make sense, then, to make your culture a priority? And given that people shape culture, wouldn't it make sense to keep it at the forefront of your mind every time you hire?

Because that's how you build a strong internal culture—you hire one. *And you don't make hiring or firing a financial decision; you make it an emotional one.* Just because you suddenly have the budget to hire someone new doesn't mean you should. Just because someone isn't performing the way you expect doesn't mean you show him or her the door right away. You have to think about how every hiring and firing will affect the collective community before taking action.

Hiring and firing should be emotional decisions because you're dealing with people, not contracts. We're all told to think "business is business," which is generally interpreted as a mandate to remove our emotions out of our decision making so that we can arrive at the most objectively and financially profitable end. Well, I disagree. Business is business when it comes to financial or contractual negotiations, but not when it comes to deciding what happens to the human beings who make your business run. Besides, there are financial consequences when you treat an individual's job prospects as a financial return on investment; they're just harder to see because they don't show up right away on the balance sheet. They're there, though, coloring the unmade profits, the missed opportunities, the lost innovation and enthusiasm that results from the low loyalty and morale that pervades companies where people don't come first.

That doesn't mean you can't fire people who aren't performing, of course. It just requires that you take more time to think through other alternatives. For example, let's say you're unhappy with someone who is extremely popular at your company because they've got great people skills. How much will everyone else suffer if you let him or her go? Is it possible they're just not in the right position, and that maybe putting them in a different department would solve your problem, increase and improve their work, and keep everyone happy?

Maybe you really need to let this person go. Could you help them find another position outside the company over the span of sixty days, rather than cutting them loose in one day? It'll cost you a lot more money, but it will salvage just as much in the form of an intact, vibrant company culture. And at some level it's just a great thing to do.

Never underestimate the power of great culture. You want outstanding results and sales and projects and awards and accolades, and you know you need great teams, great leaders, and hard work to get them. Well, how many great teams have you ever encountered that are made up of tired, resentful people? How many great leaders hate what they do? How many unhappy people are willing to give their jobs everything they've got? Not many. A great company is grounded in great culture, and great culture begins and ends with whom you hire, and how they leave.

▶ What's your best time management tip?

Hire an assistant and make him or her the czar of your time. If that's not possible, use technology apps and programs like proworkflow.com, Evernote, Calendly, Asana, timetrade.com, and even the Apple Watch.

Make time management your religion. Learn to say no to the things that keep you out of the clouds and dirt.

---

▶ What do you look for when hiring creatives?

Good creatives love their art, but great creatives who work in business love to use their art to sell. In other words, they aren't held up by romantic notions of artistic integrity. A creative who wants to work effectively and happily at an agency shouldn't care more about the craft and winning awards than the agenda. So that's the kind of person I'm looking for—someone with tons of creative talent who wants to make fantastic art, yet who understands that we're in the business of selling stuff and gets a thrill out of that, too. If we don't move product, or raise awareness for the cause, or inspire people to donate, or click, or buy, we haven't fulfilled our obligation to our client.

BOOK WINNER!

Benjamin Israel Lazarus

---

▶ Do you drug-test your employees? Why or why not?

We don't.

There is no real overwhelming reason for it. It just doesn't seem needed or appropriate, or something I have any real emotion about. I don't have any huge stance on drug culture. It just hasn't come up.

SEAN BURROWS

DIGITAL MARKETING CONSULTANT

@SeanThoughts

▶ When running a company or providing marketing services for a VaynerMedia client, how do you segment out sales, marketing, and business development? All three disciplines overlap so much, and the waters can get really muddy when one or more of those areas are clearly lacking and the others are strong.

They all work together. Being good at marketing is different from being good at sales, but a good marketing campaign can lead to massive sales. By that same token, business development is just a gateway drug to sales. Now, when all three are working in harmony, you're obviously cruising. A great example of that would be SalesForce. They've invested heavily in salespeople, they market themselves excellently for a B2B SAAS business, and they execute on business development through events like nobody else.

But not everybody is SalesForce, and that's okay. Take a look at HubSpot, which is one of my investments. Maybe not as strong with sales early on, but they crushed it on biz dev and marketing and had a highly successful IPO as of this writing.

I would argue that a business's strengths and weaknesses will always be somewhat uneven depending on the composition of its DNA, culture, and people. What it comes down to is recognizing if one of those three areas—sales, marketing, or biz dev—is bringing you down as a collective, and addressing the problem through hiring, training, re-orging, or some other solution. The good news is that unlike a car, where the failure of one cog can cause the whole system to break down, I have found that when one branch of a client's company or my own businesses isn't working, it doesn't necessarily drag down the entire organization.

The truth is that all three of them lead to the same finish line, so if you have one that is overindexing, it's possible that you can ride it home. Obviously, I'd love for you to be great at all three, but don't get too worried if one is lagging behind the other two. This all speaks back to my core tenet of betting on your strengths and not your weaknesses. I'm much more interested in you doubling down on the two things you're good at instead of the one where you're behind.

---

▶ When transitioning to a new project management role, how do you maintain high standards with your team while still keeping projects on time and on budget?

---

Use your ears more than your mouth. Take the time to understand everything that's going on in your department, and listen before trying to take control. If you see a problem, let your team explain to you what they think is the problem, and then instead of coming up with a solution, guide them to coming up with it themselves. That may require you pitching in, but you're not above getting your hands dirty, are you? Become known as the person who "gets it" and you'll always have all the information you need to make the important calls because people won't be afraid to come to you for help. Creating an open, trusting, compassionate environment where everyone knows what you expect will save everyone a ton of time and help you achieve your objectives.

As your team continues to grow, hire other great listeners. The best listeners who know how to calibrate all the data and act on it will be the winners. No one ever solved a problem alone.

▶ How do you prioritize which project to execute first?

I take care of the biggest fires where I get the biggest upside if I put them out quickly, like calming a new client or handling an employee disagreement. I focus on those immediate concerns while making sure the company vision is still clear and that everything I do will eventually help me build the company and team I want, which will ladder me up to buying the Jets. You know, clouds and dirt. And I don't worry about anything else in the middle.

▶ How can agencies make staff meetings more productive?

By cutting them in half.

Now, how are you supposed to do that when you're also supposed to be giving your employees room to talk, spending time with them, being compassionate, and all those other touchy-feely bits of advice I tend to offer?

You just do.

I swear to you it works. Estimate how much time you think you will need to cover your agenda, and then halve it.

If you give people a ten-pound bag, they are going to fill it with ten pounds of crap. If you give them a fifteen-pound bag, it's the same—fifteen pounds of crap. They will never overfill or underfill the bag. When I schedule an hour meeting with my team, we'll banter a bit and talk about a few other things we didn't plan on talking about, but we will fit everything we need into the hour. If I cut that same meeting to thirty minutes, we'll still accomplish everything that needs to be done, hands down. And we'll have saved thirty minutes, which is really what this is all about, right? Our time is valuable. When you're hustling like

I do—and which I'd like to think you do—every minute, every *second* counts.

When everyone knows they're going to lose your attention as soon as the allotted fifteen or thirty minutes are up, they prepare. No one's shuffling around papers, no one shares irrelevant anecdotes, no one talks around the point, and no one is winging it. People have spent their time *before* the meeting getting their information straight, pulling their papers together, and tightening their message because they know if they don't, they won't get a second chance.

All that friendly touchy-feely stuff I believe in? I do it, but I do it fast. Heck, I do that as I'm walking into the meeting. But the minute my butt hits my seat, everyone had better be ready to go. I'm positive that if there is any one answer that could probably benefit every single person reading this book, it's this one.

---

▶ What's one question you ask in interviews?

---

There is one question I only raise if an interview is gaining momentum and I feel like I may have found a good fit for my team. It's not just a question I love to ask, it's one I need to ask. In fact, at some level it's the only one I really care about.

"Where do you want your career to go?"

I spend most of my interviews trying to get people comfortable enough to answer that question truthfully should I decide I want to ask it. I don't care if the answer is you want to be the CEO of VaynerMedia, or you just want to move a couple of levels up and have great work-life balance. I don't even care if you want to come work for me for two years, suck up all my IP, and then go somewhere to start your own agency. I really don't. Truly. Whatever your agenda is, I'm fine with it. I just want to know what it is, so I can help us get there. You and me.

See, I'm a creature of contradictions. I welcome chaos and love to take advantage of trends and have built a business that serves as a port for companies swimming in a constantly undulating sea, but man, I hate change at the personal level. I want to keep people in my ecosystem for as long as possible, because once I like working with you, I want to work with you forever. And I know the best way to keep you close is to deliver on what you want, so the faster I can get that insight the better.

By giving people opportunities and helping them achieve what they want, I keep my relationships with my employees positive and open. Such a positive environment not only makes it hard for people to leave, it ensures I always know what's going on. This allows me to execute quicker, and together we can do amazing work faster.

I hire a lot of young people, so I know change is inevitable. People fall in love, they decide to start families, and their lives and interests evolve. And that's the way it should be. But by keeping the communication funnel open and clear, I have a better chance of finding a way to help my best talent achieve all their dreams while still working with me. And I want to start from day one, five minutes in.

---

▶ What would you do if all six hundred employees quit VaynerMedia?

---

Well, first I'd be an idiot if I didn't step back and wonder what the hell just happened. Then I would spend a lot of time going to each of the employees and apologizing to them because obviously something went very wrong. But then I'd have to take a positive approach. I'd have to decide how I wanted to take advantage of everything I've learned for the last six years. I'm an emotional guy, but I would work really hard not to react with a knee-jerk "I'll show them!" and just go out and rebuild. I'd be tempted because I'd want to show I could do it, but I think I have enough self-control to refrain from letting my emotions get the best of me. So in deciding whether to rebuild or walk away, I'd have to consider what would be the best use of my time, the decision that would get me back on track, because I'm forty years old now and want to buy the Jets. But make no mistake, if I chose not to rebuild it wouldn't be because I couldn't do it. It would be because I chose not to.

---

▶ Is the lack of chairs in your office a part of instilling the hustle in your employees?

---

No, but I wish I had thought of it. Limiting chairs to create a competitive culture? That's brilliant! Someone else should totally do it.

I actually have no hard-core tactics for instilling competitiveness. I just breed it because I'm competitive as shit, and I think people know that to keep up they're going to have to get hungry. After all, as I've said, everything stems from the top. I think it is important for everyone reading this book to understand their DNA and how they like to roll, allow their companies to ride that wave, and not push against it.

What makes me happy is that as competitive as we are, I've heard a lot of people say that VaynerMedia is one of the first places they've worked where people want to compete with the quality of their work, not at the expense of others. That tells me we're creating great culture *and* great work.

---

▶ When hiring for a team, is it better to bring in specialists or someone who can wear multiple hats?

---

You can certainly benefit from both, of course. It's always good to strike a balance within a company. And since I believe everyone should exploit their strengths, it's important for leaders and CEOs to hire people with complementary skills.

But if you have to choose, go for the jack-of-all-trades.

And if you want to enhance your marketability and value, become one.

Many would argue that by trying to be good at many things, you'll never master anything. Bullshit. If you work hard at trying to be good at many things, you'll get good at many things. And taking that attitude will force you to say yes to new challenges more often. You might be really good at something now, but why not find out what else you can dominate? Because I know it's not just one thing. We're all better than that.

Be open to adapting and evolving your skill set as your life progresses. I get so bothered when I hear people say they don't have to learn anything new because they've become so good at the thing they do. It's such a limited mind-set. And it's dangerous, too, because you never know when you'll need to tap into a new skill. There's nothing like a layoff to make you regret you didn't pick up that extra knowledge or experience. Expand your arsenal. It'll allow you to always prove your agility and your ability to offer value wherever you go. It's never too late to get better. Start moving. NOW!

---

▶ When faced with two equally qualified candidates for one position, how do you choose?

---

Two thoughts came to mind when I read this question.

**1.** I don't think there's such a thing as two people who are literally equally qualified for the same job. Someone always has a slight edge. It may not be enough to make that much of a difference, but you can use that to help you make the call. Or go with your gut. That usually works, too.

2.  If you like them both that much, consider hiring them both. I'm a big fan of hiring ahead of my growth. I would never unduly burden my payroll because I wouldn't want to lay anyone off, but I anticipate. Always look ahead at what your needs are going to be, not just the ones you have now. If you've got two candidates who can each bring you that much value, a creative solution may be in order.

---

## What three values do you hold highest in life?

---

I have more than three, but these are the three that I look for in a new hire.

1.  Patience

    I want to work with people who believe in paying things forward and doing good for others, but I want to know that they don't do so expecting immediate gratification. Because there is no immediate gratification when it comes to business. You can do amazing things, and get nothing back for a good long while. That's a really tough pill for some people to swallow. But I want to work with people who have the patience to keep going even when they haven't seen immediate results, people who appreciate that success takes time. I've seen how a lack of patience can keep people from achieving their greatest aspirations, and I want to work with those who will.

2.  Word is bond

    I've said this goes down as the greatest lesson my dad ever taught me. I want everyone at VaynerMedia to believe it, too.

When you make a commitment, no matter what, you stick to it. The best part? Every time you live up to this credo, you add one more person to your list of people who may deliver for *you* in the future.

**3.** Empathy

I hire for this one because I know it's what makes a great leader. I need to know that my managers are going to listen to their teams and work with them, not drive them, especially when problems arise. I want to hire people who look for solutions, not someone to blame. I want them to assume the best of people. It's pretty rare for people to fail because they wanted to, so it's up to a good manager to figure out what happened and then offer the support so it doesn't happen again.

**4.** Gratitude

I like people who don't take anything for granted. It makes for a really motivated worker, and generally a nice person to work with.

---

▶ When you work on projects with clients, how much is done online, for example via Skype, and how much in person?

---

I can't speak for anyone else, but I predominantly like to work through email and meeting face-to-face. I get a charge out of other people's energy, so face-to-face meetings are always more productive for me. Plus they allow me to get to know my client better and build a stronger relationship, and you know how much I value that. I hardly ever use the phone, though I am trying to push more clients into using text, and I am using Skype and Google+ more and more lately and seeing real value in it.

> ▶ If you were the owner of the Jets how would you turn around the team and make us a Super Bowl contender?

I could have put this answer in the sports chapter, but I think my answer shows what kind of manager I am in general.

As obsessed as I am with the Jets (and enjoyed my time working with them during the years they were a client) there are still things about the team unknown to me. So I'd first run an audit so that I knew what I was dealing with.

My first order of business after that would be to mandate that every two years, we draft a quarterback in the first two rounds of the NFL draft until we had our guy. We'd bring a guy in, give him twenty-four months so he got two seasons, and then if it wasn't the right fit, whether he played a snap or not I'd draft another guy, and two years later another, until I had one, because the quarterback is the linchpin of the team.

I'd also work on PR. I might do a weekly live-stream show so the fans could pound me with their anger. But guess what? I'd pound them right back. Different, right? I think I could get away with it because I am one of them, and most likely an even bigger fan than they are.

I'd execute some fun marketing ideas like sending a Jets jersey on the sixth birthday of every kid living in the New York–New Jersey area. I'd do inappropriate things like get into it with the media because I think they're out of their collective mind with the way they are handling the Jets in this city (a dangerous idea, I know, but I would do it with respect). I'd watch the games from the stands (and then probably get reprimanded by the NFL for cursing).

That's the kind of owner I'd be: methodical, obsessive, creative, combative, passionate, loyal, un-PC, and loving every minute of it.

▶ Would you support Vayner employees who wrote their own books and curated their own content streams and personal brands?

I not only would, I already have. Ask Jason Donnelly. He left VaynerMedia to go write a book, and when he was done he came back. I bought copies and gave it to people throughout the office.

I didn't do that to be nice. You can't say you care about helping people succeed and then suppress them when they actually do. And you can't be afraid that someone else will trump you. That's one advantage to having a big ego—when you think you're the greatest of all time, you're not ever worried anyone else will surpass you, so there's no reason to hold them back. I have no reason to fear anyone else's talent or keep them down. If they wind up being better than me, so be it. I believe in capitalism, meritocracy, and fairness, and that's what it should look like.

▶ How do you push your team beyond their best?

There's a right way to do it and a wrong way. The wrong way is to crack the whip and compensate for the brutal work conditions by paying people well. The right way in this one man's point of view is to appeal to their sense of guilt. (I'm not joking.)

I've already talked about what it takes to be a great manager, such as listening, getting to know your team's ambitions, and being supportive in all their endeavors, even if they don't necessarily benefit you. Now, you want to do that so incredibly well, and instill such a sense of family and loyalty, that your team would do almost anything rather than let you down. Relationships are a two-way street, but when you're the boss, and you go in about 51 percent of the way, your team will go above and beyond to give you that 49 percent back. I know it's true because I've seen it work at both of my own companies.

I didn't take home more than $30K for the first five years I worked at Wine Library so that I'd have the money to call people's bluffs. You're telling me you could really crush it if I hired some more staff? Great, here you go. Now show me. Were my feelings hurt when things didn't work out as promised? Yes, but that didn't stop me from giving people what they asked for when I could. That worked as a huge motivator, because then everyone else on the team saw their friends getting what they wanted, and they'd work hard to get what they wanted, too. It made for a very happy place to work.

A good boss is doing his employees a favor when he or she pushes a team beyond their limits, because otherwise they'd never know what they were capable of. But you have to make them believe they can do it before they actually do it. If you want people to overdeliver, you'd better overdeliver for them, too.

BOOK WINNER!

JUSTIN BROOKE
Founder of IMScalable.com

▶ How do you hold your employees accountable, aka actually do work and get results? I mean it's not like you can send them to their room, and firing them still leaves you with no work done.

There are a lot of ways that I do this and that we've done in the companies I've run.

1. Company culture. If you're able to build an environment where people really enjoy the work they're doing, believe in the mission at hand, and (most important) really love their coworkers, you probably won't encounter these circumstances in the first place. I'm often shocked to see employees at VaynerMedia who are more afraid to fail their coworkers than anything else. The best results come when employees feel like their responsibility is toward their teammates more than a charismatic boss, or a client, or even their own pride.

2. I think you *do* fire. If you're in the mind-set that firing someone will leave you with no one to do the job, then you're in big trouble. If you honestly believe you can't hire someone else to do the job, maybe you need to look at yourself more than anything else.

3. Finally, I really do think it comes down to communication. Many organizations don't actually do a good job at communicating that there is a problem in the first place, so that is on you. Sometimes all it takes is an honest conversation with that person to ask them what actually motivates them. Once the problem is agreed upon by both parties (and make sure it is!), you need to figure out what makes that person tick. You might find that a couple of extra weeks of vacation makes that person dramatically more productive within forty-eight weeks instead of fifty weeks.

At the end of the day, helping your employees get the work done has as much to do with you listening as it does with you talking.

---

▶ The dress code at VaynerMedia is clearly casual. Do you think dress affects professionalism or performance?

---

Dress doesn't impact performance or professionalism. I work with people who execute incredibly well every day, and I think they'd do that even if they came to work in their bathing suits. I think the people who disagree with me will lose because they are holding on to a tradition that is cracking as the world evolves. I want to use this book to help you recognize the subtle and not-so-subtle changes occurring in our society and how they impact the business world. Anyone who doesn't yet hear the sound of modern business dress codes changing, and quickly, is being tone deaf.

---

▶ What are your thoughts on employing friends?

---

Working with friends is the best, and it works if you practice a meritocracy.

A lot of managers will probably disagree with me. They'll say it can ruin a friendship, and that nepotism is inevitable and lowers people's motivation to work hard. To that I say, seriously? If you're in charge of hiring and running the company, are you really going to let that happen? Give yourself a little credit, whydoncha?

Rather than being a risk, there's a huge benefit to hiring a friend with just as much experience as a stranger. I hired my best childhood friend, Brandon, to work at Wine Library because I knew he was awesome from our baseball card days and I trusted and loved him. When my brother, AJ, and I started VaynerMedia, we hired a handful of AJ's friends from college and high school to get the ball rolling because we knew that these particular individuals would bring a certain energy to the company and establish a fun, awesome, hardworking, passionate, and competitive culture right off the bat. After them, we hired a few more people to round out the organization, and continued to hire as we needed.

Fast-forward, and those initial employees are now working in very different places within the organization. But as we've grown, they've been key in establishing and communicating our culture throughout the company—just as AJ and I knew they would.

The key to hiring friends successfully is simple: Be ready to enforce a meritocracy. Sometimes it can be hard to divorce yourself from your friendship and evaluate people solely on their work performance, but it is possible. I've had to fire friends. You hire friends because you think you know what you're getting, but sometimes the new environment opens your eyes to parts of them you didn't know about before. That can suck. But if you can be professional, the firing won't be as horrible as you might think. After all, if you've been doing your job right, it won't come as a shock. You'll have worked with them for a long time to try to improve performance or fix a problem, and even had a "last warning" talk in which you also ask "How do I help you?" By the time the firing comes, you'll probably both be relieved. And great friends know that you don't want to hurt them.

---

▶ Once you recognize your weaknesses, should you keep working on improving them or delegate?

---

I don't know the full answer. I had to work on getting better about being clearer with negative feedback because I led with so much honey that people didn't realize they were being told they needed to improve their performance. I needed to be more direct, and I've worked on strengthening that skill because I thought it was important. I wouldn't say I'm particularly scary, but I'm no longer a pushover, either.

Try applying the 80/20 rule, also known as Pareto's law. It's probably a good idea to spend 80 percent of your time on your strengths (though I really wouldn't mind 95/5 because I just believe so strongly in betting on one's strengths) and 20 percent on shoring up your weaknesses. We all have them. If you're not sure which one needs your attention most, ask the people who work for you, whom you work with, and your closest friends what they think. It means you have to roll with humility, but you can't fix a problem if you don't know it exists.

---

▶ Do you have any tips on delegation?

---

Sure. Once you accept that 99.9 percent of the things you deal with every day don't matter as much as you think, it's a lot easier to let other people do them. Good leaders know when to let go, and they let go of a lot because they're in the clouds and dirt.

Some people don't delegate because they're positive no one can do as good a job as they can. That may be true, but not every job needs your level of perfection anyway. You've got to know when good enough is enough. Let the bright, interesting people you hired do their jobs and make yours easier. It takes humility to accept you're not as unique or indispensable as you think, but it's also freeing.

BOOK WINNER!

GREG PESCI
SPERA, INC.
PRESIDENT & CEO
WWW.SPERA.IO
@gregpesci

---

▶ What are some of the key challenges facing freelancers today, and what tools can they use to overcome them?

---

I think the biggest challenge that most freelancers have is that while they are great at their individual specialty (design, consulting, video, etc.), they don't actually know how to run a business. The difference between having expertise in an individual skill and being a business operator is huge, and at the end of the day being a freelancer means you're running your own, one-person business.

A freelancer's biggest asset is time, so any tools or software that can help to save time is going to be huge. I mean it applies to me, too. I don't like doing the billing, following up on invoices, or managing our P&L. None of that stuff is fun for me, and it's going to be even less fun for a freelance designer. The output is the fun part. The reason so many professionals don't freelance is that they want to do their thing, but when they start getting into the goop and the gop of billing, insurance, and all the other stuff that comes with running a business, they check out. You should be looking for any and every tool that helps you save time with those tasks.

The other thing that might be helpful would be to find a business mentor, or even take business classes. Learn everything you possibly can about business management so that you can worry less about the side stuff, and spend more time on the fun stuff.

---

▶ I need to hire an office assistant, but though sales are great I don't have the capital to hire anyone. Got any creative ideas?

---

Use your social capital. Most people think money is the best compensation, but there is somebody out there who needs experience or visibility more than money. That's how DRock first started working here. He asked if he could do a video for free, he did a great job, and we formed a relationship, which led to a full-time gig. Without him, I may not have ever done the show, let alone written this book.

There are many ways to barter your services. Announce on

Craigslist and social media what money you can offer, and then add all your services free for a year. Make a video that shows why you're a great person to work with. Offer your stuff, your services, your time, or your name. Make a deal where you pay out very little in the beginning of a project but your assistant gets a sweet percentage of the final payout. Leave no rock unturned.

Whatever you do, however, make sure you can deliver on whatever promise you make.

---

▶ They say you should hire slow and fire quick. How many chances do you give your staff?

---

There's nothing worse than firing someone. I'm not usually the one who does it here anymore, but when I was I'd spend a month figuring out how to make myself feel better about it. We're not in the one-, two-, or three-strike policy here at VaynerMedia. We actually have enormous continuity, and I think part of that is thanks to the firing policy. People see that we try to handle things with empathy and grace. Also, no firing ever comes as a surprise. We work hard with people to try to help them achieve what they wanted to do when they came on board, or to help them find a better fit within the company. I think word of that effort gets around, and it makes people feel good about working here.

I don't think what's most important is to fire fast, but to fire well. It's better in the long run for everyone—you're free to find a better fit, and the employee is free to go succeed somewhere else. But if you don't have the EQ to do it well—to make it feel like a liberation and not like a punishment—find someone who does. If I hadn't had it when I worked at Wine Library, I swear I would have asked my mom to do it. She could make you see how death by firing squad could be reason to celebrate.

> ▶ How do you motivate teams of remote workers without a pay
> incentive? So far positivity and hustle are not producing resu....

Take the blame, and then start communicating better. If there are
people on your team who are not performing to their best abilities,
that's on you. But it's a relatively easy problem to solve. Arrange for
a meeting and then tell them they're not executing at the level you
were hoping for. Then ask, What can I do to help you? And then
start helping.

> ▶ What does it take to work at VaynerMedia?

It all depends on what job you want, of course. The more interesting question is, What does it take to win?

The losing players at the VaynerMedia game tend to disappear
within the first year or year and a half because they're not playing
the long game. They're either solely motivated by money, or they
have the audacity to think they're better than they are. I like bravado and confidence, but you'd better have the goods to back it up.
Admittedly, on occasion VaynerMedia has missed that talent and
the employee had no choice but to leave. I hate it when that happens, but even I know we can't always win.

What about the winners? They tend to have all the qualities
we've discussed before: empathy, self-awareness, respect for others,
amazing work ethic, and patience. They're not only good commu-
nicators; they advocate for themselves in a constructive way (hey, I
know we're not perfect). It takes hard work and smarts to succeed
here, but what trumps all of it is heart. Skills can be taught; heart
just is. If you've got it, I'm interested in working with you.

> ▶ What key factors should a Millennial-owned branding company
> look for when hiring other Millennials as it quickly scales?

Why are you intent on hiring Millennials? Lou Pearlman was a middle-aged blimp marketer before he put together two of the biggest boy bands of the nineties, the Backstreet Boys and NSYNC. He wasn't a thirteen-year-old girl, but he knew how to market to them. I am not a Millennial, but I know how to market to Millennials better than many, including Millennials. Just because you're twenty-four doesn't mean you know how to sell shit, even to a twenty-four-year-old.

The questions you need to ask Millennials are the same ones you'd ask anyone. Do you know how to market to this age group? Do you understand their behavior? Do you know how to create content that will also create the sale?

> ▶ Where would you start building a digital team in a traditional (TV/
> print) agency?

Traditional agencies that sell print, direct mail, outdoor media, or PR are all shifting to digital because that's where the dollars and storytelling are going. This isn't difficult. Hire seven people skilled in digital social, bring them into your department, and work with your CEO to integrate this new thing. VaynerMedia often starts new divisions, from live events to video production. We have to integrate them into the business and we do it by bringing in people with the right skill set. Now, how does that practice get molded into the org? I'm often hands off for the first three to six months, but then I get my hands dirtier. Leading is knowing when to step in or step back. It's just about deciding when to do it.

▶ When do you shift from hiring a freelancer to hiring someone full-time?

You should transition a freelancer to a full-time employee the moment you fall in love with that person's work and personality and know they are going to bring tremendous thunder to your business and your workday . . .

Or . . .

When you need to because your business is growing or your client is producing more stuff and why would you look for someone new when you have someone you trust and like who knows the brand right there with you . . .

Or . . .

When the freelancer falls in love with your business and keeps pushing you to let him or her join your team. It may not be a practical move to take on a hire, but do what you can to reward that passion and invest in the relationship for the long-term stickiness and ROI it will afford you.

▶ Is terminating the bottom 10 percent still a good idea? Even on a team of all-stars, someone has to be last.

This is a legendary mantra that Jack Welch introduced to the business world, and this answer came straight from the horse's mouth when he appeared on the show:

If you believe that the best team wins and that business is a game, you have to field the best players. So you have to be aware of who are your top 20, middle 70, and bottom 10. Make your top 20 feel 6'4". If they're already 6'5", make them feel 6'8". You let them know you think they're that good. Tell the middle 70 you want them to strive to be like the top 20. Tell your players at the bottom of the rankings why they're there and give them a chance to fix what's wrong. If they can't, let them go. But always love them as much on the way out as you did when you let them in.

I asked Jack whether this advice would be true for people who only had 500 employees, not 400,000 like he did when he ran GE. He said it would be even more important. Then I pointed out that a lot of people who watch my show have maybe five employees. And he acknowledged that that would be very difficult, because now you're looking at the people who got you started. But you have to do it.

Suzy Welch, Jack's wife and writing partner, who was also on the show, pointed out that there is no perfect team. There is always someone who is performing better than someone else. Instead of bemoaning the fact that you have to let go of the bottom 10 percent, celebrate everything you're doing to nurture the top 20 percent.

---

▶ As a business grows, what is the best solution for documenting policy, procedure, and process so all are on the same page?

---

There is no business on earth that won because it had a supertight handbook. Maybe a behemoth like GE should have something in place, but that's what their lawyers are there for. A company of only five hundred or so employees shouldn't have to document every little thing. As Suzy Welch said, work on building your values and culture. Make sure everyone knows the mission of the company, where they're going, and why. Hold on to your entrepreneurial spirit for as long as you can.

▶ How can efficiency and creativity better work together?

Jack Welch also pointed out on the show that to get creatives to be efficient you have to get creative. That means hiring creative people. You want everyone in your company, no matter whether they're on the account, client, or creative side, to be thinking of better ways to do what they're doing. I think one way to do that is to put your players in a position to succeed. So long as the work that gets produced is quality, I don't really care how you get it done. I've tried to get people to work within my version of efficiency, and I find that it's just better to let people do things their way. I may not like that you need to retreat to a private Zen garden, but if I like your output, why should I care? Prima donna creatives can be irritating, but if their ROI is awesome, it's worth it. A supremely efficient creative who lacks the magic is not.

One thing Jack, Suzy, and I were all in agreement about when we heard this question is that it's an awful thing to elevate the innovators in a company above everyone else. Don't put them on an altar and tell everyone else to just put their heads down and get to work. Don't let anyone's mind go to waste. Encourage *everyone* to be an innovator. At VaynerMedia we expect our creatives to be practical, and our account strategists to be creative. It works, creating an energizing sense of mutual respect.

▶ My business is completely digital. How important are real-life meetings?

The number of online tools at our disposal makes it extremely easy to allow people to work from home, or to facilitate conversations and transactions with people working across town, across the country, or on the other side of the world. But even if your company is entirely digital, you should not eliminate in-person meetings.

Why? Because human beings make decisions, not machines.

*Digital should be seen as the gateway to a human interaction*, but not as a replacement for it. You just can't get the same nuance or establish the same context via conference call or Google+ as you can in person. That isn't to say emotion can't be conveyed digitally; I get plenty emotional on Twitter and more and more on Instagram. But those exchanges don't have the same energy as an in-person one does. And it's important to keep fine-tuning your ability to read a room and people's body language. It's a tremendous skill that doesn't just make you a better boss or employee; it makes you a better person.

So whether you need to talk to an employee, client, or your boss, create opportunities to meet in person sometimes, especially if it's been a while or you have something important to discuss. Keep doing that until the robots take over. When that happens, we can reevaluate.

---

▶ How do I keep my old employees from hazing my new employees?

Be the parent. Tell them to stop or you'll fire them.

I had a similar problem at Wine Library. My staff wasn't hazing anyone per se, but they were making immediate judgment calls on new hires. Within two days, if they had decided a new person sucked, they froze that person out or made their life hard. My ultimate solution was to sit down one by one with my entire staff and tell them that if they didn't work with me to fix the problem and become part of the solution, they would be gone. And you know what? I had to fire a few people. It happens.

▶ How much of your staff's time is spent on you as opposed to other projects?

If you mean the staff that helps with my content production and the business development around it, then that entire team is part of "Brand Gary" team. Some were already working within Vayner-Media and were plucked out of the machine, and others were hired specifically for the team. I didn't need this many people when I was producing *Wine Library TV*, but now that I have so much more scale I can produce more content outside the show, and I need help to do that. This is what a production team for one person looks like. I believe the future for people with sizable audiences is less about having a PR person and more about building a modern production company around that person.

▶ How do you handle it when people miss their deadlines?

It all depends on what I expect from you. If you're a person who is usually a hard-core executor who's extremely reliable and I rely on you to be that all the time, I'm going to be pissed. If you're kind of disorganized and a little weird, and I never quite know what's going on but somehow you always make magic happen, I probably didn't ever believe you'd make your deadline and had planned accordingly. Bottom line, the level at which I or anyone else should get upset at a missed deadline will probably change depending on our expectations. If you know what someone usually brings to the table and they "miss," you have to wonder whose fault that is. Is it possible you put them in a situation where they weren't working to their strengths? It's great to challenge your strong players but you need to be fair. Put players in positions to succeed and when you put them in a spot that is challenging, make sure you remain empathetic. Above all, be fair.

---

▶ How do you diplomatically tell the boss he's f***ing it up?

I think any boss worth his or her salt will be pumped if you're brave enough to respectfully point out where you disagree, and I think it can be a win-win situation. If the boss agrees with your feedback, you've won points. If he or she doesn't and starts disrespecting you, then you know you work for a dipshit and need to look for another job. For that reason, there's no risk in giving critical feedback, especially if you don't love your job. It's a good way for people to audit their bosses and gauge whether it's wise to put their career in their bosses' hands and follow his or her leadership. I have massive respect for the people who are comfortable telling me they disagree with me. The key is to make sure you remain gracious and respectful while still expressing passion and holding true to your point of view. And of course you should go in with a good sense of who your boss is. My direct reports know they can get away with a lot more with me than they could with many of the bosses in my own companies that are below me. Know your judge.

---

▶ When trying to get your point across to meet a goal, do you prefer to be abrasive or compassionate, and why?

I'm constantly adjusting to my clients, start-ups, employees, and investors in real time. Compassion, empathy, competitiveness, warmth, straight disrespect—every situation calls for a different brew. I have neither a favorite move nor tactic. Sometimes I'll try six months of compassion and then karate-chop people to the mat because clearly that isn't working. Managing is a never-ending 365-day test-and-learn. You don't want to get into the habit of using one move over and over. It's kind of like medicine; if you use it too often, it stops working as well.

---

▶ What are your suggestions when you have to work with external partners to get the job done, but they don't share your hustle?

---

You mean like the rest of the world? Ha! If you work for an agency or a client service business, you're stuck. You have to play well in the sandbox. It can be hard for people in the trenches when I insist they be nice to a partner that's dropping the ball. But I don't think we gain much from calling people out on their idiocy. I think our work speaks for itself and that the truth is undefeated.

Here's a challenge: When you're having trouble with a partner, don't get aggressive or nasty. Win them over with kindness. Go for a drink together if you can. Build a real relationship and you may just find that they know they stink because their company stinks. When you can find some common ground and a way to align yourselves it can take some of the venom out of the situation and make you feel less resentful.

Communicate with your team. Communicate with your partners. Communicate with your clients. Communicate, communicate, communicate.

> ▶ If you have a business that is growing fast, is it more important to perfect the system or to focus on adding more people to the team?

Why can't you do both? It takes hustle, but that's the only way to get huge victories. I worked very hard on the system at Vayner-Media while hiring people and trading them up and building the team. Integrate the team from 9 A.M. to 5 P.M., and then spend 5 P.M. to 2 A.M. perfecting the system. Go all the "hell in" now or you will miss your moment. Extract all the value you can out of your day while you still can, especially if you're young. That's what I'm doing as I approach my fortieth birthday. My fund, *The #AskGary-Vee Show*, VaynerMedia, family life, my health . . . I'm pushing it all harder than ever because I know that when I'm forty-two I may not be able to do it as much. Squeeze everything you can out of the time you have right now.

# CHAPTER 16
# INVESTING

**IN THIS CHAPTER I'LL TALK ABOUT WHAT TO LOOK FOR IN A HORSE, WHAT TO LOOK FOR IN A JOCKEY, AND MY BEST HACK FOR FINDING THE NEXT HOT INVESTMENT POSSIBILITY.**

Aside from queries looking for beginner entrepreneurial advice, I probably get more emails asking me to consider investing in start-ups than any other. I have a lot of evolving feelings about being an investor. By now I've probably looked at tens of thousands of deals, and yet it's still a pretty new role for me. My investing career didn't follow the most traditional path. Most successful investors probably start small, take a few missteps, and have some success here and there before finally getting into a position to hit the mother lode. I kind of did things backward.

What happened was I started recognizing that I had been right about a lot of things like email marketing, e-commerce, banner advertising, and Google AdWords. And then one day I read that YouTube, the video-sharing platform I had long been saying was going to be huge, had sold to Google for $2 billion. It occurred to me that maybe all this "right" could probably make me a lot more money than just selling a few extra bottles of Cabernet. So I promised myself that whatever I spotted as the next big thing—it could have been a chewing gum as easily as a new digital platform—I'd try to get involved with it. That thing was Twitter.

Twitter caught my attention in 2006–2007. While everyone else was debating the value of a platform that lets you tell the world you were eating pizza, I recognized it as a communication platform that would change the world. I became bullish on Twitter and consequently became friendly with early employees. Eventually an opportunity came in the form of one who decided to sell off his stock (talk about emotion causing you to make a bad decision) and after spending some time talking him out of selling all of it, I was able to buy some Twitter stock at an outrageously low valuation.

Once that happened I stepped back and took note of Tumblr. I thought it looked interesting, and when a high school student (who is now a VaynerMedia employee) named Louis Geneux told me that everyone he knew was on Tumblr, I knew it had gone mainstream. Eventually I became friends with Tumblr founder David Karp and former president John Maloney. They were looking for marketing ideas and by 2008 I had established myself as a personality in that space. That gave me the opportunity to invest in its "D" round at a ridiculously low level that turned around substantially for me when Yahoo bought Tumblr for a billion dollars.

During that same period, maybe even within a month, my two-year relationship with several Facebook employees put me in a position to invest at very low valuations there when a member of the Facebook family decided to sell shares.

So within an incredibly short amount of time I made three investments that turned out to be enormously profitable events for me. I started off so hot, maybe it was inevitable that when I finally stumbled it would be a face-plant of epic proportions. Get this: I was actually in the room with Travis Kalanick and Garrett Camp when the idea for Uber started taking shape. You know what else? Look at the second-to-last line of the acknowledgments in my book *Crush It!*

---

**x** acknowledgments

Finally, the book you are about to read had no prayer of getting in front of you without the amazing team at HarperStudio. The fantastic Debbie Stier saw me speak at a conference and said to herself that she was going to publish me; she was right and her friendship and push and hustle during this process have made this book hers as much as it is mine. Bob Miller's vision supported this project from the very beginning when I first dropped by to hang out in his office. The second I sat down in Austin, Texas, with the fantastic Stephanie Land, I knew she was going to help me write this book. I could see it in her face. I knew my charm and charisma were not going to be enough to win her over, but after she saw I had the chops, she jumped onboard. A super-special thanks to the ladies at The Brooks Group, Caroline, Niki, Erica, and of course Rebecca; you guys are the best and I thank you for your 24/7 efforts. To Peter Klein, not only are you a wonderful father-in-law, but your insights were very helpful. And finally, this would not be the book it is without the thoughtful comments of Travis Kalanick, who gave me the perfect feedback in the late innings.

To all of these people, I am deeply grateful.

---

And still I passed on the angel round.

Twice.

If I had gone in it would have probably changed my life immensely. It sure would have gotten me a lot closer to buying

the New York Jets. I like to refer to this event as my "one almond moment," after the *#AskGaryVee* episode where I promised Vayner Nation that if anyone could guess the number of
almonds filling a big glass jar next to me on the table, I'd pay
their way to New York and they could sit next to me during the
filming of an episode.

There were 1,424 almonds in the jar.

@BoostLacrosse guessed 1,423.

Close but no cigar.

Luckily, Travis gave me another chance to invest later and I
grabbed it. And I'm sure @BoostLacrosse won't let the next big
opportunity slip away, either. The almond jar always gets refilled,
and when it does, you try again.

I learned from my mistake and was lucky enough to go on to
become part of a small group of "super angels," men and women
with personal brand awareness, like Kevin Rose, Chris Sacca, and Jason Calacanis, looking for opportunities to invest. I
later made some nice investments in companies like Wildfire
and Birchbox, and eventually in late 2013 I started a venture
fund with Stephen Ross, Matt Higgins, and my brother called
VaynerRSE, a $20 million seed fund that invests in early-stage
Internet media companies. By the time you're reading this I'll
have another one called Vayner Capital, which is a later-stage
venture fund.

I've been watching and learning, and I think we're living in
interesting times. I see a lot of young companies going for the
investments, and then instead of building up their business they
spend all their time working toward the next round of funding.
There seems to be a disturbing lack of patience and scrappiness
out there in investment land, to the point I've changed the way
I consider businesses. In fact, I'd go so far as to advise a lot of
businesses to reconsider going for the VC money. It's useful, to
be sure, but I think it can make people lazy. The company whose

founders have made great things happen on a shoestring and spent every dime and drop of sweat on building the best product they can before reaching out for VC dollars—that's the company I've got my eye on.

---

▶ What should I focus on with the companies that I invest in?

---

Entrepreneurs often struggle with making the transition to investor. We're so used to running the show, and all of a sudden we have to step back and watch other people execute. It's not easy. In the beginning I didn't even realize jockeys could completely screw up an investment; I figured the horses they were riding were such magnificent beasts the jockeys were almost just there for the ride. Boy, was I wrong.

When considering whether to make any investment, make sure that the idea looks phenomenal on paper *and* that it is in good hands.

---

▶ You've said that sometimes you invest in horses (companies) and sometimes in the jockeys (founders). What do you look for in each?

---

If I don't believe in the upside in your market, I'm not going to believe in your start-up.

That said, when looking at a horse, I'm looking for companies that are built on concepts or ideas that are only about two to three years away from hitting mass consciousness. In 2006 and 2007 that was social media. Today I'm looking less at social networks and apps and more at things like smart tech. For example, who is going to win with the smart toothbrush that stops when you have fully brushed your teeth? Or smart pants? Who is going to win in a sector like e-sports? I also think there is a lot of potential in consumer packaged goods as companies try to make healthier versions of everything we already have. Mobile commerce is also interesting to me. Virtual reality. I'm looking at trends. So when I'm looking at horses, I'm following my own intuition, which has rarely served me wrong, to help me see what is gaining traction and will soon be mainstream.

At this point in my career I am spending more and more time vetting the CEO and team, especially if I'm considering an early-stage investment. Jockeys come in all shapes and sizes, even more so than horses. Entrepreneurs often struggle with making the transition to investor because we're so used to running the show, and all of a sudden we have to step back and watch other people execute. It's not easy. When I first started investing, I overvalued anyone who was techy. Oh, you can develop? Cool! I also kept looking for people who looked like me. Are you a good operator? Are you hungry? Are you competitive? Then I started seeing all the ways businesspeople can be successful—with operational strength, motivational strength, financial strength—and I realized I didn't have to look for my clone. I started spending more time getting to understand the jockeys' strengths. I want to know they are self-aware enough to team up with people who fill out their weaknesses. I also want to know if they've got the stomach for business. When things aren't working or times get hard do they know what to do to pivot the business? Can they be good wartime generals *and* peacetime generals? The last seven years have been boom years for founders. But it's easy to be a general when there is no war being fought. Wartime generals have to deal with a crumbling economy, money drying up, a massive competitor. If my horse's jockeys don't have that, I'm going to think twice before investing.

---

▶ What's your stance on investing in competitive companies?

---

When I was an investor in Gowalla and there was a chance to invest in Foursquare, I didn't. The cost of competing with each other is much lower than it used to be, but investing in a direct competitor just seems like a jerk move. Period. As I see it, the bigger problem is what happens when companies pivot. I'm investing in companies that aren't competitive, but as an entrepreneur I can see how they could each make a move that would bring them into the same orbit. And then what would I do?

The only thing anyone can do is approach investments with openness, honesty, good intent, and the understanding that the scenario I just described above is possible. In fact the only reason I avoid it, and I suggest you do, too, is that if you make it a habit, you will hurt your reputation and no one will want to deal with you. Earn a reputation as someone who is trusted and transparent, and every opportunity will find you. So to put the issue to bed, I am very down on the practice.

---

▶ You talk a lot about upcoming companies and predicting their success. Where and how do you find these companies?

---

There are three things I do every day that you should do, too:

1. Read Jason Hirschhorn's newsletter *Redef.* Hirschhorn is one of the great curators of our time.
2. Start following Techmeme, an aggregator, and Re/code, a blog. Also create a Nuzzel account. I skim mine every morning.
3. And here's my best hack: I go to the iTunes app store every morning, click on the apps tab, and look at the top three paid apps to

get a sense for when things are bubbling up. I watched a lot of the big platforms like Yik Yak and Snapchat grow organically through this channel before Techmeme and Re/code even wrote about them.

---

▶ What usually prompts you to walk away from great opportunities?

---

My intuition. It allows me to walk away from bad opportunities that may look good on paper. I'm not an analytical thinker, and it's not often that the data tells me an investment is going to work. I taste and observe, and if I don't feel it's a good investment, I don't do it. I think many more people who read this have to find a good balance between their number sense and their gut. It's a science and an art, and anyone who tells you otherwise has a vested interest or just doesn't get it.

---

▶ How do you balance risk and reward?

---

I always value reward over risk. When I invested in Meerkat it was obvious that Periscope was going to launch within the week, and it had the advantage of being backed on Twitter's infrastructure. In fact, Twitter shut a lot of Meerkat's virality down within Twitter before I made the investment. Instead of looking at what was wrong I looked at what would happen if they could make the right moves, and the upside was tremendous. I didn't worry because the upside was so great. Remember Facebook's attempt to slow down Snapchat with Poke? Blockbuster was going to go after Netflix. Wal-Mart was going to crush Amazon. The leader doesn't always win when they are playing the other guy's game.

▶ Does instability with China and the macroeconomic environment
   affect how you see the world?

When I first started getting involved in investments in the mid-
2000s, companies were valued at $2–3 million, even if they had
pretty strong seasoned entrepreneurs. Currently it's not unusual
for kids fresh out of school to get an $8–12 million valuation.
That is aggressive inflation and it only happens during good
times.

I have no way to know where China's market will be by the
time you are reading this, but instability within any of the world's
top four economies, let alone a top one or two like China, is absolutely going to affect the way I think about investing. If the
stock market collapses, and the Facebooks and Googles are now
worth half the price, that usually leaves all the other companies
that were using those companies as a barometer overpriced in the
current rounds they are trying to achieve. The effects of instability will definitely trickle down, all the way down to angel investments.

▶ How beneficial do you think patents are in being able to set a
   start-up apart from the competition?

I've been viscerally against playing the whole patent game, but
I'd be naïve not to recognize that there is value in it. A lot of
companies have sold their IPs and their patents over the last
half decade for sizable change. However, as an investor it's not
something I look for. In fact, often during pitches, if someone
says they have a patent, my next question is usually, "Patent or
patent pending?" The answer is overwhelmingly "Patent pend-

ing." Patent pending doesn't mean anything except some paperwork has been filed. Most people use it more as a sizzle, a tactic to sell me on the company, than something meaningful. I tend to be interested in more consumer-based products than extremely technical ones, so a patent is not nearly as valuable to me.

▶ Why don't you invest in space, biotech, or life sciences?

Because I failed science class from fourth grade through my senior year of high school. I think it's super-important to invest in areas in which you have intuitive strength or where your interests match your knowledge. And that is just not the case for the sciences and me. I would be shooting blind in those sectors. For that reason I will always stay away from them.

▶ How does geography affect your investment decisions? Is where founders or their businesses are located important to you?

I consider it a bit, but I don't value it as much as some of my Silicon Valley contemporaries who have totally bought in to the Silicon Valley brand. I'm a big believer that great businesses can be started anywhere. Facebook was started in Boston. Pinterest was started in Pennsylvania. Snapchat was started in Los Angeles. Why would a company need to be in Silicon Valley? I'm pretty passionate about the incredible stuff happening in middle America. And Berlin. And Asia.

Location would only be a variable if I saw that a company needed heavy infrastructure. Then I'd have to consider the fact that they'd eventually have to move to San Francisco because that is where a lot of developers live. I have to consider geography when I look at U.S. companies trying to get into Europe, or vice versa, mostly because they each have an astounding lack of understanding for the foreign market they're trying to penetrate.

For the most part, however, the horse and jockey is way more important than where the race is taking place.

---

▶ **Will you ever play in syndicate platforms like CircleUp or AngelList in the future?**

---

I have an AngelList account. I respect that platform and it's a great place. But I tend to lean toward doing far fewer deals that are far more meaningful. Though I don't see it as a growing trend for me, I would encourage anyone who is reading this to check out those platforms. AngelList has a lot of cool stuff going on.

---

▶ **What should companies expect from their investors at each stage of investment?**

---

Expectations are dangerous. Every start-up and investor relationship is different. Some investors are extremely hands-on, some are hands-off, and I've heard founders time and time again complain about both.

Ideally, founders and VCs should have a conversation about their expectations up front. That's what I did as I started extending myself with VaynerRSE even as VaynerMedia continued its hypergrowth. My conversation with a lot of our investments was pretty consistent. I would say I could be the backbone, but my team was going to be way more hands-on than me. Ninety-five percent of people were fine with that. A small amount weren't, and that was okay, too. My reputation and remaining a man of my word was more valuable to me than any deal. I passed on an investment that is now doing extremely well because I didn't feel I was going to be able to deliver on the multiple hours a month that would be required for me to make the investment. It's admittedly hard to watch it do so well, but I'm at peace with my decision because I knew I wasn't going to be able to live up to the company's ask. What's important is that everyone lay out his or her variables and not overpromise.

---

▶ Should founders always be the ones that end up running their company when and if they reach a billion-dollar valuation?

---

Absolutely not. As a matter of fact, I would argue that few founders should be running their companies at that size. It's been very impressive from afar to watch Ben Silverman and Mark Zuckerberg run their companies from start-up to that billion-dollar valuation. It obviously can be done, but they are the outliers.

The skill sets required to take a company from zero to ten million, let alone zero to a billion, are very different from the skill sets needed to run a company once it has actually achieved that mega-dollar valuation. The founder of one of my most successful deals no longer runs the company, because he just wasn't capable of operating it at its new, bigger scale and size. It really exploded when we put a more seasoned CEO in place. The company literally would have been out of business under the founder's watch, and now it's on its way to becoming a substantially large business with millions of dollars of value. I'm not even sure if I should run a company that big. I could probably run a $500 million company but once you get into the billions territory, you start getting into different kinds of dynamics. You have to know what you're good at.

# CHAPTER 17
# SELF-AWARENESS

---

## IN THIS CHAPTER I TALK ABOUT REACHING HIGH WITHOUT DELUSION, THE BIGGEST DECISION I´VE EVER MADE, AND WHETHER IQ OR EQ IS MORE IMPORTANT FOR SUCCESS IN BUSINESS.

---

This chapter means a lot to me because I think the topic of self-awareness doesn't get enough attention. And yet, if there's one thing that's helped me win over the course of my career . . . well, I've said that about hustle and gratitude and all kinds of other traits discussed in this book, haven't I? Whatever. This is another characteristic that has really worked for me. If I could sell a formula made up of gratitude, empathy, and self-awareness, it would be my billion-dollar coconut water idea.

My self-awareness is one of the reasons why I can comfortably say outlandish things and make hyperbolic statements. I know what people think of me, and I know that the same things that draw people to me turn others off and keep them away. I'm okay with that, because I think I can help more people and get my point across better when I'm my unfiltered self.

Knowing how you come across to others can often give you an advantage as an entrepreneur. Take sales, for example. You can set the tone in a scenario, anticipate how other people might react, and thus be prepared to address their concerns and questions even before they've been able to articulate them. It's a really valuable tool to have in your communication tool belt, and it's something I look for and admire in others.

Self-awareness is underestimated now, but I know someday when I'm in my fifties, sixties, or seventies, it will be the subject matter of the day. *If there is a chapter in this book that you would read twice*, I'd ask that this be it.

---

▶ What are some easy ways to become more self-aware?

---

There's one hack, and it's asking people straight up to tell you your strengths and weaknesses. These people have to be the five to twelve people who know you the best or work with you the most. You have to create a safe zone within which they can do this, of course. No one is going to be honest with you if they think you'll make them pay for it later or if they love you too much. You also have to be prepared for them to tell you things you may not want to hear or that you disagree with. That's why you have to gather a diversity of opinion. If you hear enough people say the same thing, whether it's that you're too kind or too aggressive, you'll eventually have to accept that it could be true. In fact, embrace the people who tell you you're full of crap. Double down on those relationships, because they're the ones that will help you improve the most.

Get yourself a thick skin. I hate reading bad stuff about me, but I can handle it. I respect it, accept it, understand it, and I try to learn from it. If you're aggressive about getting the feedback, and man or woman enough to "eat it," you can make changes in your interactions with people and your approach to business that can pay off in big ways.

---

▶ What's the most common mistake founders make when building a consumer-focused business?

---

There are so many goddamn mistakes, but the biggest is when they delude themselves into thinking they are significantly more talented and special than they really are.

No one wakes up and says "I'm going to be an NBA player today," but everyone today—the young and hungry, and the old and hungry—is deciding on a whim that they're going to be a consumer product innovator, start-up founder, or cofounder of a consumer product company. The audacity is ludicrous and stunning to me. People underestimate how hard it is to build a consumer app and create something sticky that people care about. It takes a special talent, yet career students, corporate people, and bright-eyed hustlers think somehow they're going to understand consumer behavior and scratch that itch for a consumer product better than anyone else. So the mistake? Not having the self-awareness to know they're not good enough to do it.

That said, if you can afford the risk, I say go ahead and try, just as I would tell anyone to try out for the Los Angeles Lakers if they allowed it.

---

▶ It's good to understand our talents and weaknesses, but I fear we'll get trapped into a mind-set of telling ourselves that there are things we can and can't do. Poet Robert Browning said, "A man's reach should exceed his grasp." I want people to try lots and lots of things. I don't want people to tell our children what they are and aren't good at. How can you incorporate that idea into your discussion about self-awareness?

The person who asked this question, speaker and social media strategist Ted Rubin, was absolutely correct: People should reach high. But nothing I see in the market today indicates to me that people have a problem holding themselves back from trying whatever idea pops into their heads. Ideally, of course, people would blend a healthy sense of confidence with self-awareness. But I think we live in a culture that encourages us to believe we can be good at everything we set out to do, especially in the U.S. market.

Modern parents are telling little Stevie, "You can do anything you want!" Except Stevie sucks at basketball. They do the same for kids who want to be singers or engineers—or entrepreneurs. You're just not always going to be able to do everything you want. I think it's a good thing to remind people to evaluate their strengths *and* their weaknesses because not enough people are acknowledging they may have the latter.

Since not many people are willing to have that conversation, I think it's okay for me to push that message out a little harder than I might otherwise, and not hedge with Ted's valid point. I do the same thing when I bash TV advertising. It's not that I don't believe it has a purpose or value, but I don't need to advocate for it because 99 percent of the market already does, and it is grossly overpriced. TV doesn't need me. Self-awareness does.

What people don't realize is that the process of forcing yourself to be self-aware requires drinking a shitload of humble Kool-Aid. It's insane how much humility has been instilled into me by the market and has balanced my ego and self-esteem. I get why people think I'm full of myself, but what they're seeing is the postgame of a long period during which I learned to stay away from what I'm not good at so that I only talk about the things that I know I'm better at than most people. Everything should be in balance, so when the market is leaning so strongly in the direction of "Everything Is Awesome!" I think there is an opportunity to talk about how some people need to understand they suck.

Now, here's the thing. If you do suck but you love the thing you suck at, do it! If you love singing more than breathing, go for that singing career. I would just like it if you could go for it with the full realization that you're most likely going to wait tables for your entire life. You can't be disappointed if you go in with your eyes wide open. I'm not immune to FOMO, but I knew that to do what I do I'd have to leave a lot of fun and leisure on the table. You always pay a price for doing what you love. That's just life.

---

▶ Do you have any tips for presenting your consulting services to a potential client? PowerPoint? Video?

---

How should I know? Are you good at making a PowerPoint? Can you make a better video than anyone else? Or are you the kind of person who can just walk in and close the deal? Ask your business partners or employees, if you're not self-aware enough to figure out for yourself what you're good at.

This question is one I could never answer without knowing you well. What works for me doesn't necessarily work for you. Look inside yourself (or get others to tell you what they see): The answer is predicated on your God-given ability or on the skill you've worked hardest to master. Many of you do so many things better than me it makes me want to vomit. There are sooooooooooo many ways to present. Go with the one that lets you shine.

▶ How does humor play a role in business, if at all?

It does, and it plays the same role it plays in all of life—by easing tensions, greasing wheels, making people feel good. Wouldn't you rather do business with someone who makes you laugh than with a stick in the mud? A gift for humor happens to be one of the most attractive personal traits, and maybe one of the rarest. Remember the outpouring of grief over Robin Williams's death? People who can use humor to show us the world in a way we'd never have noticed on our own are special. I use humor inspired by stand-up comedy in my keynotes because I think it helps people remember (and enjoy) my talks more. I also use it to drive difficult HR conversations, and leverage it when I'm selling to clients.

As attractive as a sense of humor is, though, it's no more important than the other ones people are attracted to: caring, empathy, self-awareness, kindness, and beauty, among others. But if you know you've got it, use it.

▶ What was the biggest decision in your life that made you successful today?

It was the day I made the choice to suck at school.

Fourth grade. Mr. Mulnar's science class. I got an F on a science test. To make shit worse, I had to get it signed by my mom. To avoid being punished, I hid it under my bed, where it sat for two days until my conscience got the better of me and I showed it to my mother.

Until that moment, though, I was in hell. I distinctly remember sitting in my small bedroom, crying and trying to make sense of why I was having such an intense reaction to this test. And then it hit me, the thought that changed everything:

"Screw school. I'm a businessman."

I made the conscious decision to eat the pain four times a year when report cards came, to eat the pain of failing pretty much daily. Who cared if everyone thought I was a "loser," a kid without a shot? I knew better. I saw something different. Even at that young age, I was self-aware enough to realize what I was born to do.

It's not that I didn't care. I went to every class. I was respectful to my teachers. I just decided that I would be better off honing my skills and concentrating on what made me happy and what fulfilled me. I learned about selling baseball cards, which then became wine, which became WineLibrary.com and VaynerMedia and everything that makes me so immensely proud.

That moment marked the first time that I decided to fight what society expected of me and deliver on what made me happy.

And you should, too. Bottom line: Stop doing things that make you unhappy. I've been preaching this since my first book came out, and long before that. Sure, it sucked to get those report cards every quarter, but sometimes you have to take a thousand punches before anything good happens. Not everyone will understand what you're doing, and the more you work, the more chances you have to be disappointed. Or even to be the disappointment. But don't let those moments fool you. An instance of failure could be a huge opportunity.

Pay attention. Learn to be self-aware. One F on a test got me started. Countless bad report cards got me going. And if I could go back, I would fail every single test all over again.

---

▶ What was the toughest thing you've ever had to do for your career?

---

Historically, my answer has always been that it was leaving the Wine Library and starting my venture in VaynerMedia, but that's not the whole story.

Truthfully, the toughest thing I've ever had to do professionally was decide that I was okay putting myself out there.

Many people have forgotten that the first ten to fifteen headlines ever written about me in the media were essentially all "Wine Wiz Kid Builds Business." All of a sudden, all these entities I'd always had huge respect for, like the *New York Times* and the *Wall Street Journal*, were respecting me. It felt great.

But not long after that, I realized that there was a certain path I would need to take if I was going to get a bigger reach and gain a larger audience. And I was pretty sure there would be consequences. Sure enough, as soon as I started really letting people into my mind-set into business, not wine reviews, and communicated it in the way I do, people stopped talking about me as a great business operator—someone who made huge profits by realizing trends and executing on them—and instead described me as a "self-promoter," a "social media guru," and an "author."

In the eyes of those entities and people I'd always admired, I'd taken a step back (or two or three). There was a lot of eye rolling from "the establishment" that looked down on me for my self-promotion, as though it somehow undermined the success I had created until that point. It wasn't easy to know that my choices would cause some people to dismiss me and everything I'd accomplished. In fact, it continues to be something I struggle with, because I really enjoy being respected, as does everyone, especially when you work so hard. On the other hand, in a weird way I like the fact that people's prejudices against me cause them to underestimate me. *In entrepreneurship, the truth is undefeated.* Ultimately, if I execute multiple hundred-million-dollar businesses and make smart investments, it's all "net-net." You might not like that I don't dress up, or that I curse onstage, or that I self-promote, but if I execute, you just have to "take it."

Once I was able to accept the fact that I was going to enhance my accomplishments and live at ease by being me, at the expense of the establishment's respect, I was able to carry on and create everything I have today.

---

▶ How do I keep low self-confidence from keeping me from succeeding?

---

Self-esteem is the ultimate drug of our society. When you have it you give yourself the audacity to dream big, and when you do that, the little things stop mattering and anxiety cannot cripple you. I'm probably the least anxious person I know, even though you might think I should be, with all the responsibilities I carry on my shoulders. It's just that I have such strong self-esteem. (Thank you, Mom, you are truly amazing.) I'm absolutely sure that I can handle whatever comes my way.

I wish I could give people who struggle with this issue a rah-rah "you can do it!" answer, because without self-esteem, I'm not sure they can. That said, if you are self-aware enough to know that you lack confidence, you could definitely execute to get more. You need to do research and think hard about what you can afford to do. A lot of people would probably benefit from seeing a therapist who could help them work through whatever is keeping their confidence down. At the very least, start working to surround yourself with confident, positive people. Be as determined to get that self-esteem as an addict jonesing for a hit.

▶ A lot of small businesses fail because they refuse to accept when they're not good at something and insist instead on doing it themselves. How would you suggest telling someone they need to stop?

It's easy to know you need to outsource when you need A-level work and you're an F. It's a lot harder to see when you're a B. Here's the clue: If you try, try, and try but don't get any better, hire someone who's an A. There's no point in wasting energy on that struggle when it could be better used to enhance things you're already good at.

Now, let's say you know someone who thinks he's an A, or at least who thinks with enough practice he can become an A, but after a while it becomes clear that he clearly isn't and won't. Do you just let him flounder? I don't think so. I say call him on it. I do this all the time. I'll see a tweet and respond to tell the account holder how he or she could have done it better. I'm very polite and try to provide value.

▶ Do you think it is necessary to have an outgoing personality to be a successful entrepreneur?

It's never been less important.

Don't believe me? Think about all the successful entrepreneurs whom people talk about every day. Zuckerberg. Evan Williams. Kevin Systrom. David Karp. If those names aren't familiar to you, maybe you'll recognize these: Facebook. Twitter. Tumblr. Pinterest. Instagram. Ringing some bells now? While I don't know for sure they each identify as introverts, I do know they're absolutely not the kind of people who outwardly self-promote by today's Internet standards.

In the past, most of our connections were made through things like networking events or conferences. That setup made it absolutely necessary for young entrepreneurs to be outgoing and put themselves out there. And if they couldn't, they often found it necessary to bring someone on board who could. But technology has changed the game, and now your first impression doesn't have to be made face-to-face. You can shape your persona through your online interactions and presence. Meeting people in person is still important, but there are many other ways to build a company, talk to people, and make connections in the business world, all without leaving your desk. We are in the glory days of the introverted entrepreneur.

There is still plenty of room for the extroverted entrepreneur like myself, of course. And thank goodness for it, because I could never try to fake being someone I'm not. I'm very good at representing myself authentically online, but I know my strengths, and I know that I can get ten times more when I can meet people and bring my energy to the table face-to-face.

So introverted entrepreneurs, don't fake it. Bet on your strengths. If you prefer to sit all day at your desk and focus, do that if it's working for you. Never make the mistake of thinking that you need to be louder or more outgoing, or fake a bigger personality. This is a tremendous time for you to build a company. The ball is in your court, and social media and technology have put the whole game in your favor.

---

▶ How do I overcome my people-pleasing nature?

---

Why would you want to?

Society has long taught us that wanting to please people is a flaw and that it makes us weak. But it's not a weakness; it's a strength. I should know, I've built my entire world on it.

What is wrong with wanting to give? Being positive? Making sure everyone around you is happy? It blows my mind that people would want to label these as weaknesses, especially when I have seen firsthand how much ROI these actions offer when you use them to build a business. The only time people pleasing is a weakness is when you don't know how to ask for something in return or you only do it to ask for something in return.

You can give, give, give all you want, but if you never step up and ask for something back, you're not going to win. When you give someone something they need, when you make someone's dream a reality, in a sense they owe you. Their gratitude will make them very open to doing something for you when the time comes. *But you have to ask.* Nothing will ever happen if you don't just step up and *ask* for what you want, whether it's a sale, a connection, or a reference.

It's a tremendous personality trait to want to make others happy. Just don't forget to look out for yourself.

▶ You get very personal when building your brand with the public. How personal is too personal? Where do you draw the line?

You draw the line where you feel you should. I like getting personal because I think it helps people feel closer to me, which helps me build my brand but also allows me to get to know my fans better. Getting personal is one of the reasons I love doing *The #AskGaryVee Show* so much. But I've got limits. I'm willing to put out a picture of me on the toilet, but I don't share pictures or really any information about my children. Some people go nude; some won't show their belly button. You've got to go with your gut. Also, remember that you've always got the right to change your mind. What might be too much last week might not be tomorrow, and vice versa.

▶ What do you think is more important in business, IQ or EQ?

They're both important, of course. I know my IQ is kind of average but that my EQ is off the charts, so that's where I go all in. It's been the foundation of my success and allows me to give back to my community, which gives me leverage. It allows me to form instant relationships, which is quite the advantage in my line of work.

I hear that a lot of people try to emulate me because my way looks fun and sizzly, but my way won't work for you as well if you're putting it on like a costume. You have to do you. There are plenty of people who love data, math, and tech and have happily made tons of money on their IQ. (I wish my math skills were as strong as AJ's! They aren't even close.)

Whether you're all EQ, all IQ, or like the majority of people a nice mix of both, the important thing is to be aware enough of your composition to capitalize on your natural gifts.

# CHAPTER 18
# GARYVEE'S GUIDE TO PUBLIC SPEAKING WITHOUT SHITTING YOUR PANTS

---

## IN THIS CHAPTER I TALK ABOUT PUNCHING PEOPLE IN THE MOUTH, HOW TO GET AWAY WITH F-BOMBS, AND STICKING TO WHAT YOU KNOW.

---

Fun fact: I did not give my first public speech until 2006, when I was thirty-one years old. It was at an Internet conference, and I really didn't know what to expect. But the second I took that stage my world was never the same. Sometimes I wonder if my real talent is public speaking, not building businesses. I enjoy it almost as much. There may be no greater high for me than that second right before I walk out onstage; it feels like home. It's no secret that I like to hear myself talk, and this gives me the perfect excuse, but I really do tremendously enjoy connecting with my audience. I'm so grateful for the opportunity to speak to so many people on a regular basis.

If you've done a good job of building your brand, there is a good chance someone will ask you for an interview, or to sit on a panel, and eventually, if you're really good, to host a conference or deliver a keynote address. When this starts happening to you, you'll know you're on your way. It's not only fun, it's lucrative. I love it. I really freaking love it. I hope I can make you love it, too, if you're like I was and unaware that it was even in your skill set.

Given how many times I'm asked to speak per year, and the somewhat—how should I put it?—colorful way I tend to express myself, it's no surprise I've gotten a number of questions about public speaking on the show. I hope these answers will help you prepare for your moment in the spotlight.

---

▶ How do you prepare for an important keynote?

---

I know some people are absolutely terrified by the idea of speaking in public. If that's you, and you're growing a business, I hope you'll get some help from a counselor or coach. Some people even attend acting, improv, or comedy classes. Finding a way to free yourself from your fear of public speaking is an extremely worthwhile investment, because if you succeed, it sets the potential for an enormous boon to your brand and business.

The benefit of doing keynotes or talks is tremendous. You can reach new audiences you might not have encountered. Build your credibility. Take time to articulate your ideas in a longer format. And public speaking opportunities often give you the chance to meet other influencers and cool people, as well as learn a bit more about yourself by seeing how you communicate differently in various settings. Take the first opportunity you can get. It's a great experience.

Some people have to write out a script and memorize it word for word before they'll feel comfortable up on the stage or at the podium. Some people practice with their friends. Others prefer to improvise. Me? Well, my preparation is a little unconventional. It works for me, but I'm not sure it would work for everyone. Whatever. You asked.

Eight minutes before I take the stage, I'm doing my everyday stuff. I'm checking email. I'm joking with a friend. You'd never know I'm about to give a talk. I find that continuing my routine activities helps keep me calm.

Six minutes before showtime, I get into a weird place. I become extremely focused, like a boxer about to hit the ring. But I don't review any notes. I don't frantically start rattling through the speech to make sure I know it by heart. Those last-minute tendencies people have to want to fix something or change something can be really destructive. The day you find yourself in this moment, have confidence in yourself and go with your plan. You've worked hard for this. You're ready.

Then, right before I go out onstage, I think about punching every audience member directly in the mouth.

Seriously.

Though not literally, of course. I don't want to inflict harm on anyone. But when I'm onstage, I'm hyperfocused on bringing my audience value and so I'm in a sort of aggressive attack mode. I know it sounds strange, but I feel a weird mix of love and aggression for the people in the seats, because on one hand I'm so grateful for their presence and their support and interest, yet I'm also determined to send them away with a powerful message ringing in their ears. I'm like a boxer in a crazy zone before the fight.

Except unlike a boxer, I can't physically grab people's attention. I have to demand their attention with my voice, and convey my story in a way that keeps them rapt. Here is where showing your emotion is a good thing. Go ahead and get excited, or pissed, or frustrated. Show the audience how you feel about your topic. People respond to honesty and emotion. You'll look strong and convincing. Most important, you'll be almost impossible to forget.

So that's how to prepare for an important talk. Trust me, the first one is the easiest one you'll ever do. Know why? Because you're only as good as your last talk. You've got nowhere to go but up. The second you take that stage, you're wiping the slate clean and reaffixing your brand in people's hearts and minds. Treat each event as your last at bat, and make it an amazing one.

---

▶ How do you get away with so many f-bombs onstage?

---

I think the answer is twofold. First, I mean it. I'm not just throwing curse words out there to shock you, I'm really feeling each and every one. It's not a tactic, I'm just in the zone when I'm up on the stage. As I mentioned earlier, as a kid I idolized Richard Pryor, Chris Rock, and Eddie Murphy, and their influence translated directly into the way I deliver keynotes. But although there is a little bit of a stand-up quality to my speeches, I'm not acting up there. That Jersey boy is all me, and I think even when they're a bit taken aback by my penchant for profanity, most people in my audience respect my authenticity.

Second, I get away with dropping f-bombs because I just don't fucking care if I catch flak for it. In fact, I use the f-bomb all the time to vet people with whom I do business. How you react to me tells me a whole lot about you. If you're operating at such a micro level you can't get beyond my language to hear the bigger message I'm trying to communicate to you, you're just not someone I want to do business with or take on as a client. You're never judging me half as much as I'm judging you.

▶ As a speaker, you rarely use filler words and you hardly ever lose
your train of thought onstage, or in front of the camera. Can you
provide insight into how you've nurtured your public speaking
chops?

I've had a lot of practice since the first time I hit the stage in 2006,
and here is the biggest secret I have learned for a flawless presentation: Talk about what you know. Don't let people suck you into
a debate about a topic in which you're neither interested nor well
versed. For example, I try not to answer questions about foreign
policy or currency like Bitcoin. The only reason my opinion matters about anything is that I am a practitioner and have grounded
my execution in strong research and experience. I'm not providing
value if I start spouting opinions based on nothing more than a few
clickbait headlines. I stay in my lanes of expertise where I spend
my time honing my craft. If you're comfortable with your subject
matter and speaking from the heart and from experience, you'll
always sound like a pro.

# CHAPTER 19
# MUSIC

---

## IN THIS CHAPTER I TALK ABOUT THE NUMA NUMA SONG, NEW REVENUE STREAMS, AND MAKING YOUR FANS FALL IN LOVE WITH YOU.

---

I would have lost an enormous amount of money if a year ago you had told me that I was going to write a book called *#AskGaryVee*, and one of the chapters was going to be about music. I would have made a bet against that for money that matters. Yet as Stephanie Land, my writer, and the rest of the team and I worked to pull together the material for the book, we discovered that I had answered a number of questions about music. Who knew?

Most people who care about the art form do not respect my relationship with music. I have no musical talent and my contemporaries often disrespect my taste. One of my favorite things to do is put a favorite song on continuous loop and listen to it for five to seven hours. I once listened to Bone Thugs-n-Harmony's song "1st of tha Month" through the entire train trip from Boston to New York—and I didn't take the Acela. While making the final edits of this book I listened to Drake's "Back to Back" on loop. But you'll also find Lionel Richie and Cyndi Lauper jams on my iPad.

This is fun for me. I don't have amazing passion for the indie or the hip-hop scene, but I am excited to see how many musicians have real talent mixed in with entrepreneurial DNA, and I'm passionate about seeing how the changing marketing and communications landscape has provided opportunity for them.

Think about it. Would anyone have ever heard of "Dragostea din tei" if it weren't for Gary Brolsma? You're probably thinking you still haven't heard of it, but you have. It's more commonly known in this country as the Numa Numa song, and Gary Brolsma is the guy who uploaded a home video of himself lip-syncing to it onto the Internet back in 2004. The song went on to become an internationally bestselling single, and while the band who wrote it, O-Zone, split up, Gary Brolsma endures and, according to his website, continues to make music and videos. Carly Rae Jepsen, whose new pop album is being called one of the best of the decade, had been writing and recording songs in Canada for several years before Justin Bieber and Selena Gomez first tweeted about her catchy song "Call Me Maybe" and created the famously goofy YouTube dance video to go along with it that turned her into an international star. So you know how I'm always saying that you don't want to obsess about how many followers and fans you have, but rather about *who* your followers and fans are, and that the quality of your content and engagement with them is everything it should be? That's why.

It used to be that in order to get any attention you had to make a thousand demos and pray that some music producer would bother to listen and sign you up for a record deal, after which you were at the mercy of the label. But now aspiring musicians have far greater control over their careers, and many more avenues they can take to get their music heard. They don't have to please record labels anymore. They just have to please their fans.

Do you have any idea how many bands and artists have been able to break out and become profitable because they knew how to use social media like Vine and YouTube to reach their audiences? These are the same bands that would never have been able to get so much as a meeting with a major label fifteen years ago. For sure there are fewer artists who go platinum, but the long tail has gotten even longer and allows a greater number of performers to make money.

That's why I don't understand why so many people continue to bemoan the fate of the music industry and complain that musicians can't get a fair shake. They sure as hell can. If they hustle, that is. They just have to stop thinking of themselves as artists and start thinking of themselves as a business.

---

▶ Since music itself doesn't create income anymore, what advice do you have for musicians wanting to make their living playing music in the twenty-first century?

---

Let's get some perspective—throughout history, maybe 1 percent of all musicians, singers, and songwriters ever made it big. Most professional musicians worked their whole lives making the best living they could doing what they loved, while supplementing their income doing work that they did not love. But they don't have to take that second or third job anymore. Just like many other entrepreneurs, artists can make a perfectly livable income through AdSense, YouTube ads, sponsored social media content, and Beatport sales, which leaves them more free to devote their working hours to honing their craft, distributing their music, engaging with fans and music venues, and creating their own opportunities to perform live. In fact, according to a *New York Times* article called "The Creative Apocalypse That Wasn't," "More people are choosing to make a career as a musician or a songwriter than they did in the glory days of Tower

Records, with as many as forty-six possible revenue streams available to them."[*]

Musicians have to implement a proper content strategy on social media and build awareness of their brand and product, same as any entrepreneur. Where is your audience? If you're trying to reach new music lovers, you need to go where they are. If you're not on Snapchat, YouTube, Vine, Instagram, and SoundCloud, you basically don't exist to the average twenty-five-year-old. Get over there now.

Your presence won't be enough, however. It's not sufficient to make some Vines, throw your music up on DistroKid, and wait for the sales to roll in. You have to cultivate community. That's what the best music stars have always done. Madonna, Michael Jackson, Justin Timberlake, the Grateful Dead, Phish—is their music *that* much better than anyone else's? Yes, to a point. But one thing that is unquestionably true is that these artists beat the odds by going well beyond merely putting out music and building an extremely engaged and loyal community.

Most musicians think their art is their priority, but your audience needs to be, too. Show them you care. Start doing things for them. Use all the platforms at your disposal to knock on their doors and say, "Hey, let me in." Live streaming offers musicians today a spectacular way to connect to fans, and Facebook Live, Meerkat, and Periscope have created a new pipeline they need to expose and use. You can play for people live. You can take requests. You can talk about the process that went into the creation of a song or piece of music. You can test new material. Imagine the behind-

---

[*] Steven Johnson, "The Creative Apocalypse That Wasn't," *New York Times Magazine*, August 19, 2015, http://www.nytimes.com/2015/08/23/magazine/the-creative-apocalypse-that-wasnt.html?_r=0.

the-scenes access you can offer. Imagine the connections you could make. You'd have fans for life! Once people love you, it's easy to sell them your stuff.

Create music, create content, create community, and create revenue streams. If you're a musician, that's the path that will allow you to support yourself with your art.

---

▶ As a private music teacher I have limited hours to teach. Thoughts on how to increase my income and brand?

---

Of course I do.

There are entire industries that have been transformed by tech, allowing people who work on opposite sides of the globe to connect and collaborate. Who says your students all have to be in your time zone? There are doctors who treat patients, and accountants who consult with clients, via Skype. Why couldn't a music teacher do the same? Offer classes on Skillshare. Take a page from online education and start marketing yourself to people who don't have easy access to good music instruction. Find the need and fill it.

Another strategy would be to monetize the hours when you're not teaching. As hard as teachers work, they of all people should have the most time to crush it when they're not in the classroom or with students. Teachers usually find their schedules open up a lot during the summer, so that's another time when you could get a lot of initiatives going that could carry you throughout the year. Start putting out content—blog posts, videos, podcasts, anything—about music, teaching, cultural events, and any other topics that are even tangentially related to your business and give you a chance to show who you are and build trust. Use Twitter Search and engage with people who love music, or who have kids who love music, or who might be interested in music classes, or even to connect with other teachers. Offer tutorials on Spreecast or Meerkat (I'm an investor), start a YouTube Channel, and take advantage of Google hangouts. The options are endless for creative entrepreneurs.

Does all of that sound like a lot of work? It is. How people react to the prospect of so much work is really what differentiates between those who build successful small businesses and those who eventually give up and go work for someone else. If you love the work—if the idea of putting yourself out there and sharing your love for your art and reaching more and more students gets you excited—then there's no reason why you can't make this work for you. If you're overwhelmed by it all and just can't imagine giving up *Game of Thrones* or the many other activities that take up hours in our days, you're really not cut out for it. Your talent is what it is, but the level at which you increase your income and brand is limited only by the scope of your ambition and willingness to hustle. Nothing more, nothing less.

---

▶ I'm a music producer. How can I use social to promote my content?

---

When this question came in, we decided to take a look at this music producer's Twitter account to see what he was already doing. You know what we found? He'd posted a remix of a Rihanna track eight times in twenty-four hours. That's a bit much. Overwhelming, actually. You want to put out content, of course, but you want to put out a variety of content, and you want to do it with purpose. Otherwise you start to look desperate.

So, the answer to improving your social, whether you're a music producer or a mustard seller, is, as always, to listen to your audience or the target audience and produce great content, in that order. Get your best work up on SoundCloud and other music platforms, and then start looking for opportunities to listen to people and then engage with them to the degree that they decide they want to check you out.

Someone in the music scene might go old-school by joining some music message boards and becoming an integral part of that community. If Rihanna's music inspires you, you could use Twitter Search to find every single person who recently tweeted about her music and start jamming with them, sharing why you love her work, too, and how it influences yours. Be interested and interesting and more than likely they will check you out to learn more about you. You might even set aside a few days to concentrate on this strategy. If you do, consider this tactic: Change the URL on your Twitter profile to that of your SoundCloud account so it links directly to the track you want people to hear. If people love it, they're going to share it. If they share it, it has a chance of gaining more attention from more people and maybe even have something pop, aka go viral. Get that viral loop going and you can get major brand awareness. All your efforts should go into creating great art, making it as easily available as possible, and engaging with the people who might want to hear it. If you're truly skilled, your fans and their word of mouth will start doing much of the social work for you.

---

▶ I'm holding back tears and my heart is heavy because the Seahawks lost and I bet $225. That's like four Xbox games and an Arizona iced tea. I've listened to Drake, the Weeknd, Jhene Aiko, and even PartyNextDoor, but the pain is too much. How do I cope?

---

I'm an extremely happy guy in general except when the New York Jets do something stupid. And then for a few hours I feel like I'm drowning in quicksand. When you're feeling this low, do what I do: play a heavy rotation of two songs, Bone Thugs-n-Harmony's "Tha Crossroads" and Taylor Swift's "Blank Space." Put them on loop, repeating each about seven times before switching to the next. Drown your sorrows. Then take the pain and carefully put it in a little compartment near your heart, and let that be an engine for the revenge you will strike against your enemies.

---

▶ How would you suggest an indie artist use his or her marketing money when royalty checks come six months later?

---

Simple. Be patient. You can't do anything if you don't have money, so you wait for it, and then you execute.

Come on, you didn't really think that was all there is to it? Use your time to hustle and make some other money! Look at the royalty checks as gravy. Go out and play shows, get another job, go garage sale'n' and flip the stuff you buy on eBay. Whatever it takes! If this is your dream, if you want to be a famous and rich artist, or even just a working artist, sitting on your ass waiting for your check before doing any marketing seems idiotic.

Read the answers to the first two questions in this chapter and you'll see what you need to do while waiting for your money to come in. You should also go back to Chapter 2, "Starting Out," and reread every single question and answer. If an entrepreneur can figure out how to market a product that's still six months away from a finished prototype, you can figure out how to market the music that is probably as much a part of you as the air you breathe.

# CHAPTER 20
# SPORTS

---

## IN THIS CHAPTER I MAKE A PREDICTION ABOUT THE DALTON DEAL, REVEAL WHAT TEAM I'D BUY IF I CAN'T BUY THE JETS, AND EXPLAIN THE PARALLELS BETWEEN TENNIS AND BUSINESS.

---

Unlike music, sports are an enormous pillar of my life. It's my real passion besides business, and factors into all of my ambition and determination to buy the New York Jets. It's relevant, too, because over the last decade the sports industry has become very interesting to a lot of entrepreneurs, and the landscape around it, from communications to business, has expanded and is evolving rapidly.

This chapter may not have the most teeth in it, but if you want this one man's 360-degree point of view, we gotta go here. I hope you'll enjoy reading it as much as I enjoyed answering the questions.

---

▶ What do you think of the Dalton deal?

---

In 2014, quarterback Andy Dalton signed a six-year, $115 million contract with the Cincinnati Bengals. And even though he crapped the bed in the playoffs, I thought it was a good deal. Quarterbacks are tough to come by, especially redheaded quarterbacks. The New York Jets haven't had a top 15 quarterback in 25 of the last 27 years, and I would rip my arm off for Andy. I have a feeling he will have that playoff run that all the Bengals fans are looking for. We'll see who was right.

---

▶ With the NFL in London this week, what do you think about sports franchises moving to other cities or countries?

---

This question was posed the day after the Jets lost their game, and my answer reflected my mood. At the time I said that some sports franchises should move to faraway places, like as far away as possible. Now that a little time has passed and I'm less disappointed, I still think it's interesting to think about a world in which teams play in other countries. I am also super-curious to find out what city in the United States will be next to get its first professional team (Oklahoma City?) and in which sport.

---

▶ If the Jets never come up for sale in your lifetime, and another NFL team does, would you buy that team instead?

---

I don't want to answer this question. I've gone back and forth with this. In the end I think I would focus on the Knicks, and after that a random other basketball team. I just can't see myself owning another football team.

---

▶ Do you see parallels between tennis and business?

---

I'm not as good at tennis as I wish I were, but I enjoy it a lot. The best thing about it is that because the matches are made up of multiple games and sets, even when you're down, you're not necessarily out, because you've got time to watch your opponent and gauge his or her weaknesses and strengths. Once you figure it out, you can come roaring back. I've done it. Nate Scherotter, my former assistant and the CEO of my last book, has never beaten me in a game of tennis, even though twice he has had me down 5-2. How did I win? I reacted to what was happening, took a step back to observe, made the necessary adjustment, and started targeting his weaknesses. I evaluated Nate exactly as I would if I felt threatened by a competitor in business.

It's like Mike Tyson said: "Everybody's got a plan until they get punched in the face." You can strategize and plan ahead all you like, but once you're on the court, or in the ring, or on the field, you'd better be ready to adjust and improvise. The same goes for business. You created a plan, you set a path toward success, and then suddenly someone copies your product for less. Someone is better than you. Nobody wanted your stupid app. Time to adjust or die.

Entrepreneurs need to have the emotional composure and the intestinal fortitude to make real-time adjustments and come back from the brink. Those qualities don't hurt in a game of tennis, either.

# CHAPTER 21
# WINE

---

## IN THIS CHAPTER I TALK ABOUT HOW TECH BRINGS NEW VOICES INTO OLD INDUSTRIES, I MAKE SOME WINE RECOMMENDATIONS, AND I TELL YOU WHAT TO DRINK WITH KIMCHI.

---

You didn't think I could write this whole book and not mention wine, did you? In this one man's point of view, what has happened to wine in the last half decade since I stopped being as intimately involved with it is nothing short of transformative. So many fun things have happened. Wine has grown to become a standard in American culture. Rosé has finally established itself in the United States. That makes me smile quite a bit. People are trying lots of different wines. That makes me smile, too. But the thing that really makes me smile is how many new voices have emerged. I have enormous respect for Robert Parker and *Wine Spectator*, the two powerful voices that dominated the industry long before I entered the field and throughout my early wine career. They were monumental and served a real purpose for their time. Yet what a great evolution to see how many new voices have been able to emerge because of social media and tech. New apps where people can leave reviews, blogs, hundreds of thousands of pieces of content put out by bright new personalities in the wine community, especially on Instagram, Twitter, Facebook, and Pinterest. It's been inspiring and exciting to be able to learn from so many different perspectives in addition to incredible thought leaders like Jancis Robinson, *Wine Spectator*, and many others. As in all other sectors that provoke passion in so many, we're living in a time where we have access to better debates and more original stories, which I think allows consumers to enjoy a richer exploration of a beverage and cultural touchstone that's been around since the beginning of time and will be around when most of us are gone.

---

▶ What wine bar or restaurant would you recommend to a first-time visitor to New York City?

---

Any establishment that has been smart enough to get on my reservations app, Resy. (JK.) Gotham Bar and Grill, Rosemary's, Minetta Tavern, Toro, Estela, Scarpetta, Carbone, Marea, Charlie Bird, and Balthazar, among others, are all great choices. I'm also a huge fan of a wine bar called Terroir.

---

▶ Tea, coffee, or wine?

---

The answer these days is water, but in my heart it's wine, then tea, then coffee. And root beer, too.

▶ What wine goes with kimchi?

We Eastern European immigrants are big on pickled foods, too. High-acid whites would be good, or oily thicker whites. So I'd recommend a Falanghina, which is a white wine from Italy, or from the United States a Santa Barbara Roussanne or Viognier. There is also a wine we produced exclusively for Wine Library called The Neighbor 2013 Sauvignon Blanc, which is super-creamy for a Sauv Blanc, and if it's still around by the time this book comes out you should find it and try it!

▶ On Fridays we drink wine. What's a good drinking-home-alone-bottle-to-yourself wine?

I'm a big white wine fan and I'm obsessed with Italian whites, non–Pinot Grigio. Look for things like Fiano, Soave, Greco de Tufo, and other white varietals from Italy that a lot of people don't know about and don't recognize the quality of. For 8–22 bucks you can get an enormous array of tremendous high-acid wines that still go great with cheese if you get hungry. Some suggestions:

2012 Bertolani Spergalino Secco Colli Di Scandiano Di Canossa
    Frizzante
2013 Girotondo Chardonnay Delle Venezi
2012 Mesa Giunco Vermentino
2014 Costa Alessandro Roero Arneis

▶ When someone gives you a horrible glass of wine, how do you
   politely get rid of it?

I made a big effort to be the anti-snob of the wine world and my
mom raised me right so it's natural for me to be polite. I guess my
way of politely saying your stuff is crap would be to suggest that if
you like this (swill) you might consider trying this other wine (that
is not swill). Sometimes people don't know what's good because
they haven't been exposed to anything better.

Actually, I like trying the occasional glass of bad wine because
it makes me appreciate the good stuff so much more. And the
same could be said for times when I'm asked to judge someone's
content or social media presence on *#AskGaryVee*. Often it's crap,
and yet it's my job to point out how it could be better without
tearing an entrepreneur or marketer down so viciously, he or she
never wants to try again. And seeing the crap makes me appreciate it that much more when I see others executing their social media strategy and content well. Because producing quality,
whether wine or webinars, takes major commitment and effort.
And I respect that.

▶ Is the high-end wine business a complete hoax?

Wine is as much of a hoax as art, high-end restaurants, stock prices,
or movie stars. Are movie stars really worth all those millions?
Well, does everyone have their talent? Probably not. And when
they draw audiences to the movie theater, they're supporting an
entire creative industry that puts thousands of people to work. Am
I worth the money I get paid to do speaking engagements? I used
to wonder, but now I know the answer is yes, because my time and

expertise is valuable. If people didn't get anything out of my talks no one would be willing to pay my fee. But people do because from their perspective, I'm worth it. The same goes for wine. I wouldn't expect someone who is satisfied with a $10 bottle of Cupcake to believe a Château Latour is worth the $800 or even the thousands of dollars it goes for in the right vintage. But for someone who appreciates what goes into the creation of a spectacular vintage, or even the story behind it, and will savor it, that money might be well spent.

The reality is that so long as you haven't experienced the difference between something high end and low end, it's hard to see what the big deal is. But in most cases, all it takes is one ride in first class, or one game in the front row of a stadium, or one sip of a Châteauneuf-du-Pape, and you'll wonder how you ever doubted its value.

---

▶ What's your favorite city in the world to drink wine?

---

Wherever my friends and family are. I'd be just as happy drinking wine in Newark as in an Austin hotel lobby, or the parking lot outside a Jets game, or inside a cave in a Tuscan winery. My happiness is always about the who, not the where.

---

▶ How do you tell the difference between all the wines in the store?

---

Buying wine based on a label crushes my soul, as does buying based on the shelf talkers (although Wine Library puts them up because they sell wine). The best way to buy wine is to form a relationship with your local wine seller and help them get to know your palate. If you can't do that, try a different varietal every time and see what you like best. When you haven't tried something you can't judge it. Once you have, you form an opinion and you can start making better decisions.

# CHAPTER 22
# THE PERSONAL, THE RANDOM, AND THE WEIRD

---

## IN THIS CHAPTER I TALK ABOUT MY SPIRIT ANIMAL, MY FAVORITE ROOT BEERS, MY BIGGEST FEAR, AND WHO SHOULD PLAY ME IN MY BIOPIC.

---

*The #AskGaryVee Show* is supposed to offer a 360-degree perspective of how I work, live, and think. I already live my life out in the open, so I'm often a bit surprised that there are still things people don't know about me and are curious enough to ask about. But there are quite a few, as it turns out. Which is good and makes sense because of course there are many topics you should be paying attention to. And amid all the conventional questions about running companies, investing, branding, marketing, and general business development, there are occasionally some, um, unusual inquiries. We like to respect every type of question, which is how some of these oddballs made it onto the show. I'm also flattered that some people want my opinion on these random topics. I always find it interesting to hear what's on people's minds. I hope you enjoy reading this fun collection as much as we enjoyed putting it together.

---

▶ Legend has it that on your first date with your wife you told her you would marry her. We want to know the details. And also, what dating advice do you have for women in their twenties?

---

Lizzie and I are married because the Jets won on the Sunday night we were supposed to go out for the first time. If they had lost, I would have canceled. But they didn't, and so I drove into New York City for what turned out to be a three-hour date at an awesome spot in Washington Square Park. She lived on the Upper East Side, and I lived in New Jersey. After dinner I dropped her off, and two minutes afterward I called her on her cell. She wasn't even in her apartment yet. And I said, "Can you believe this is it?" We talked during my forty-five-minute ride home, and then until about four in the morning. We were married within the year of our first date.

And now we have a daughter, and it has completely changed me. I meet so many strong, smart women through my work, and it blows my mind that one day my daughter will be one of them. What dating advice would I give a young woman coming up in the world? The same advice I'd give a man: Think about your legacy. Live on the offense. Don't be afraid to show your feelings and go for what you want, whether it's a job or a relationship. It's possible you'll get rejected, but it's more likely you won't. Better to experience the brief, temporary pain of rejection than to live forever with sad regret for all the things you were too scared to do.

▶ Does it bother your wife that you constantly spin your ring on the show?

All my straitlaced friends who don't travel are on their third rings. Me, I don't lose anything. I'm dramatically less careless than you might think. I can be chaos and practical at the same time. Lizzie is way too big picture to worry about silly things like that. I don't think she minds me spinning it on the show.

▶ How do I get the cute old lady who keeps accidentally calling my house to stop? I just want to nap . . .

You called her "cute," which means at some level you like getting these calls. Flip the script and go on the offense. The next time she calls, try to engage in a twenty-five-minute conversation with her and form a relationship with her. Bringing her deep into your heart may bring value to your soul. Who knows, it may lead to something meaningful for both of you. Relationships are everything. And I think everyone reading this can tell that I featured this question because I almost always believe that things you do in life can be applied to business and vice versa.

▶ Why is your phone always in the shot?

Because my phone is an extension of me, just like it's probably an extension of just about every human being who owns one. Few people are more than an arm's length away from their phone, even when they're showering and sleeping. Eventually we will embed our phones into our bodies. Yes, we will be like robots. I have it near me because I need it to be a human. Think about that statement!

---

▶ Cake or Pie?

I don't eat them much anymore, but I am obsessed with blueberry and apple pie.

---

▶ Center or edge?

Edge.

---

▶ What is your favorite pair of sneakers of all time?

Hands down the 1985 Patrick Ewing Adidas. I'm a huge Knicks fan. The ones I hated the most? Every single pair of Air Jordans. I hate Michael Jordan. Every one of us should!

---

▶ What is your favorite holiday tradition?

Going to my parents' house in Hunterdon County, New Jersey, for Thanksgiving. Birthdays used to be sacred in our family, but then my dad screwed that up a few years ago by taking my mom to Italy and now we don't share all of them together (yes, that's a fun zing at my dad). So now we make sure the whole family get together at Mom's on Thanksgiving. We've all got to be there for the football games. AJ and I are usually doing something crazy, my sister's kids are there, extended family . . . it's the best.

---

▶ My husband is a "big-picture" kind of guy, but so is his wish list. Any advice on Christmas shopping for this type?

---

Make something that is one-of-a-kind, something that is not scalable. I know exactly what I want: one-of-a-kind experiences. Here's the greatest gift Lizzie could ever get me: She could interview every person I ever met, or come to VaynerMedia and record everyone telling me I'm the greatest. It's easy to spend money; people will appreciate the time, effort, heart, and soul you put into a gift far more.

---

▶ If you could clone yourself, would you?

---

Easy as they come. I would, 100 percent. I wish this tech existed because I would send the cloned version to spend every waking moment with my family. No, wait, I meant at work? Uh-oh, is that Freudian? Maybe I do love my business more than my family? Not possible. I'd love to take the equal version of me and accomplish the two things I love most at the one time. Man, I hope I see this technology before I go.

▶ Do you wish you had done more or focused more on just one thing when you were in your mid-twenties?

I did focus on just one thing, and it was Wine Library. I wish I'd gone out and had more fun, hooked up with some girls. It's actually unfortunate how focused I was on the hustle and building my career when I was still so young. I'm pumped about my life and I'm happy, and I would never change a single thing, but it's human to look back and see in retrospect how you could have done things differently. But I made choices that served me well. I learned the skills, discipline, and focus that allow me to run a company while juggling a whole lot of other fantastic things at the same time.

▶ What's the hardest thing you've had to deal with in the past five years and how did you get through it?

Hands down, it was leaving the routine and day-to-day operations of working in the family business and easing off *WLTV* and *Daily Grape*. I just didn't realize what an emotional experience it would be to transition into a new chapter of my life that also profoundly changed the dynamics between my father and me. I got through it the way I get through everything: I kept communicating with everyone involved or affected.

▶ Are you ever scared before you do something big, even something not business related?

The only thing I'm really scared of is reading in public. I am an atrocious reader. It's even affected how I run my business. In 2015

I started creating only 5–7-minute meetings with much of my staff because I don't read fast enough and therefore wasn't reading their emails in full ahead of time.

Even reading to my daughter, Misha, is hard. If I were asked to concoct a fabulous story off the top of my head, I'd be good with that. But *Goodnight Moon*? Oh, God. And the Haggadah at Passover? I'm a nervous wreck.

One of the reasons I didn't accept the offers to do TV shows is I didn't want to have to read off the teleprompter. And even when I did my wine Web radio show on Sirius for nine months, my first commercial read was a disaster. It was probably the worst thing I ever did publicly. Then Sam Benrubi saved me by coming into the booth and saying, "Do what Howard Stern does. He can't read, either. Just read it to yourself and do your thing." So I read it through once to myself, figured out what Stella Artois (now a VaynerMedia client) needed to be delivered with that ad, and then I did an incredible read. Truly, the second reading was insane.

I'm scared of snakes, a little of heights, and ultimately of dying. But reading in public? Please don't ever make me do it.

---

▶ What's your spirit animal?

---

I originally answered that it was Ram Man from *He-Man*. But now that I think about it, you know who it really is? My wife, Lizzie. She's the best.

---

▶ Are you the person behind the #TomShady billboard?

---

I wish I could take credit. It wasn't me.

▶ If you could have a bionic body part, which body part would it be and what powers would it have?

---

I was cohosting the show with Casey Neistat when this question came in, and I'll bet Casey's answer came as a surprise to a lot of viewers:

"I do have one. My right leg from the knee to the hip is made of titanium. I was twenty-six years old, lying in the hospital with my leg broken in twenty-seven places, when the doctor said, 'You'll never run again. You can catch up with a taxicab, but that's it.' Prior to getting my bionic limb I wasn't much of an athlete or a runner, but since getting my metal leg I've run twenty-two marathons, four Ironman Triathlons, and countless other races."

As for me, I would go with ears. I'm not joking. One of the things I enjoy and think I do well is pay attention to more than one conversation. I'm often at a dinner table or at a conference, and I'll be fully immersed in a conversation but still able to listen to two or three other side conversations. Often when I talk to a group of forty or fifty I'll hear someone whispering to a friend or colleague and then incorporate what they said into my talk while looking at the person. It usually freaks them out. *I don't think people listen enough.*

---

▶ What's your favorite airport? LGA? JFK? SFO?

---

Small ones, like in Des Moines; Greenville, South Carolina; Montana; Arkansas; Chattanooga, Tennessee; the Vermont airport . . . the ones where you can roll up and be at your gate in four minutes without precheck. I know the big ones—LGA, LAX, JFK, SFO/L, Newark—better than I know my own office. They've become my home. The people there are my friends. The coziness that I feel at an airport is disturbing. Super-disturbing!

▶ Would you ever automate your position, delegate to as many
people as it takes, and fully engage in your family and life?

Absolutely not. Of course I love being with my family, but I would
suffocate if I couldn't work to create the things I want to create. I
want to build companies and commerce and be a salesman and put
out content. I love the process, the grind and the climb. I love what
it's going to take to get to the point that I can buy the Jets more
than I'm going to love actually buying them. Most young entrepreneurs want stuff—the watches, the cars, the planes, and the bling.
I just want the pain, the gratitude, and the happiness that come
with the work.

▶ Do you work on your birthday?

I hate my birthday because I hate getting older with a passion. I've
worked on every birthday of my entire life, including when I was a
teenager and my dad would drag my ass to the store on the weekends. I've given speeches on my birthday. I've attended conferences
on my birthday. I'm 100 percent all in every day of the year. You
want to do what you love on your birthday, and I do.

▶ What food(s) have you added to your new lifestyle that you are
enjoying the most?

There are no new foods. My trainer Mike and I went to the supermarket and I told him what I liked that was conceivably healthy,
like mangoes and shellfish. Luckily for me I like pretty much ev-

erything, so this new regimen has not included any additions. It's been all about subtractions.

---

▶ Why don't you watch your own videos? Ego or time?

---

Time. I know what I did.

---

▶ What value do you find in knowing a foreign language?

---

My Russian is English-accented. I failed German twice and the only reason I graduated from high school is that my Spanish teacher, Señora Kennedy, was the greatest of all time. You need to pass two years of language in New Jersey, and since I had already failed out of German, I needed a miracle to pass Spanish 1 and 2. God was good to me and gave me a teacher who had a hard reputation but clearly was smart as shit because she could see who I was. She called my mom and said, "I'm giving him a 'C' for charisma, but he doesn't even know how to say hello." She knew I had "it." Big shout-out to Señora Kennedy!

I think the business value of learning foreign languages is going down. I think tech is coming where we'll be walking around with earpieces or some other tech that will translate to us while we're traveling. For now, our phones do it.

▶ What's your travel schedule like to and from the office? Car, train, Uber, walk? How do you spend that time?

I live on the Upper East Side in New York City and work on Twenty-Fourth and Park, so my commute is a straight shoot in the morning. I travel a lot to JFK airport so I'm always buckled up in the back of an Uber, a black car, or taxi. During my commute I call my mom and I call Brandon at Wine Library to catch up on the day and strategize (I talk to my dad and sister more spontaneously during the day). I check my email and Twitter and look through Instagram. I check up on my fantasy baseball team (whereas of this writing I am still in the running). I check Nuzzel for news. I check for NFL news when the Jets are in it. Every morning, that's what I'm doing.

▶ Star Wars or Star Trek?

I don't like Star Trek at all and Star Wars is the only sci-fi thing I like. In 1981 my parents bought me two Star Wars figures for my sixth birthday, and I remember being blown away because we were still poor, and I was stunned they would do that for me. Star Wars was a big part of my culture. I was a chaotic kid, and I'd lose my light sabers right away. In 1983 I was super-pumped for *Return of the Jedi*. I was there at midnight in 1999 for Jar Jar Binks and I wasn't mad at him. I will be there on Christmas Day 2015 to see the new one.

► What's the fastest way someone can piss you off?

Despite my intensity I'm a love and Zen kind of guy, so it takes a lot to piss me off. Hypocrisy, cynicism, complaining . . . Man, if you complain about stuff it drives me up the wall.

► What's the most significant thing you get out of your show?

I video blogged every day for five and a half years, and it feels really nice to be back in the game. It's fun for me. But by far one of the best parts about this venture is that it has drawn together a little family of characters who are each becoming an integral part of the show, much the way my cameraman Mott was back in the days of *Wine Library TV*. India, Stunwin, Staphon, Zak, DRock—I so appreciate that they care enough to help me create the shooooooooow!

► What should I get my mom for Mother's Day?

Your new strategy needs to be recognizing that the mothers are on Pinterest. So go there and see what she's pinning, and buy it. Poke around her other social media sites like Facebook. If that doesn't work, call your mom's best friend or your aunt, because they will always know. That's the kind of effort you need to put into buying gifts for the people you love.

▶ You've repeatedly mentioned your love of root beer over the years. Why root beer specifically, and any we should give a whirl?

I grew up drinking Coke and root beer and loving it. Incredibly, I'm about to hit a one-year mark of no soda thanks to the efforts of my trainer Mike. But if you are looking to try something wonderful, Henry Weinhard's is incredible root beer. I'm also a big fan of Hosmer Mountain in Connecticut; Pirate's Keg in Rochester, New York; and Thomas Kemper. Virgil's is an entry-level root beer and often easier to find than the others.

▶ Do you ever have dreams at night about your business?

All the time. I go to sleep and tell myself to dream about Jets Super Bowls and instead find myself in a meeting. Not that you can remember many of your dreams. We actually looked it up and people dream four to six times per night, but we remember hardly any of them.

▶ What's the best thing that's happened to you this week?

I got this question in the summertime, so I had spent that weekend watching my kids play outside at a house my wife and I had rented for the season. So if you consider Sunday the beginning of the week, it was spending time with my kids. It felt different. I saw a preview to the next four or five years with them that really excited me.

▶ What environment is best for you to have successful business meetings in? Conference room, restaurant, in-flight?

Anywhere possible at all times. I will sell and "biz dev" and make the action happen in the bathroom, on the toilet, outside, at the game, anywhere. A funeral parlor. It doesn't matter. I'm comfortable in all environments.

▶ Do you believe in aliens?

I do. I even think there's another GaryVee in a different galaxy. I just want to know if he's crushing it or a loser.

▶ If you could go back to your twenties, would you prioritize health, or was neglecting it necessary to get where you are today?

I know I always say I don't regret a thing about the way I've lived my life, but I guess I lied, because I do wish I had prioritized my health more. I should have slept one hour less, played one hour less of *Settlers of Catan* with my brother and brother-in-law, Justin, worked one less hour, done less of a whole lot of things so that I could make room for that one hour per day to prioritize my health. So if I could go back and start working out and eating the way I am now, I would.

▶ What do you splurge on?

Experiences. LeBron's first game back in Cleveland against the Knicks because AJ is a huge fan and it will be something we can attend and remember together when we're older. Vacations with my family. Paying for my friends to go on trips when they couldn't afford it. I splurge on spending time with people I care about.

▶ Back in the old-school days of hip-hop, were you East or West Coast?

Biggie changed my music life so I was East Coast. But here's a curveball: During that era I was a bit more Cleveland. I was all in on Bone Thugs-n-Harmony. *Take me to the crossroads every time, East 99 is where you'll find me.*

▶ If it weren't for the Fourteenth Amendment, would you run for president?

This question exposes a dark, selfish part of me. The single reason I don't already have an eye on politics is that the presidency is out of my reach. I am not willing to play a game in which I can't be the ultimate winner. If the amendment changes, I'd go for it. I pride myself on the fact that I eat pressure for breakfast. And if you look at presidents' hairlines, you see they age fast in the office. I'm already losing my hair, so we're good there.

▶ My bro has been dating a girl for two years and refuses to
acknowledge their relationship on social media. Red flag?

Your brother is in deep shit. Any relationship that is two years old and
hasn't been acknowledged on a social platform is scandalous. Period!

▶ Did you have any bucket-list items that you wanted to complete
before you turned forty?

I don't have a bucket list.

I don't want to climb any goddamn mountain or jump out of a plane
or meet a specific person or hit some random goal. I'm just not that
dude. I really only have two goals in life, and guess what? I've already
completed both of them. So I guess you could say I had a bucket list, but
I already finished it. And before I turned forty, too. Not bad.

Now some of you might be thinking, What about your goal of
buying the New York Jets?

I've never been motivated by the end result of a long-term investment. I'm all about the climb, and the battle that comes with it.

I live my other major goal every day. It's at the core of every
business I've ever created, and is what gets me out of bed every
morning: I gain leverage daily.

Guess who you meet on a climb? People. Many on the same
route as you. Find those who fascinate you, who challenge you,
and who help you look forward to getting started every day. Treat
them well, provide them with value, show them why you're worth
keeping around, and you'll get tremendous return. I find the individuals I think I can jam with for the next fifteen, twenty, thirty
years professionally, and I bring them into my circle to make them
the next generation of operators.

I don't believe in bucket lists. If there's something you want to do or accomplish, don't put it off until you're almost dead. Go do it now!

---

▶ In the first thirty seconds of someone meeting you, what do you reveal about yourself?

---

That I'm different. But I don't reveal it with words. I don't have to talk (although I'll admit it's rare for me to stay silent for very long) because I'm so filled with energy. Forget thirty seconds: I can set the tone of a conversation within thirteen seconds. No one meets me without figuring out very quickly that I'm not your average dude.

---

▶ What actor would you want to play you in a movie about your life?

---

The person who's going to play me in a movie may not have even been born yet because I'm a slow grinder and 99 percent of the world still has no idea who I am. In twenty-five or thirty-five years, when a movie about my life does get made, I'd like to be portrayed by whoever is the most attractive actor of that era.

---

▶ Do you watch your own videos?

---

I have never watched a whole episode of *The #AskGaryVee Show* or any of the thousands of episodes of *WLTV*. I know what's on it— I'm living it.

▶ What historical figure would you have lunch with if you could, and why?

Nobody. I know that's an awful answer. It's insane how little I want to meet famous people. Which doesn't mean I don't find people fascinating. I do. Like Winston Churchill; wrestler "Macho Man" Randy Savage; Pete Rozelle, the former NFL commissioner. (Hey, I read his book! That probably brings the total number of books I've read up to nine! See Chapter 3.) Walt Disney. But the truth is, if it were the month of August and you told me I could have dinner with any historical figure or I could watch the Jets' first preseason game, I'd rather watch the preseason game. Maybe I'm broken. Maybe it's ego. Or maybe when given the choice, I'd rather spend my time bringing value to the people who pay attention to me instead of paying attention to other people. For sure I would pass on every historical figure just to have dinner with the three grandparents I never got to know.

▶ What was your first or most embarrassing screen name?

One of my AOL chat names was GeeNutz.

▶ Would you rather have a pet dragon or be able to turn into a dragon?

I'd turn into a dragon called Revis Island.

▶ I'm curious to know how you feel about the way you've touched
and inspired people over the years.

I think a lot of people think they know me well because we've been interacting for so many years. I'm probably a little more real, even tangible, than other online personalities because the engagement is so important to me. And yet, some people probably still see my intensity and hear about my commitment to buying the New York Jets and figure that money means more to me than anything. But it doesn't. Money means much less to me than the fact that I've been blessed with a communication style that allows me to talk about what I believe in my soul with such conviction I can actually help people improve their lives. It blows my mind to think about how many people have been affected by *Crush It* and some of my other books and videos, even in small ways. So I feel thankful, and I feel that I've got reason to be proud if this is the legacy I get to leave behind.

▶ When have you been happiest in life?

Right this second. And it's true regardless of when you are reading this.

It's the truth. It was the truth when I answered this question back on episode 37, too. Because I'm a collector of good people and good moments. The birth of children. The Jets beating the Patriots in the playoffs. Getting standing ovations at important business conferences. I'm all about momentum and clout. Every day that goes by in which good things keep happening, and there is no sickness or sadness in my family, feels like the next big day. All I have to do is just keep building on each day, one after the next.

You know, earlier I listed my biggest fears, but I forgot to mention this one: I'm afraid that eventually the climb will be over and I will become bitter when I realize all the things I wasn't able to capitalize, all the moments I missed. That's why I pray that I'll never actually reach the other side, and that my life can always be about the climb. I hope I feel that way up until I take my last breath.

So, yes, this moment is the happiest in my life because with every encounter, every adventure, every experience, ultimately everything always gets collectively better. That is, it does when you choose to focus on the positive, which I definitely do. You should try it.

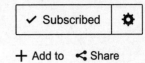

▶ **QUESTION OF THE DAY**

---

I have a ton of strengths. What's the best way to drill down on the best to move forward at a faster pace?

---

Shut the fuck up, pick the one you like best, and start winning.

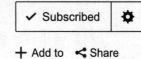
▶  A FEW WORDS FROM THE REST OF THE CAST

---

YOU SEE STEVE UNWIN AND INDIA KIESER
IN FRONT OF THE CAMERA ALMOST DAILY, SO
WE THOUGHT WE'D ASK A FEW OF THE CAST
MEMBERS WHO DON'T GET MUCH SCREEN TIME
TO OFFER US THEIR THOUGHTS ABOUT THEIR
FAVORITE MOMENTS OR CLAIMS TO FAME ON
THE SHOW.

---

**Staphon Lawrence—Video**
**@staphonlawrence**

Episode 45 was my first time sitting in on the show and actually meeting Gary. The prop for this episode was a jar full of almonds. Gary decided that for his question of the day, he wanted people to guess how many almonds were in the jar. Of course being the new guy, I was the one who would have to count them and I spent my first official day, outside of orientation, counting almonds. Good times.

## David Rock—Video
## @DavidRockNYC

*Don't edit this, DRock!* I'm sure if you've watched/listened to the show you've heard Gary shout this to me. Working for Gary has definitely been a change of pace, but in probably the most valuable way possible. I've learned that speed is super-valuable and quality is subjective to that. Gary values authenticity over everything, and it's not often that you find someone as scrappy and fast as Gary; he's super-entertaining. Ever since day one I've loved the energy that he brings to the camera. It makes my job that much more enjoyable.

One of my favorite "editing" moments was the birth of the Share Monster in episode 129. *"Share! DROCK do something there, like, actually you know what, I want you to create something right now, edit this and we'll use this all the time Shaaare-Monsterrr!, and when you edit it, use fire and crazy stuff Shaaare-Monsterrr!"*

When we were starting I would always get frustrated with the "bad audio," especially in episode 5, and Gary would remind me that it's okay and we just need to learn how to get faster, so since then I've strived for a quicker turnaround time while still making slight improvements to the quality of the show (we've gotten great audio now, whew!).

If you want to go and create your own videos, I want you to stop getting caught up on what camera to buy, and what mic has the BEST sound. You don't need the BEST to start. Grab your iPhone, hold it at arm's length, and start, and whatever you do—provide value. This is No. 1.

Wanna see something really cool? Check out episode 1 of

*WineLibrary TV*, then skip ahead to episode 598. See how Gary's personality shifted from quiet and reserved to outgoing and absolutely entertaining? *He found his voice.* Now for a more recent example, check out episode 1 of *#AskGaryVee*, then check the most recent episode . . . let me guess, you see that same difference? He had to find his voice again.

Why the big difference? We began to find our cadence; we evolved. As we continued to crank out episodes we were able to make slight adjustments little by little and we continue to do so.

You are probably asking, "Aren't you a videographer?" and "Don't you want it to look good?" Of course I do, and it will keep getting better because I'll get faster. But I want you to recognize that this situation applies to every aspect of life. Sometimes we overthink things and you need to just start. Get feedback and continue to make changes. You'll get there if you put in the work. You can do it. It's possible.

## Andy Krainak—Growth Hacker
## @krainak

My claim to Vayner Nation fame is that I've been on what many consider the best episode of the show to date, episode 118 featuring Gary's father, Sasha. In it, Gary's dad jokes that I made Gary famous via Facebook ads and Gary promptly corrects him: "No, Dad, I made Andy famous." It was a special episode and I know everyone enjoyed watching his dad talk about GV growing up and how quickly kid Gary was able to give back the money his dad had lent him to start selling baseball cards. "Like that," Sasha said, snapping his fingers. I'm consistently taken aback by the always-on energy and gusto GV brings, not just to the filming of the shoooow but to all the executional details. The texts that I get from Gary at any day or time with strategy/execution commands followed up with "ATTACK!!!"

"ASAP!!" "Yayayayaya" not only fire me up but always give me the right perspective on what hard work and passion look like. Hopefully all the watchers and podcast listeners have learned as much about execution and hustle from the #AGV show as I have.

## Andrew Greif—Design
## @andrew_greif

So you're telling me you've never heard of Rich Uncle Millford? Oh, well, neither had I up until the moment I was called in to the show (out of the blue) to create this one-of-a-kind character Gary imagined up that I knew nothing about. But on the next show he appeared on a T-shirt and everyone could finally put a face to the name, and it's definitely my favorite shirt design so far.

## Alex De Simone—Business Development
## @TheRealDeis

A large part of my job around this book was to get it into your hands, so I thank you for making the purchase, or for kindly accepting it from someone I'd presume to be your new best friend ☺.

At the writing of this blurb, I'm approaching a full year's time on "Team Gary." Prior to joining VaynerMedia, and subsequently Gary's team, I thought I knew who Gary was—an author whose books I'd read, a public speaker whose videos I'd consumed.

Boy, was I wrong.

In my days before being on team GV, the show (and consequently Gary) not only served as a companion for my once two-hour commute to and from Long Island, but also a lens into who the captain was steering this beautiful and ever-expanding ship we call VaynerMedia.

Now that I've been a part of Gary's team for quite some time, I've come to realize that both Gary and The Shoooowwww are much more than just a semi-regular video series/podcast hosted by a guy I call my boss.

Although we are very much a close unit, the roles we on Gary's team fulfill vary quite a bit, which lends our respective day-to-day to be naturally autonomous. The show, in my opinion, is what brings us all together. It serves as the glue, the core of our relationship as a team, as we all contribute to its existence, be it through its preparation, production, or distribution.

And for that, I'm forever grateful.

Not only am I indebted to the friend I also call my boss, but also to the show that's fostered lifelong relationships with the "dopes" I get to share it with.

## Zak Moy—Designer-in-Chief
## @Zakmoy

Like all things in my Gary-centric world, working on the production team of a show was not something I planned to tack on to my résumé. In early 2014, Gary declared to Steve and I that 2014 would be the "Year of YouTube" and he would return to doing video content. And, in true Team Gary fashion, that idea was put on the back burner. It wasn't until a few months later when DRock was hired that the spark was reignited and, before I knew it, we had a show to produce on top of everything else we do. Yikes!

Aside from bringing the show art direction and working on visual assets, my early roles in the filming of the show have also included emergency voice-overs, temporary question-asker/hunter, and secondary cameraman. But those were the early days, and I've been too busy with other responsibilities (like designing this book) to go to every filming. Now I only appear on the show when GV wants to point out my choice in attire (e.g., pixel sunglasses and Pokemon hats) or when he needs to know what font something is. My behind-the-scenes stance is probably why I can't recall a favorite moment.

But I'm cool with that because I think the true beauty that we (the cast, the crew, the viewers) have experienced with *The #Ask-GaryVee Show* is that it has presented all of us with the opportunity for growth. Gary and the show's energy have pushed me through more doors than I expected as an early twenty-something and I couldn't be more thankful for that. The show was definitely not planned to be part of my "clouds" or "dirt." Perhaps it's the "gray" that GV talks about—that middle part where all the magic happens.

# ▶ THE #ASKGARYVEE SHOW PROP-WORD PUZZLE!

Every episode, the team puts three or four whole minutes of thought into what prop is going to sit on the table to give me something to play with. This puzzle is a list of our favorites from throughout the run of the show. See if you can guess the answers without referring to the episodes!

As soon as you finish, post a picture on Instagram with the hashtag #AskGaryVeeProps. The first person to do so will get something awesome.

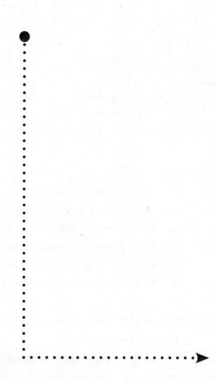

## ACROSS

3. Ep 59—Keeping Gary in shape
4. Ep 76—The original GaryVee giveaways
6. Ep 32—Baller's nickname
8. Ep 97—Needed for jabbing and right hooking
11. Ep 87—The book that started it all
13. Ep 123—Budweiser on a diet #client
14. Ep 105—The book before this book, short for
15. Ep 120—Good for home runs, home security
21. Ep 34—Go-to gourd
22. Ep 101—@locomodem's construction material of choice

23. Ep 51—Tenuta San Guido's star Super Tuscan
24. Ep 11—Kingly headwear
25. Ep 135—We can't ride it, but it's cool to have around

**DOWN**

1. Ep 20—Necessary for long wine tastings
2. Ep 95—Quintessential Napa blend
4. Ep 117—Crossbreed-centric eighties cartoon
5. Ep 62—Tom Brady's weapon of choice
6. Ep 44—Reply hazy, try again
7. Ep 91—Some toys just want to watch the world burn
9. Ep 41—Home-team headwear
10. Ep 52—Pro wrestler who was also a regular on *WLTV*
12. Ep 73—Ephemeral messaging app
16. Ep 53—Gary just loves to give these away
17. Ep 45—The official snack of *#AskGaryVee*
18. Ep 5—The reason VaynerMedia employees have cavities
19. Ep 54—For kids who play the long game
20. Ep 71—Just _____ away from your dreams

# ▶ INDEX

## ▶ ABOUT THE AUTHOR

**GARY VAYNERCHUK** is an entrepreneur, tech investor, and CEO of one of the fastest-growing digital agencies in the world. Host of *The #AskGaryVee Show*, Gary was named to both *Crain's New York Business's* and *Fortune* magazine's 40 Under 40 lists, as well as *BusinessWeek's* list of the top 20 people every entrepreneur should follow on social media. He lives in New York City.